Vienna in the Age of Metternich:
from Napoleon to Revolution 1805–1848

by the same author

AUSTRIA:
PEOPLE AND LANDSCAPE

VIENNA IN THE
AGE OF METTERNICH

from Napoleon to Revolution
1805–1848

Stella Musulin

Westview Press   Boulder, Colorado

Published in 1975 in London, England,
by Faber and Faber, Ltd.

Published in 1975 in the United States of America
by Westview Press, Inc.
1898 Flatiron Court
Boulder, Colorado 80301
Frederick A. Praeger, Publisher and Editorial Director

Printed in Great Britain by Ebenezer Baylis and Sons, Ltd.,
The Trinity Press, Worcester, and London, Great Britain

Library of Congress Cataloging in Publication Data

Musulin, Stella.
Vienna in the age of Metternich.

Bibliography: p.
1. Vienna—History. 2. Metternich-Winneburg,
Clemens Lothar Wenzel, Fürst Von, 1773-1859.
I. Title.
DB854.M87 1975 943.6'13'040934 75-19264
ISBN 0-89158-501-x

'Who speaks of victories? Survival is all.'
(Rilke)

Contents

Illustrations

Plates

Illustrations

The author is grateful to the following for permission to reproduce photographs in which they hold the copyright: the Art History Museum, Vienna, for Plate 12; the Department of Tourism, Municipality of Vienna, for Plates 1, 2, 5, 18, 24, 25; the National Library (Picture Archives) Vienna, for Plates 3, 4, 6, 7, 8, 9, 10, 11, 13, 14a, 14b, 14c, 16, 17, 20, 21, 22, 23, 26, 27; the War History Museum, Vienna, for Plate 19.

Maps

HABSBURG FAMILY TREE

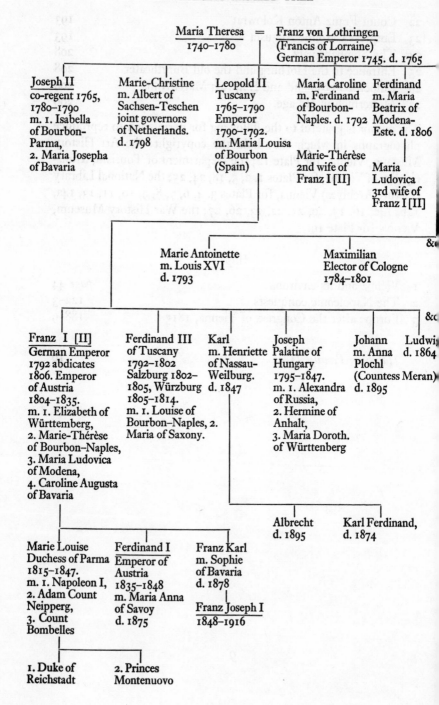

1
An Empire at Bay

The early years of the nineteenth century found Napoleon in an almost unassailable position both at home and abroad. In his first Italian campaign he had snatched the wealthy cities of Lombardy and Tuscany from the Austrians. In the Treaty of Campo Formio in 1797 Austria also relinquished the coalfields of Belgium but made herself partner to a rape by accepting a share of Venetia. Then King Ferdinand of Naples lost his crown because Queen Marie Caroline, who tended to dominate her degenerate husband in affairs of state, was a Habsburg, a daughter of the Empress Maria Theresa, after which Napoleon turned his attention to the Pope for whom he had in mind a role something like that of a court chaplain. These initial conquests in Italy, while not wholly unwelcome to the people themselves, sowed the first seeds of the Risorgimento.

In 1803 Napoleon embarked on a rearrangement of the political map of Germany which, too, was to have enduring consequences. Having annexed lands on the left bank of the Rhine, he compensated the German princes concerned at the expense of others. The Act of Mediation, signed in Paris, suppressed the independence of 123 states; this was a preliminary factor in the ultimate emergence of Germany as a major power in Europe and a rival to France.

At home, the First Consul's position was now unchallenged. After his cold-blooded murder of the young Duc d'Enghien in March 1804 he was as safe from the Bourbon princes as from any suspicion of royalist sympathies. Two months later he placed the imperial crown upon his own head. It was, he believed, the crown of the new Charlemagne, and in Milan he added to it the crown of

Lombardy. His idea was to resuscitate the Holy Roman Empire, but under the hegemony of France, and he did not omit to ensure the presence at his coronation of the Bishop of Rome. But while the Holy Roman Empire had long been an object of mockery, while it was totally ineffective, it was not dead. For centuries, the Habsburg emperors had worn that crown, and the coronation regalia remained, as it still does, in Vienna; the ruling Habsburgs were emperors of the Holy Roman Empire, not of Austria. To counterbalance Napoleon's action, Franz II now took a fateful step and assumed the title of Emperor of Austria. It has been said that this was the most stupid thing he could have done. Could it not be read as implying that he reckoned to lose the German imperial crown anyway and was looking round for an alternative? Was it not a hint to Napoleon, an implicit declaration of intent to withdraw the Habsburg influence from Germany, to abdicate from a time-honoured primacy, leaving the field open to Prussia? If this were so, it would still leave room for a more positive interpretation. The standing of the Habsburgs in the world rested upon the Austrian realms. In pronouncing himself Emperor of Austria Franz bound the imperial title to the hereditary *Casa d'Austria*; he was, as it were, withdrawing it to a safe place rather than leave it to the whim of the German Electors.

Two years later, in 1806, Napoleon set up the Confederation of the Rhine. Touching the coastline between Denmark and Prussia in the north, the Confederation broadened to fill the whole area between France and Belgium on the one side, and Prussia together with the western frontier of the Austrian monarchy on the other. By force of arms, by humiliation and by bribery: in his subjugation of the German states there were no weapons which Napoleon would not bring into use as required. He had bribes in plenty, as the redistribution of the mediatized princedoms cost him nothing, and we can assume that the newly promoted kings of Württemberg and Bavaria paid for their own crowns. He was helped, too, by the notorious disunity of the member states of the Holy Roman Empire even in its better days, and there was the Germans' jealousy and suspicion of the Habsburgs to play with. When, in 1740, the 23-year-old Maria Theresa had called upon the signatories of the Pragmatic Sanction to honour their word, Bavaria, backed by France, had been the first to deny her right to the throne of her father,

Karl VI. Thus it was not altogether surprising that, regardless of the ethnic and cultural ties linking that southern German state to the western provinces of Austria, Bavaria fought on the side of Napoleon. Significantly, the only protest against the Act of Confederation signed on 12th July, 1806, was made by George III in his capacity as King of Hanover. The rest swept off into the French camp. Now, Emperor Franz had no alternative but to lay aside the crown of the 'Holy Roman Empire of the German Nation', and he did so. The whole business was unconstitutional from start to finish, and it is this that was to make the task of constitutional lawyers so perplexing. There is a theory that Franz, first Emperor of Austria, only renounced his title to the German part of the old Empire and that in him its soul went marching on. And this was roughly the conclusion reached by the Congress of Vienna, but its authenticity is doubtful. Nevertheless the mystical power of the old Empire was by no means dead; it was, after all, the only potential link between the German states.

To turn back to 1805: the Emperor of the French intended not only to walk in the steps of Charlemagne but in those of Alexander as well. He wanted Egypt, the Middle East, India. Command of central Europe was essential if he were to conquer his arch-enemy, Protestant England, and to ensure the effectiveness of the continental blockade against Britain he must also control Italy and the Iberian peninsula. Equally, with Germany and most of Italy in his hands, he could embark on conquest of the enemy to the east: Catholic Austria. Yet what in effect brought him to Vienna were considerations of prestige rather than of strategy.

For two years, an army of 210,000 men had been lying draped along the western coast of France watching the winds and tides. But with Nelson and Cornwallis keeping an eye on the French and Spanish navies it was impossible to bring together sufficient ships to transport and protect an invading army. Meanwhile the Czar Alexander I, shocked by the murder of the Duc d'Enghien, had entered into an alliance with England which Austria joined, and in September 1805 Austria delivered an ultimatum to France. More relieved than alarmed, very much in contrast to his Foreign Minister Talleyrand who made frantic efforts to prevent a fresh outbreak of hostilities, Napoleon hurried eastwards.

The reign of Franz, last Holy Roman Emperor, first Emperor of Austria, covers the years from 1792 up to his death in 1835. The death of his father Leopold II after a reign of only two years marked a watershed in the history of the Habsburg monarchy because it ended a long period of social progress. Leopold's mother the Empress Maria Theresa (1740–1780) was on most counts one of the greatest of monarchs and not one of the female sovereigns of Europe can easily bear comparison with her. As a reformer she is mainly remembered for introducing primary education throughout the realm. In her later years she was assisted as co-regent by her son, later Joseph II, a man of the Enlightenment who combined to an extraordinary degree a burning desire to improve the condition of his peoples and a facility for offending the susceptibilities of all classes. In 1782 his sweeping interventions in the life of the Catholic Church brought Pope Pius VI rushing to Vienna. An essentially tragic figure and like his mother a strict moralist, Joseph lacked her instinct for the emotional and spiritual needs of the people. He died childless and was succeeded in 1790 by his brother Leopold.

Maria Theresa's children were to be found on thrones all over Europe: to mention only those who come into this narrative, there was the joint governor of the Austrian Netherlands, Archduchess Marie Christine; Queen Marie Caroline, the wife of King Ferdinand of Naples; Queen Marie Antoinette; and Grand Duke Leopold of Tuscany (later Emperor Leopold II). Under Leopold, and subsequently, Tuscany was a model state. It was said of it that 'Under a liberal administration, Tuscany basks in smiling serenity.' It was heart-warming, said an Italian writer, to observe the contentment of the people, the country's flourishing trade and the constantly growing population. 'This was the result of loyal adherence to the principles of administration given to the country by this incomparable sovereign.' The writer went on to draw a most unfavourable comparison with the Papal States which enjoyed the same soil, the same climate, the same radiant, life-giving sunshine.[1]

It was one thing to rule smiling Tuscany, another to carry on quietly with the Josephine reforms where they were on the right lines but drawing back where Joseph II had gone too far. But

[1] Domenico Demarco, *Il tramonto dello Stato pontifico.*

Leopold, essentially a moderate man, gave every promise of being far more successful than his brother had been. Perhaps it was partly because he was a happier man. For Austria, his death in 1792, probably of peritonitis, was a disaster of the first magnitude. Contemporaries could see the ineptitude of Leopold's eldest son and heir Franz, they could see more easily still the mediocrity and worse of his closest advisers at the outset of his reign. Only future generations were able to realize that in 1792 half a century of reform—patchy, proceeding by fits and starts but fairly consistent—had come to an end. From then on, such was the traumatic effect of the French Revolution on a nervous and suspicious nature in which neither the steadiness nor the brilliance of his immediate forbears were there to act as a counterweight, Franz was to fear and resist change in any form. The rigidity of the Metternich régime—one question which will be worth looking into is how justified it is to use this time-honoured term—led on to the Revolution of 1848, and in its turn the trauma was passed on to the young heir to the throne, Franz Joseph I, whose reign was to last for sixty-eight years, ending in 1916.

Franz's confidence in his brothers varied in inverse proportion to their intelligence and ability, but his relations with them were also greatly strained by his susceptibility to intrigue. The two brothers who are unforgotten in Austria today are the soldier Archduke Karl, Napoleon's principal adversary, and Archduke Johann, the maker of modern Styria, husband of Anna Plochl the postmaster's daughter from Aussee. Both of these archdukes were infinitely superior to their elder brother in intellect and ability, both were natural leaders and their lives were to be darkened by the clouds of envy and suspicion issuing from the throne. Like their immediate ancestors, they too were pre-eminently reformers. Archduke Johann had one foot in the era of the Enlightenment, the other in the industrial revolution. What would have happened if one or the other had chanced to be the firstborn son?

Archduke Karl's talent for the 'arts' of war was of the highest order; it was his fate to have to answer the challenge of a military genius. But he was no wager of aggressive war and his views on the suppression of ideas by force were the same as those of Leopold II, and he never revised them. Leopold II had firmly believed in the principle of non-intervention, he was convinced that ideas could not be defeated by force of arms and he thought that for foreign powers to march into France would merely rally the French behind such leaders as might emerge. There can be very little doubt that if he had lived events would not have followed the same course. Some of the more conservative contemporaries of Karl and Johann believed, and a historian in our day has flatly said, that either of those men on the throne of Austria would have been a disaster. Both were too brilliant, too erratic—too clever by half. There was one contemporary above all others who not only thought this but took action on it: throughout Metternich's long term of office from 1809 to 1848 he ensured that neither of them acquired any influence in affairs of state. The fact that he was not wholly mistaken in his judgement, that even the Emperor Franz's paranoid suspicions of Karl and Johann were not wholly without foundation, deepens the tragedy as, for us, it greatly enhances the interest of the relationship between these Habsburg brothers. To be a Habsburg, male or female, was never altogether easy. As the dynasty moved towards its sixth century it became increasingly difficult; this is one of the main threads in this attempt to bring out a few significant aspects of life in Vienna during the Napoleonic wars and up to the end of the age of Metternich. Another strand which becomes recurrently visible is the nature of the police state to which all, from the Emperor downwards, had to adapt themselves, the nature of the stress which it placed on all classes and its effect on the way people thought and behaved.

The backcloth to this book is provided by Vienna itself where the head-on clash between Napoleon and the House of Habsburg took place. Twice Napoleon occupied the capital of the Habsburg Empire. During 1809, for Austria a climactic year, two major battles were fought within earshot and even within sight of Vienna, on a plain called the Marchfeld which has seen some of the decisive battles of western civilization. Here Charlemagne defeated the Avars; in 1278 the Battle of Dürnkrut assured the supremacy of Rudolph of Habsburg and of his dynasty and dispelled for all time the danger that Austria might simply become an appendage of Bohemia. In 1529 Suleiman the Magnificent laid siege to Vienna, and in 1683 the bogey of Islamic conquest of the West was laid when the allied armies poured down from the Kahlenberg to the relief of the besieged city.

The Vienna Basin lies where the last ripples of the eastern alpine range come to rest. A few miles to the north and north-west, well beyond the Kahlenberg, that line of hills which looks down on Vienna much as Fiesole does upon Florence, the Bohemian massif begins. The shelf along the edge of this plateau is the shore of an immense primeval sea. East of Vienna the country is as flat as a table, geographically speaking the plains of Hungary start here. In Roman times, the focal point of this eastern area of Austria was the L-shaped junction where the River March, descending from the north, meets the Danube near Hainburg. At this spot two very ancient trade routes meet: the River Danube and the Amber Road from the Baltic to the Adriatic. At that time the Danube marked the *limes*, the northern frontier of the Roman Empire. Since the late Middle Ages the main traffic between Bohemia (Czechoslovakia) and Italy has passed in an almost direct line to the south through Vienna. As a trading post, Vienna came to enjoy remarkable privileges. Whether the goods in transit came by water and were to proceed by the same means, or whether a transfer were to be made from road to water and vice versa, everything had to be unloaded on the spot and bought and resold by Viennese merchants. An easy life—but only so long as trade flowed, and this was not always the case. These two characteristics of Viennese commercial life persisted for centuries: entitlement to a share of all that passed one's door without personal effort or risk, but on the other hand a lack of security. The consequence was a so-called 'pensioner mentality', a love of state monopolies, of guilds, charters, *konzessionen* and all forms of protectionism, which continues to this day. The Viennese tradesman's idea of hell is a town where anyone, without by your leave, can put a notice on his door saying 'A. Novotny, Ratcatcher', or 'Susi Müller, Dressmaker'. Civic independence was only to be thought of in times of acute emergency such as the Turkish sieges and when under attack by Napoleon. Then, in the absence of the Emperor, his Court and most of the quality, the citizens were left to get on with it and their behaviour was exemplary. At other times the Habsburgs have been liable to execute the mayors of Vienna; four examples come to mind.

B

The withdrawal of the Turks from eastern and south-eastern Europe during the early eighteenth century under the hammer blows of Prince Eugen of Savoy at last freed Vienna from a frontier position to which, tragically, it has now returned. From being an outpost of the West it became the pivot of a monarchy which Talleyrand saw as 'a combination of ill-assorted states, differing from one another in language, manners, religion, and constitution, and having only one thing in common—the identity of their ruler', by A. J. P. Taylor as 'a vast collection of Irelands'. On a smaller scale both comments might apply to Hungary *vis-à-vis* the other ethnic groups: the Magyars were a minority in their own country but showed little tolerance towards their 'inferior' neighbours. Austria's major injustice towards Hungary however lay in arresting the industrial development of the country in order to maintain Hungary as a permanent granary for the more advanced areas. The same short-sighted protectionist mentality in Vienna was to erect customs barriers against Germany behind which Austrian factories could shelter from the industrial explosion in the Ruhr.

Finance was never Metternich's strong point. A member of an old Rhineland family who remained an outsider in Austria all his life, he displayed an aristocratic disdain for economic realities which the two Archdukes Karl and Johann found incomprehensible. Yet they lacked his political vision. There was no way by which they and Metternich together could have worked in unison towards the defeat of Napoleon and afterwards towards the reshaping of Europe. For a generation, the decisive element in the foreign affairs of the monarchy and to some considerable extent its internal affairs as well, was the relationship between Clemens Metternich and the Emperor Franz I.

2

Napoleon at the Gates

In one of the rooms in the Schatzkammer hangs a full-length portrait of the Emperor Franz I.[1] His brooding glare as it follows the visitor round the room is anything but agreeable; it is icy and a trifle menacing. This is Napoleon's 'Papa François', and although their ages were only ten years apart, Alexander I of Russia jovially called him 'Papa' too. *'Der gute Kaiser'*, ladies would write mechanically, time after time, in their diaries. 'Il passe pour bête', it had been said, 'mais ses sujets l'aiment.'

Born in 1768 to Archduke Leopold, Grand Duke of Tuscany, and his wife the Spanish Infanta Maria Ludovica, by the time Franz was six the future Emperor Leopold II was beginning to be seriously worried about the character and personality of his heir—the eldest, as it turned out, of sixteen children. Franz's uncle the Emperor Joseph II, one of the most complex and controversial figures ever to wear the crown of Charlemagne, was no less concerned, and a stream of letters passed between the Hofburg in Vienna and the Palazzo Pitti in Florence, a correspondence in which the boy's tutor Count Colloredo joined. 'Reserved, delicate, anxious, it is his pleasure to deceive his elders and betters,' wrote his father. 'Much egoism', wrote Colloredo when Franz was twelve, 'likes to dissemble in all that he undertakes; mistrustful and jealous.' He was strangely apathetic. 'To me he seems lazy', commented the sovereign

---

[1] As Holy Roman Emperor he was Franz II until his abdication in 1806. In 1804 he adopted the title Emperor of Austria whereby he became Franz I. To avoid switching to and fro and consequent confusion he has been called Franz I throughout.

in the Hofburg who wasted nothing, words least of all. 'Does anything please him?' 'He accepts everything', said his tutor, 'with excessive, forced indifference.'

Tutor and pupil moved to Vienna, and Franz, at 17, took over the suite of rooms in the Hofburg which he was to occupy for the next 50 years. Joseph II tried to look on the brighter side. 'As to his character: rather slow, hypocritical and phlegmatic . . . nevertheless his mind is not devoid of energy and system . . . to all appearances he has worked with diligence and has acquired no little knowledge. For his age he is not ill-informed both in theory and in practice, yet it is all mechanical, as though taken at dictation, with no ideas of his own, no personal style . . . Yet this is an important matter.' The Emperor said much the same to old Kaunitz, the statesman who had served his mother Maria Theresa and himself for so many years. It was essential that the boy be shaken out of this fearful lethargy. What, Colloredo was asked, did the fellow do when left entirely to himself? Well (and all the tedium of an archducal existence can be felt in the tutor's reply)—'he wanders up and down, and he looks out of the window to watch what is going on outside.' Joseph II drew the boy into his own company, took him along on official occasions, talked to him, tried to draw him out. This was not altogether ineffective. But leave him to himself, and 'at the first opportunity he is once again a block of wood set down in the middle of the room, with absent mien permitting his arms and legs to dangle, and in this pose, if he were not desired to arise, he would remain until the morrow.'

How much the heir apparent's leaden temperament was inborn or to what extent it can be blamed on Franz de Paula, Count Colloredo, it is not easy to say. The child was certainly overworked, as was often the case among royalty and nowhere more than among the Habsburgs. Maximilian I was put through such a stern curriculum that he developed a nervous speech impediment, but the eighteenth-century passion for learning, combined, in this case, with over-anxiety on the part of the adults and a rather dim-witted pupil, was likely to have its effect on both temperament and character. Add to this a sense of personal inadequacy, a growing realization that his brothers were intellectually more highly endowed, more able, more popular, the mystique of his ancient dynasty, a feeling that he was borne up by the divine right of kings, produced in the adult a rigid mind which, while hardly daring to move beyond its own narrow confines, demanded unquestioning loyalty where a more self-assured man would have taken this for granted and set some value on ability and qualification for office. Colloredo, on the other hand, was described by Count Andreas Razumovsky, the Russian ambassador in Vienna and patron of Beethoven, as a man of 'extremely limited intelligence', moreover 'a byword for his lack of ability', slow-witted and ponderous. Rigidly and unimaginatively conservative as he was, it was certainly due to his influence that Franz, shocked to the marrow by the violence and brutality of the French Revolution which he attributed wholly to the philosophy of the Enlightenment, acquired and retained for life a deep distaste for intellectual freedom, for the press, constitutions, and for everything which smacked of liberalism, as well as an almost pathological fear of secret societies.

Immediately on his succession in 1790 Leopold II brought the new heir to the throne into the councils of state, a wise policy not unusual among the Habsburgs which might have been imitated with profit by royalty elsewhere. Franz had to make reports on particular branches of public administration, and his father, who was greatly concerned to pursue and also to stabilize his predecessor's programme of reform, must have been struck by the tart, governessy tone of these memoranda. For Franz, although quite devoid of imagination, had a quick eye for bad administration but no understanding whatever of the human element as a contributing factor. To him, complaints by civil servants of bad pay or strangling bureaucratic usage merely showed their disloyalty to the throne; they should review their attitude afresh, a task in which they would be best assisted by regular attendance at Mass. Insubordination in the army must be suppressed by creation of statutory examples. The young Archduke was galvanized by the challenge which his work provided. All apathy left him, he drafted and redrafted and at last on 1st November, 1791, he laid his masterpiece before his father: Franz's very own New Police Constitution.

This significant document is the cornerstone of the whole repressive system which was to last for over half a century, and although Metternich's name would come to symbolize the system, as he only came to office in 1809 he is innocent of paternity. The principle it lays down is that one of the main functions of the police is to watch for 'reprehensible, dangerous meetings, clubs or however such petty societies and secretive guilds may term their conventicles'. This emotionally loaded text meant Freemasonry and—with less precision—Jacobinism, but its elasticity is such as to make it applicable to anything which the government happened to dislike. Franz reverted to the subject again and again. In 1797 a law was promulgated expressly forbidding all 'secret societies' and containing the remarkable statement: 'Clandestine congregations conflict at all times with the fundamental principles of a well-regulated state police; may their original purpose be never so benevolent and noble, their degeneration and consequent threat to the state are to be anticipated.' The issue was brought up once more in 1801. Worried by the thought that his civil service might be infiltrated by Jacobin revolutionaries, while the higher ranks and even his immediate associates might be committed to the ideals of Freemasonry, Franz now introduced the *eidliche Revers*, a declaration to be made under oath by all ranks of the public service that they had no connection with secret societies at home or abroad. Five years later the measure was extended to the universities: from professor to doorkeeper, everyone had to take the oath. Later still, membership even of learned societies in foreign countries required the personal permission of the monarch. Originally, the oath was meant to be repeated annually, but the cumbersomeness and near-impossibility of such an undertaking daunted even Franz, and the declaration was incorporated in the regular oath sworn on entry to the service. Whether or not the archdukes were all required to take the oath is a matter of dispute, but this could well be so as a document signed by his brother Archduke Joseph who was Palatine of Hungary has survived. At all events, this pathological mistrust of his brothers was to cause endless distress within the imperial family, and dissension in the private sphere was to exert a baneful influence on public affairs.

If we try to understand the mentality of this last Habsburg to wear the crown of the Holy Roman Empire as he was in the opening years of his reign, and to picture the situation in which he was placed, the tragic effect of his father's early death in 1792 becomes very evident. Those were frightening times, and the young prince, though no physical coward, was easily alarmed. The French Revolution, the years of the Terror when the rattle of the tumbrils, the thump of the guillotine could be heard throughout Europe, paralysed with horror the minds of men whose nerves were much stronger than his. And Franz, of whom as a boy it had been said that the only thing on earth which could make him move was fear of unpleasantness, determined that, whatever the cost, the germ of revolution would not infect his subjects. The cost was to be a high one.

The first major shock of his reign was the execution of Louis XVI and Marie Antoinette, an event which may have sent a tremor of guilt through the conscience of the 25-year-old sovereign as there can hardly be much doubt that the responsibility of the Hofburg for their death is heavy.

It was after the Battle of Neerwinden, one of those innumerable actions during the 1790s which are forgotten by all but specialists in the period, that the French General Dumouriez crossed over to the Austrians. Having lost the battle he could look forward with complete certainty to a court martial in Paris, and he waited, in fact, just long enough to snatch up the four commissars plus the Minister for War Beurnonville who had come to arrest him, and took them along as a sweetener. Archduke Karl met the party on 6th April at Mons. At once, the plan was born to hold them as hostages for the French royal family, and the Austrian commander-in-chief, Prince Coburg—it clearly never occurring to him that his government could let such an opportunity drop—lost no time in opening up negotiations with the other side. Before an answer came from Vienna the Directory had agreed: the royal family would be released in exchange for Beurnonville and his four commissars. Meanwhile, however, Franz and his advisers were wringing their hands over questions of principle and precedent. What was the significance of such an exchange? Did it not imply recognition of the government in Paris? If so, then was not the Hofburg according legal status to the Revolution as well as to its dreaded offspring, constitutional government? The ball of argument bounced hither and thither, to land at the conclusion that such a dangerous precedent would never do; it would jeopardize the principle that the *status quo ante* must be restored.

So the plan failed. It was a curious form of mental contortion to sacrifice the legitimate sovereign in the interests of the principle of legitimacy. Did Franz, or did he not, want to take the only chance there was to save his aunt's life? Probably this simple proposition never occurred to him.

It is difficult to escape the impression that at this juncture decision-making at the apex of the monarchy was unusually slack. The Foreign Minister, Baron Thugut, was soon to be the one man in the Emperor's immediate entourage who knew what he wanted and usually achieved it, but at the time we are speaking of Thugut had only been in office for three months. In the meantime the Habsburg Empire was largely run by two men who leaped straight from the imperial schoolroom into high office. On the death of Leopold II, Count Colloredo was appointed to a dual post specially created for him, that of Minister to the Cabinet and the *Konferenz*, roughly the equivalent of the Privy Council. He had perhaps not yet, as Friedrich von Gentz was to put it in a letter to Pitt ten years later, 'become a byword for imbecility', and he was certainly neither an uncultured nor an ill-intentioned man, but his mental processes and in particular his views on current affairs were any-thing but subtle. Hofrat (Councillor) Schloissnigg had been taken on—in spite of being a Freemason—to coach Archduke Franz in law. Determined to remove the stain of his masonic adherence and soon realizing that Franz was bored to distraction, Schloissnigg took the far-seeing decision to cut formal instruction to the bone and to play games instead: blind man's buff, for example, which in those days was a great favourite among young people at parties but would be inclined to pall, one would think, as a twosome for tutor and pupil. They also dabbled a little in various handicrafts. In the generally prevalent dislike of Schloissnigg there may have been a touch of snobbery; 'the "two emperors"', said a contemporary, 'ruled the Empire with a power subject to no constraint, and although both lacked the necessary ability, Schloissnigg was also wanting in integrity. Their creatures alone were advanced in the public service, two posts in the inner Cabinet being occupied, for example, by nephews of Schloissnigg whose command of the language was far from complete.'

It was in the summer of 1794 that the police, repeatedly exhorted to search for subversive plots, did at last uncover what appeared to be a nest of genuine 'Jacobins'. The conspirators had been indulging in a lot of wild talk, they had not yet in fact done anything, and while it is doubtful whether they would ever have become a danger to the state, what is certain is that their sentences—of death and life-long imprisonment in the dungeons of the notorious Spielberg —created an unpromising precedent in two ways: they were pronounced retrospectively, in accordance with a law which was quickly passed to fit a crime which was not on the law-books at the time it was committed. And, for a generation to come, this handful of men was to provide a precedent and an excuse for an even tighter control on the part of the state police. Even a woman of such undoubted loyalty as the writer Caroline Pichler (it was said that even her poetry had a strong flavour of the civil service) lamented the way that this affair poisoned the air of Vienna during the last years of the eighteenth century. 'People began to use the expression *Jacobin* very frequently, but applying it not alone to such persons as subscribed to the principles of the French Directory. Excessively loyal and orthodox opponents used it to stigmatize those whose sole offence had been to give expression to some idea of a free-thinking nature; "c'est le mot pour perdre les honnêtes gens" said a friend of our family.' But she added, showing that 'free-thinkers' were not a rarity in Vienna: 'A follower of the rules of religion, loyal to the Imperial House and wishing for peace and public order, now stood accused of being an aristocrat, a bigot, an enemy of all enlightenment.'

In these early years of his reign Franz's subjects found him unimpressive. The German actor and dramatist August Wilhelm Iffland gained the impression that the Emperor enjoyed a certain popularity among the general population simply as the current Habsburg, but that the middle classes, civil servants and smaller landed nobility thought him a bending reed. The senior nobility mocked him. More seriously, he made no impression on the army: not until it had been fighting the French for two years did Franz show himself anywhere near the front—and then only under pressure. By contrast, the Emperor Joseph II spent the whole campaign against the Turks at the front. If Maria Theresa had not been incessantly pregnant one can be sure that in her time she would have done the same. Franz II was developing slowly. Colloredo, who to do him justice, on being appointed to the highest government office did protest that he was entirely unqualified for it, was still begging his sovereign to work harder, to play less, and show himself more to the public as his great forbears Maria Theresa and Joseph II had done. From time to time another senior official, Count Saurau, would add his own sharp comments. The whole court, said Saurau, is held in disfavour by the public because of its lack of contact with the townsfolk, its inordinate and—having regard to the times—improper love of pleasure and the undignified nature of its entertainments. The All-Highest Himself (no conceivable translation can be found for the personal pronoun *Allerhöchstderselbe*) must be insistently urged to show more respect for public opinion; if Louis XVI and his Queen had followed this principle they would not, Saurau opined with some justice, have lost their crowns and with them their heads.

Inordinate love of pleasure, undignified pastimes? Franz's circumstances had altered since the days of blind man's buff with Schloissnigg. In the meantime he had married. His first wife was Elizabeth of Württemberg, but as she very soon died she need not detain us further, nor for that matter did her death detain her widower for very long, as within six months of her death he was married to Marie-Thérèse, a daughter of Queen Caroline of Naples. Among the Habsburgs interrelated marriages were so frequent as to be normal practice; the Queen was a daughter of the Empress Maria Theresa.

Marie-Thérèse brought gaiety and laughter to the court of Vienna such as had not been known for half a century. Laxenburg Castle, that Gothic horror resting on an island in a large pond a few miles to the south of Vienna, is almost solely associated with her. After her time Franz only used the place for the sake of the air which he thought more salubrious than that of Schönbrunn. Here at Laxenburg Marie-Thérèse organized amateur theatricals in which she often took a leading part, as well as those Chinese shadow plays which were the fashion of the moment. She loved the fun of dressing up, not only to act a part on the stage, but also as a disguise, and here the celebrated masquerades, the *Redouten*, gave her her chance. Her reign marked the heyday of a particularly Viennese institution, ultimately it would lose its specific piquancy and turn into a fancy dress ball like any other. People of all classes were admitted to the *Redouten* provided that they were dressed for the occasion and masked. It was always a characteristic of the Viennese, which strangers looked upon as a rather oriental trait, to invest their capital in jewellery and then to display it: a dazzling necklace might lie on the creamy bosom of a princess, a courtesan or a butcher's wife. And as every better-class courtesan was certain to be there, together with the court and society, the diplomatic corps, spies native and foreign, war profiteers great and small and an army of anxious mothers and daughters making a last dash at the marriage market, opportunities for intrigue, dangerous flirtation and deception were legion.

The Empress would not have missed a *Redoute* for anything. She possessed that coquettish delight in contact with the general public which so many royal personages have felt before and since. 'Masked to the teeth,' recorded Countess Lulu Thürheim, a delightful and intelligent observer of the times she lived in, 'it was her pleasure to harangue persons of lowly station. Sometimes she would even dance . . . with some artist or handsome singer. She would then disappear into the corridors of the Hofburg, firmly convinced that she had been recognized by no one, notwithstanding that a man wearing a police cockade had remained constantly within ten paces of her.' The Archdukes and even the Emperor, she added, greatly enjoyed being teased by ladies of society and others. Franz I, in spite of his suspicious nature, would wander among dense crowds unaccompanied by anyone except a detective who had to keep his distance, and he had no objection to being jostled or even, on one occasion, to being nearly swept off his feet and pressed up against a wall.

There is plenty of evidence to show that in circles close to the throne this craze for popularity and the often childish pleasures of the Emperor and his consort was thought to be a bit overdone. And yet it was out of sheer good nature that she would receive almost anyone who wished to speak to her. There were no formalities. It was well known that she would give away all that she had in the way of loose cash, distributing, when the money ran out, brooches, diamond pins and so on, and the entrance to her apartments was often the scene of unseemly confusion while her women of the bedchamber fought a running battle with beggars and bearers of petitions. The diarist von Schönholz recalled his private audience with the Empress Marie-Thérèse. As she was not dressed she came across to the rooms of her Lady of the Bedchamber, Antoinette, Countess Wratislav, just as she was, 'in an unadorned morning cap and an outer garment of a light, yellow and red printed silk, known in the trade under the name of "flander" and in general use for house dresses, a linen kerchief about her neck, simple as any woman of the bourgeoisie.' In another key, odd stories used to go the rounds in connection with four musicians who played every evening at Schönbrunn, often with no one present but Franz II and his wife. High jinks were suspected. True or not, Marie-Thérèse had her favourites, such as a singer called Simoni: the two would stroll through the grounds of Schönbrunn arm in arm, much to the disgust of the townsfolk who considered that the Empress was demeaning herself. But the consensus of opinion among the great families was that she was not unfaithful to her husband, and it is true that they must surely have known: how could she have done anything which went unnoticed by her ladies, in particular the appalling old gorgon Wratislav?

Whether or not the cheerful, carefree young Empress with a penchant for sexy games and an endearing dislike of formality permitted Signor Simoni to take liberties behind the bushes at Schönbrunn, there were still other aspects to her character. Her jealousy of Archduke Karl was caused by envy of his popularity in the army and among the population in general, and she did not care to see his intelligence and ability put Franz at a disadvantage. As long as the two brothers lived there would be plenty of people at court to busy themselves creating and deepening the dissension between them, but in her time Marie-Thérèse played her part with her insistence that Karl was pro-French, and—inevitably—a Freemason. Her influence ended with her death from pneumonia in 1807.

If a graph were to mark Archduke Karl's relationship with his brother the Emperor, it would show gradual ascents, sudden peaks, high plateaus and violent plunges into deep valleys whose flat, broad floors led to the foot of the next slow, uphill gradient. It was a relationship which had something in it of classical Greek tragedy.

Karl was the fifth child of Leopold II, then Grand Duke of Tuscany, and Maria Ludovica. He was born in the Poggio Imperiale in Florence but his youth was spent in the official residence, the Palazzo Pitti. He was a delicate child, and by the time he was eight he was occasionally suffering what his anxious attendants called 'attacks of nerves'. Now and then he would 'see things', and more alarming still, would go off into prolonged faints. In short he was mildly epileptic, and his parents came to the rather inevitable conclusion that the only possible career for him was the Church. But there was no hurry, and when he was 20 the suggestion was made that he should go and live for a time with his uncle and aunt in Brussels and continue his studies under their general supervision.

His aunt, the Archduchess Marie-Christine, favourite daughter of the great Maria Theresa, ruled as joint governor of the Austrian Netherlands with her husband, Duke Albert of Sachsen-Teschen, a man of considerable intellectual stature to whom Vienna owes one of the greatest collections of prints and drawings in the world, the Albertina. Today, Marie-Christine is mainly remembered on account of her tomb, carved by Antonio Canova in 1805, in the Augustinerkirche in Vienna; it is the most important monument in the Empire style in Austria. The couple were childless, and they soon decided to adopt Karl whose letters to them both, and after her death in 1798 to Duke Albert, show a remarkable degree of easy intimacy and affection. And yet Marie-Christine had been guilty of a deed which is quite astonishing for its well-meaning tactlessness. Her brother, the Emperor Joseph II, was married to Isabella of Bourbon-Parma. Her contemporaries did not find Isabella beautiful, but she had very lovable qualities, and although Joseph realized that he was unable to arouse in her the passion and profound tenderness which he felt for her, he did believe that she loved him. She had in the meantime become an intimate friend of the Archduchess Marie-Christine, and unfortunately she took her into her confidence in letters which revealed that she found Joseph's lovemaking a considerable strain. The couple had only been married for three years when Isabella died of smallpox. Seeing her brother's despair, her own affectionate heart wrung with compassion for him, Marie-Christine now came to a decision which makes one doubt, if not the purity of her motives, at any rate her intelligence: she showed the letters to Joseph. 'Well may his tears for the Lost One have been staunched,' comments Caroline Pichler, 'but bitterness and contempt for all womankind took root in his breast, better judgement permitting but few exceptions, all the rest being considered as mere dolls or objects of sensuality.' Admittedly, the authenticity of this story is dubious; we only have Frau Pichler's word for it, and how did she know? Certainly, however, Joseph II suffered an emotional disaster which threw him right off balance.

When he married Maria Josepha of Bavaria it was solely for reasons of state and it would have been much better had it been left undone. From the outset he humiliated her before court and public by his ostentatious neglect: it was obvious to anyone who walked beneath the windows of the imperial apartments that a screen had been set up to separate her part of the balcony from his. And the walker below might even be lucky enough to see the Emperor climb out of the window and edge his way round the screen so as to avoid having to walk through their joint sitting-room from which a door led on to the balcony. This totally undeserved treatment of his normally good-natured and attractive consort who was highly popular at home, did nothing to improve relations between Austria and Bavaria at a time when such relations mattered acutely; it is one of the many puzzles in the character of that greatly gifted monarch.

On the arrival of Archduke Karl in Brussels his uncle and aunt encouraged his enthusiasm for soldiering, and at once officers were seconded to his establishment who were qualified to provide him with systematic instruction. For his part Franz was thankful to know that his brother was willing to adopt a career in which he might be of infinite service to the monarchy. The best brains in the Austrian army, all the facilities that he could need must be placed, said the Emperor, at his disposal. He must be kept clear of those endemic intrigues which lacerated the senior ranks of the army, and perhaps—who knew—he might become that great leader of men for whom the enemies of Napoleon were waiting. Karl's preparation for high command took approximately five years, but for most of this time he was absent from the army in the post of Governor-General of the Netherlands. In 1796 the army was more than ready for new men at the top. The field-marshals had held their batons for too long, their ideas were rapidly becoming out of date, just how rapidly the unnerving adaptability of their principal adversary was making painfully evident. It would always be Archduke Karl's opinion that the Austrian system, whereby speed of promotion usually stood in direct relation to precedence in the Almanach de Gotha, was a mistake. But in his case it was a different matter. Royalty, it was thought in the Hofburg, stood above considerations of self-interest, on the other hand their identification with the survival of the Empire and of the dynasty was total.

Hardly had Archduke Karl taken over command of the army on the Lower Rhine than he received a personal letter from the Emperor which contains the essence of all the bitter conflict which was to follow in years to come. 'Abstain from intervention in whatsoever form of business not of a military nature, particularly in the realm of politics; you have enough to do with military activities. Experience teaches us that persons in command who have concerned themselves with the former have wrought nothing but mischief. . . . Know no other duties than those which pertain to Our House and the Monarchy, to whom the Empire and all persons must yield precedence.'

Karl could never say that he had not been warned. And yet his very proximity to the throne was to aggravate the normal tension between the throne plus politicians at home, and the Commander-in-Chief in the field. In his time, Prince Eugen of Savoy had suffered almost unendurable frustration in the service of the Habsburg dynasty. But now the man in command at the front was to be the brother of an Emperor, who, while he gave the orders, had if anything less knowledge of the art of war than his Foreign Minister. Moreover, in intelligence, in intellectual grasp of events and circumstances, Karl was greatly superior to Franz; he would never—a very rare, almost unique quality in a military commander—be able to confine his thinking to the contexts of his profession. His inward eye saw not only his men, he saw the burned-out villages, the trampled crops, the war-weariness of the people. And he saw the economy as a whole.

Image-building and prestige: how much they may take precedence over common sense he was to find out during the first weeks of 1797. In the actions at Emmendingen and Schliengen the French under General Moreau had been driven back across the Rhine, but two fortresses in Germany were still in French hands: Kehl and

Hüningen. In vain did Karl point out—his view was upheld by
members of the War Council in Vienna, including the ageing Field-
Marshal Lacy—that as a ceasefire on the Rhine front had been
suggested by the French both fortresses must shortly capitulate,
whereas to take them by force would be a slow business inevitably
involving great loss of life. But Foreign Minister Thugut thought
otherwise: there was to be no talk of a ceasefire and the attack was
to be made. Karl did what he was told, with the results that he had
foreseen.

So Thugut had his sensation, and from the point of view of his
war party he was probably justified. In newspapers and broadsheets, on medallions, pictures in shop windows, Karl was now the
'Saviour of Germany', and while it would be too much to say that
the Austrian government was in a position to steer public opinion
from the Adriatic to the North Sea, all the same Kehl and Hüningen
were part of an exercise in war propaganda founded on awareness
of a pressing need to find a counterbalance to the star in the West.
At this juncture Franz was genuinely grateful to Karl. 'I cannot
sufficiently thank you and felicitate you,' he wrote, 'also My confidence in you has at all times been so unbounded that there is
nothing in which I can say you nay, being, as I am, persuaded that
all your undertakings are praiseworthy. By reason of the happiness
that you have caused Me, as well as by your actions, you have
brought joy to My government . . .' A personal letter using the
familiar 'thou' form, rather touching in the clumsiness of its structure. Unfortunately, a letter of this kind, full of brotherly affection,
was frequently followed by an ice-cold douche from the Hofburg;
Franz notoriously swung hither and thither according to whoever
last had his ear, and already his innately suspicious mind was beginning to mistrust the public hero whose aura might come, as come it
did, to rival his own.

All neuroses, all malice apart, there was a genuine and apparently
insuperable conflict of principle between Thugut and Archduke
Karl which, hardening and broadening into two hostile camps,
would persist long beyond Thugut's fall. On the one side: conquest
of the French Revolution by force of arms at whatever cost. In the
words of Thugut: 'My will is to continue the war until I am in a
position to dictate the terms of peace, even though the Emperor

himself and the State should go down to their destruction!' By contrast, this was the very cataclysm that Archduke Karl feared if he were continually forced into campaigns before his attempts to modernize the army had had time to take effect and while the monarchy continued to stagger along the road to bankruptcy. By temperament, and it was for this reason that the war party's mistrust was not unjustified, he tended to parley at the first even remotely favourable opportunity. It was thus that the wholly grotesque situation was to develop whereby the commander in the field became the leader of the peace party in opposition to the Foreign Minister. But it is also worth repeating here that if Leopold II had lived, Austria would probably not have entered the war against Napoleon, at any rate until forced to do so. Both he and Prince Kaunitz were opposed on principle to armed interference in the internal affairs of other nations.

The decision, which was now made, to send Karl down to the crumbling Italian front was a gamble: the prestige, the glamour, the ability of the young Archduke were deliberately thrown into the balance. 'Take with you whom you will and transfer generals and other officers from the Army of the Rhine and vice versa at your discretion,' wrote the Emperor. Karl should search out and eliminate all the sources of disorder so that plans could be made for the forthcoming campaign. But what Karl discovered when he got down to Tarvis was a state of affairs undreamt of in Vienna: an army in a state of disintegration, hiding, as soon as news of the approach of enemy forces reached them, in the woods and ravines of the neighbourhood. 'Until now,' said Napoleon, hearing that Karl had been posted to Italy, 'I have been conquering armies without a commander; now I am hastening to fight a commander without an army.' During the campaign in Germany, Napoleon had watched the pattern of the Austrian's tactics with great interest and some approval, but he now swung round: 'He has made mistakes at every step,' he reported to the Directory from Italy. 'He fell into every trap which I continually set for him. . . . This has cost him dear, and would have cost him more still had not his reputation impressed me to some extent and prevented me from recognizing certain errors which I at first attributed to his clear-sightedness, only to find that this did not exist.' More objective, and worth noticing because of the shadow which it casts forward to the fateful battles of Aspern and Wagram, is the comment that instead of forcing a decision in one powerful action, Karl had given his opponent a fresh chance to restore the balance.

Two despatches from the Hofburg told Karl that the Emperor wished to discuss the situation with him in person once he had had the chance to assess it, and Karl set off for Vienna and had actually reached the Semmering when a courier arrived with instructions to turn back. Used as he was to the ways of the Hofburg and to the Emperor's moods, and being within two hours' ride of the city, Karl disregarded the rebuff and continued his journey. He was coolly received, and after a few polite enquiries as to his brother's welfare, Franz stepped into a carriage and was driven off to Laxenburg to supervise the planting of some trees. Something did lie behind this offhand treatment of the 'Saviour of Germany': a suspicion that the Archduke might overstep his prerogative by insisting on an end to hostilities on the Italian front. Exasperated, Karl returned to his headquarters where all he could do was to carry out as orderly a retreat as possible.

The bitter tone of his despatches at this time, his feelings of shame and dishonour at having to fight in rearguard actions with totally demoralized troops, are perhaps a trifle excessive in their self-pity, though the diction of the time must be allowed for. But the Emperor's retort to the effect that if Karl had not left the army when he did to go to Vienna it would not have been defeated, was as illogical as it was malicious. Nor was Karl allowed to carry out the negotiations for the Treaty of Campo Formio which took from Austria Belgium and Lombardy and the left bank of the Rhine from the Swiss frontier to beyond Andernach and Mainz, but ceded Venice in exchange. Secretly and in haste Karl left the southern field of operations.

The lull in the Napoleonic wars during the last three years of the eighteenth century saw Archduke Karl mainly at the headquarters of the Austrian armies in Prague, engaged in the task of reorganization but always surrounded by a network of intrigue unusual in its intensity even for the higher ranks of the Austrian army. Since Karl was allowed and expected to express his views on military affairs but must never touch on anything even remotely 'political', parallel streams of correspondence resulted between Baron Thugut or other members of the War Council, and officers on Karl's staff. Of these Count Bellegarde was not even under the Archduke's orders, and the situation bore more than a slight resemblance to the political commissars of the Russian army since the Revolution. Unconsulted and not even informed on major questions of policy—during the period of Austro-Russian co-operation the question of an armed entry into Switzerland was under discussion—Karl's health began to deteriorate, and this provided Thugut and the anti-Karl clique at court, including the Empress Marie-Thérèse, with the excuse that they sought. The Archduke had, it is true, twice asked to be relieved of his command, but this was not because he really wished to be rid of it, he was simply worn out by the strain and he needed leave and a chance to recuperate. Archduke Karl was one of those people who, often apparently on the verge of collapse, recover remarkably fast when the strain is removed, and more than once he came back from his country estates completely restored to health much sooner than it suited his brother.

Since nothing that took place at the Hofburg was ever simple and straightforward, the problem now was how to remove this uncomfortable man without appearing to do so. Certainly he must ask for his release, he must in fact lay down his command, and the public should preferably consider him to be abandoning the patriotic cause for his own comfort. 'I only beg of you', wrote the Emperor, 'to express it in such a manner as to avoid the appearance that I had issued a command that you come hither . . .' Karl came to Vienna and lived in the Palais Kinsky which his aunt Marie-Christine bought and gave to him. To her brother, the Elector of Cologne, she wrote: 'He has remained just as he always was, unassuming, friendly, wise, only much more serious, almost sad. When you look at him you can hardly believe that this is the hero who by his ability has saved the monarchy . . .' But Franz asked for agents' reports, and was told: 'All the evidence shows . . . that the soldiers idolize him, they place the greatest trust in him and for his sake they spare themselves no exertion; it is also true that the soldiers say: "Ah, he is here, now all will be well." '

It was clearly not going to be easy to find someone to put in his place, and the incompetence of Thugut and Franz in all things military is reflected in their delusion that although he possessed the necessary personal magnetism and the ability to turn a rabble into an army, Karl was a man who could be manipulated like a puppet. A less awkward servant of the crown might, they thought for a time, be found in another brother of the Emperor's, Archduke Joseph, Palatine of Hungary. This was a man who loved his glasshouses and other hobbies and was to be of service to Hungary while acquiring no merit in the Hofburg for so doing, but his military talents were not easily detectable. And admittedly the idea was soon dropped, but the practice of using archdukes as figureheads had by no means yet been abandoned.

The new century opened. In April Napoleon overran southern Germany, pushing back the armies of Karl's incapable successor, General Kray. Crossing the Grand St. Bernard into Italy, on 14th June Napoleon defeated the Austrians at Marengo and appealed to Franz to make peace: it is not France, he declared, which is upsetting the peace of Europe, but Britain. And Britain, behind the backs of the continental Europeans, is engaged in seizing world trade and the seas for itself. This approach was skilful, because anti-British feeling was strong, and not only among admirers of Napoleon throughout Europe but among his opponents as well. This was not the familiar prejudice on the grounds that 'They pay while we fight the battles' which was silenced to some extent by the Peninsular War. Nor was it confined to indignation that Britain was master of the trade routes of the world. It was this, but also something more which late twentieth-century mankind would apply to outer space and to the ocean floor: a growing sense of moral outrage that any one nation should gain something very like exclusive rights over the high seas. Two years later Friedrich Schiller would write that England was trying to close the 'kingdom of free Amphitrite' as though it were its own house, while the author Christoph Martin Wieland would write to the Swiss historian, former tutor and friend of Archduke Johann, Johannes Müller: 'Freedom on the continent and humiliation of the haughty islanders who trumpet their "Rule Britannia" so defiantly in our ears and by their assumption of supremacy and sole command of the seas not only threaten an infinitely more oppressive and ruinous universal monarchy than that which we have to fear from Napoleon, but do in fact practise it, is, according to my innermost conviction, our most important and pressing purpose, upon which end all desires and all our strength should be brought to bear.'

'To encourage the troops', as the records have it, the army in Germany was now placed under the command of Archduke Johann, who, though of course essentially a figurehead, found himself in an unhappy situation. No more than eighteen years of age, faced with a disunited, jealous and scrapping staff, innocent of all but the most elementary military knowledge and quite without experience, he was nevertheless titular Commander-in-Chief and could not wholly deny responsibility for what lay ahead. Public opinion and posterity would associate his name with any battles to come. Archduke Johann wrote anxiously to Karl, who replied with a series of long letters crammed with advice and clearly trying as best he could to buoy up his younger brother's spirits. Whether or not even the presence of Karl himself could have helped matters is questionable, and perhaps it was as well that his reputation was not put at risk. So far, Napoleon had seen nothing to make him change his views on Austrian strategy and tactics. The War Council still planned each campaign in advance, with a tolerable eye for the terrain involved but with little regard for the mobility of the enemy—and Napoleon's armies moved much faster than standard manuals of instruction allowed for, sometimes more than twice as fast. 'On the whole, they are unaware of the value of time,' said Napoleon, and they seemed never to learn from experience. He himself kept his troops together, carried out reconnaissance at the first ray of dawn and only then made his dispositions, while the Austrians moved their forces separately over different routes, and too often assumed the French forces to be where they were not. (Later, the classic example was to be the situation at Ulm, where Mack was eagerly pursuing forces which were in process of surrounding him.) And now, after the French triumph at Marengo, came the Battle of Hohenlinden, resulting in the total defeat of the Austrian army, general demoralization and wholesale desertions. For the young Archduke it was a dreadful experience, the memory of which would never leave him. By the terms of the Treaty of Lunéville Austria lost, for the time being, its last foothold in Italy. Thugut was dismissed.

Now at last, Archduke Karl was given the supreme command.

Strangely enough, neither the dismal situation in Italy nor his illness and absence from the field of action had done anything to diminish his reputation. On the contrary, during the dark months after Hohenlinden and Lunéville the Archduke became a moral rallying point. 'In Archduke Karl,' said Princess Eleonore Liechtenstein, 'reside all the honour and good reputation which remain to us.' And August Iffland, 'Only one bond held the monarchy together, one name alone held back the explosion—Archduke Karl.' But—'This prince,' wrote the French ambassador in Vienna, Champigny, 'revered by the public, respected in Germany, held in esteem throughout the continent, was not beloved of his family—he was too big for them.'

Was the Empire on the verge of an explosion? The Archduke certainly thought so. In a memorandum to the Emperor he declared that the economy was in a worse state than that of France on the eve of the Revolution, and he diagnosed a pre-revolutionary situation which could not fail to explode sooner or later. There was certainly a prolonged crisis of public confidence in the government. While the whole of Europe lay in the grip of inflation, here there was chaos in the public administration as well. Archduke Karl, now President of the War Council with the rank of Field-Marshal, had a look round and found thousands of sacks lying about in innumerable cellars. In each sack, pushed in anyhow, there were files, documents, bills from every theatre of war. He discovered that no attempt had been made to assess the cost of the campaigns since the outbreak of war in 1794, and indeed how could there have been in view of 154,000 unpaid bills and 33,000 unsettled claims, petitions and so forth? To find any particular document was an almost impossible task. The Archduke's civil assistant Matthias von Fasbender (a native of Trier whose sudden rise to power caused intense ill-feeling among the senior officers and the aristocrats close to the throne whom he liked to keep waiting for hours in his antechamber) found a no less disastrous situation in the civil departments. Incoming files were entered in a register, but a custom had crept in whereby not merely the number and title or subject of the file were recorded, but practically the entire contents of the files were copied out as well. This alone resulted in an accumulation of more than two hundred folio volumes per annum. In the meantime the original files were kept

happily in circulation for years together, and there was no end to the
indexing and cross-indexing which accompanied their progress. The
most insignificant matter, if once it had to be brought before the
Imperial Majesty, would pass through the hands of forty-eight
persons in the War Council alone, while a summary of its contents
would need to be registered in and out, copied, etc., some twenty
times. Fasbender discovered a long-winded minute from General
Command H.Q. Lower Austria, asking for comments on a proposal
to keep a cat because mice had gained a footing in the attic of Headquarters and were nibbling at the files.

The programme of army reform would clearly take some years to
put into effect and a start was now made by abolishing life-long
service. A system of training for officers and non-commissioned
officers was also brought into force. But above all, an attempt must
be made to free the Emperor from detail and matters of low priority
—at any one time there might be up to two thousand official papers
waiting for his decision. By August of the same year the decision
was taken. The old State Council was abolished and a *Staats- und
Konferenzministerium* put in its place. Divided into three departments, Foreign Affairs, Home Affairs and War, this was the summit
of the civil service and the heads of department would report direct
to the Emperor, who, with an uncluttered desk, would be in a position to take immediate decisions. It seemed that a new era had
dawned. But there is an Austrian saying that bills should not be
totted up without consulting the innkeeper, and this scheme left
the mentality of the sovereign entirely out of account. Franz did
not want the details of administration to be kept from him; he enjoyed them because trivial problems were within his grasp. What he
hated was taking decisions, particularly on matters of policy; but
equally, he disliked delegating authority. By temperament he was the
typical middle-grade file-pusher, delaying a final decision for years,
by which time the problem had either solved itself or the ruling was
inapplicable.

Of inestimable value in relations between sovereign and people
was the Habsburg tradition of accessibility. Right down to the ex-
tinction of the monarchy anyone with a deep sense of grievance
could, and did, say '*Ich gehe zum Kaiser.*' Franz was famous for his
approachability, and anyone could go to his audiences without

regard to class or position. His air of kind, gentle concern earned him much affection, and only his senior civil servants—and perhaps not even they—realized that no single exception to a regulation was ever made throughout the reign of Franz I. The most that ever happened was that the petition would be passed on with a request for information. All things considered it was amazing that anything ever got done. There were no channels of intercommunication between the departments, and the Imperial Will was expressed with sublime disregard for previous directives and with so many qualifications that it would be a bold man who would have dared to say that he now knew what it was.

Civil servants are not bold men. An Austrian historian considered that the higher ranks in Vienna at that period contained plenty of first-rate organizational talent. But incessant petty reorganization with no basic improvement, the manner in which the Emperor would vent his fury on any convenient victim, the miserable pay and the grinding frustrations of the administrative machinery, resulted all too often in total discouragement and sullen unwillingness to take any action more hazardous than the addition of a few words to a file before it continued on its rounds. 'It is the tradition here', said a sufferer, 'that no important business is ever brought to a conclusion. Instead, it revolves in an eternal circle of lamentation, vapid experiment and ink-slinging without end.' Archduke Karl thought that it would be immensely difficult to raise the standard of the civil service 'when the educational institutions are in a state of dissolution—not one single university which could lay claim to a modest reputation. What can be expected of public servants when men are appointed to ministries who openly boast that they have read not a book nor a newspaper in thirty years?'

In the meantime, Franz had quickly become bored with his new centralized government machinery, council meetings were convened at less and less frequent intervals and his brother's brave new era, hardly begun, soon petered out.

Failure on this home ground had an effect on Archduke Karl which can easily be imagined: his health deteriorated once again, the attacks of epilepsy recurred, and at one time he was so ill that he received the last sacraments. At such moments of profound discouragement another side of his character would come to the surface.

It was a habit of his, from time to time, deliberately to withdraw into 'monastic isolation'.[1] Now he was going through a phase of increasing introversion and insecurity and was in a mood to take criticism very badly. Archduke Johann noticed that he had become touchy and all too inclined to take any adverse comment on his suggested reforms as a personal slight. Even the man who had taught him all that he knew about war, General Lindenau, was not spared. In the characters of the two brothers, the Emperor Franz and Archduke Karl, there was more than a touch of similarity.

The reluctant warrior submitted another report to the Emperor in which he urgently warned against a resumption of hostilities until such time as the country's finances were on a better footing. Archduke Karl could only think of the cost of war in terms of men and material and the strain on the economy: high prices, the growing flood of paper money (the French soldiers called the Austrians 'paper soldiers') and its evil consequences—hoarding of coinage and flight abroad—all this would soon be aggravated by the inflow of Austrian currency from the territories ceded to Napoleon. The Archduke was overruled, because as Prince Karl Schwarzenberg put it: 'The whole Ministry wanted war: the State Chancellery because in its mental poverty it saw no other way out; Finance because it was more convenient to hope for a *deus ex machina*; the Court Chancellery because its chief executive hoped and believed that he would thus best serve His Majesty's pleasure.' This is perhaps a biased view, although it is true to say that, on the whole, the government was pressing for a resumption of hostilities while the army was almost as disinclined for war as was the population as a whole, and it was the war party at court which now pressed the Emperor into joining the new coalition under the Younger Pitt, following the example of Sweden and Russia. Schwarzenberg's evident contempt shows the opinion of men of his calibre for the Emperor's closest advisers. When he sacked Thugut after the Peace of Lunéville Franz replaced him by Count Ludwig Cobenzl, a polished courtier who possessed some knowledge of the workings of political and diplomatic routine, but whose whole statesmanship, the publicist Friedrich von Gentz told William Pitt, consisted 'in the concealment of his own total nullity. He has no principles, no

[1] Manfried Rauchensteiner, *Kaiser Franz und Erzherzog Carl.*

character, and lives politically from one day to the next.' With his red hair turning white, high, broad forehead and chalk-white complexion, Cobenzl reminded people of a cat, and his presence was not made more dignified by a fat, flabby body of medium size, drained of all vitality by many years of dissipation, and a slight squint in his small, twitching, piggy eyes.

Franz I now ordered his brother to draft plans for the campaign of 1805, and General Karl Mack was quietly told to do the same, adding a general appreciation of the situation and prospects. Mack was that officer whom Napoleon had described as the most mediocre man he had ever met, inflated with presumption and conceit, over-confident, incapable and, for good measure, unlucky as well. Mack's report cast a warm, rosy light over the whole scene: the army, its training and equipment, the economy—it was all so much better than Franz had been led to suppose. Delighted at the good news, the Emperor immediately relieved his brother of his responsibilities, and handed over the task of preparation for war to Cobenzl and Mack. Franz I himself took over supreme command and Karl was packed off (this was clearly not to be the decisive area) to Italy while the figurehead over Mack was the Emperor's brother, Archduke Ferdinand of Tuscany.

Karl reported: 'The army lacks money, bread, horses, provisions and men.' Pontoons and other material needed by the engineers were also in short supply, and even boots. Many infantrymen were 'running around' inadequately clothed and without serviceable rifles. No one was interested; all eyes were on General Mack.

One of the greatest days in British history, the Battle of Trafalgar, and perhaps the most ignominious defeat of Austrian arms, at Ulm, were separated by only 24 hours, and it was an element of the ridiculous which made it so hard for Mack's officers and men to bear. Confronted, admittedly, by 200,000 well-trained and armed adversaries while his own army was only half the size and badly equipped, Mack now totally mistook the situation. While the French were advancing he thought it was a 'retrograde movement', and while he fondly believed that he was in hot pursuit of Napoleon, part of his army (23,000 men) was being quietly encircled. Archduke Karl was in Italy; a week later he threw back an attack by General Masséna at Caldiero. Archduke Johann was guarding the Tyrol. Neither of the brothers could possibly place his army in the path of Napoleon, and the road to Vienna lay open.

The scene now shifts to the capital, on a day in the early part of November 1805.

Loading up was in full swing. On the Josefsplatz over a hundred horses were assembled, many of them already harnessed to every sort and kind of cart and carriage. Bags, sacks, boxes, crates and trunks were streaming out of the Imperial Palace—the Hofburg— through the wide open doors of the riding school. The Empress's ball dresses had evidently not been forgotten, and on another wagon a number of objects were heaped up which on closer inspection turned out to be a forest of boot-trees. Carts piled high with the goods and chattels of the citizenry were rumbling down the Kärntnerstrasse, and the government had even made provision for those who were unable to make their own arrangements to send what valuables they might possess down the Danube by ship. As it turned out there was really nothing very serious to be afraid of, and among the well-to-do who spent several weeks cooped up in excruciatingly confined quarters in Budapest, many would afterwards agree that it would have been better to stay at home; at least they would not have been robbed by their neighbours.

Meanwhile by some oversight the entire contents of the arsenal had been left where it was. Where treasure is on the move, however, fable quickly joins it, and there was much talk of a box which fell from a coach as it swayed along the road to Hungary and burst open to reveal gold coins. Did Franz I, warned that Napoleon might try to rob him of his crown, really say, 'Oh well, I should still be the richest man in Europe'? He almost certainly said nothing of the kind. But whatever bullion the impoverished treasury possessed did leave for Hungary under military guard on 5th November, while priceless manuscripts and incunabula from the imperial library together with the treasure of St. Stephen's Cathedral had gone ahead to a secret destination in Hungary a week or two earlier.

Except for the incompetent Maximilian d'Este who was left in command of the garrison, the imperial family had left Vienna and so had most of the aristocracy. It was already becoming very difficult to leave the town. Horses were scarcely to be found,

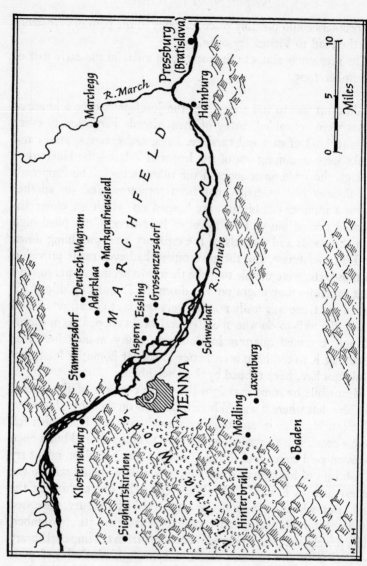

1. Vienna and its environs

coachmen demanded 200 gulden for a carriage and pair to drive to Pressburg, a boat cost 400 gulden for the trip, the roads to the east were crowded and to flee towards Moravia, to Brünn and Prague, was highly inadvisable as the countryside was full of Russian troops. In any case, the road surfaces to the north were vile, and by 8th November all horses had been requisitioned.

Napoleon was at Sieghartskirchen, the last post-chaise station west of Vienna; on 9th November Joachim Murat with the main body of troops entered St. Pölten. The decision not to defend the city had been taken long ago, but although by the night of the 11th the glow of camp fires could be seen on the hills surrounding the capital nothing of all this appeared in the newspapers. Vienna had capitulated and Napoleon had been asked to take the town under his personal protection before the public was provided with any information whatever. 'The state of ignorance and mystery is almost incredible,' wrote Dr. Henry Reeve, a young English physician. In view of the official doctrine on the purpose and function of the press, this state of affairs was, on the contrary, perfectly credible. Newspapers were there to protect the government from all tiresome opposition in the way of written criticism. Leadership of public opinion was not called for, since the primary duty of every citizen was to be calm. It followed from this that, assuming a state of unruffled *Ruhe*, submissiveness and unquestioning loyalty to the reigning house, 'it is not called for', says a memorandum on the desirability or otherwise of daily newspapers, 'that subjects be put in mind of their sense of duty with any frequency, far less daily.'

A news vacuum of this order provided Napoleon's superb propaganda machinery with ideal conditions. One of the first harbingers of defeat in the swoop upon the capital of the Habsburg empire in 1805 was the arrival from Paris of a francophile Austrian, Josef Georg Wiedemann who would turn up again, equally ominously, in 1809. Immediately he took over the editorship of the *Wiener Zeitung*, and a stream of leading articles, written or commissioned by him, poured from the presses into the hands of the Viennese who never in their lives had dreamed that journalism of this quality could exist. In proclamations and broadsheets, as well as in the pages of the *Wiener Zeitung*, the Viennese learned that the French had come as liberators. Austria's paralytic administration, absolutism, the privileges of the aristocracy, unjust forms of taxation, obsolete laws: without being too precise and without threatening the institution of monarchy or the Emperor in person, the impression was conveyed that Napoleon would bestow a constitution on the Austrians which would give them freedom. The imperial councillors, readers were assured for good measure, were all in the pay of England.

To begin with Napoleon held his army in check. Draped across the suburbs, the soldiers were forbidden to enter the walled town at night, although some did manage to gain a foothold and climb in, a fact which makes quotation from contemporary reports on the crumbling state of the fortifications superfluous. Now the march-through began, and the Viennese—showing, the invaders thought, rather indecent curiosity—hurried along to watch. In spite of general mobilization for the age-groups between 16 and 45, so many occupations were exempted that, even without the refugees from the Tyrol in their distinctive national dress, the streets would have been almost as crowded as ever. There was no finer sight in Europe at that time than Napoleon's *grenadiers à cheval* with their high caps and flashing cuirasses. All these troops, the observers saw, including the infantry, were well clothed and armed, and while the drawn swords of the cavalrymen were unpleasant symbols of armed conquest, the hunks of meat impaled on the bayonets of the infantrymen or laid upon their knapsacks spoke another language again. All day, all night and all the next day, the French army marched through Vienna, or so it seemed to Dr. Henry Reeve who failed to notice that Napoleon was playing the time-worn stage army trick. With a much smaller contingent to garrison the town than was generally supposed, the French command did all it could to preserve the illusion by marching men out at one gate and in at another, to the joy of those who soon began to recognize their faces. The same ploy was used with the Austrian prisoners of war.

All the same, to quarter and feed 34,000 men in the city, suburbs and adjoining villages was a task which was going to fall principally on the Viennese housewives. To begin with some hoped to get away with snacks such as bread and cheese on which to begin the day, but these offerings the men flung into the street to the accompaniment of indignant demands, in a variety of patois, for a decent breakfast. What the French had in mind, their hosts—no mean trenchermen themselves—soon found out: coffee, ham, sausage, roast veal, tongue, poultry, cheese, fruit, cakes and wine. The invaders, the Chief of Police told his relations the Thürheims who had fled to Budapest, were like all others of their kind: 'demanding, thieving, shameless—in short, unpleasant guests'. On the whole this was an exaggeration. In spite of the general discomfort caused by overcrowding, once the soldiers had eaten their fill and caught up on their sleep, tempers cooled and fraternization could begin. Many an officer was soon spending his evenings in some quiet middle-class drawing-room, taking part in readings from French plays and novels or joining in a duet at the piano with the daughter of the house. All things considered, no one would have thought that this hostile occupation was the first entry of a foreign power to Vienna since the time of Matthias Corvinus 300 years earlier.

Napoleon, his own crown not yet quite firmly fixed on his head, was wooing the Viennese, and with some success. His psychological warfare had something on which to build: soon after the turn of the century '*der Eipeldauer*'[1] was noticing the amount of Bonapartist talk to be heard wherever people met in public, to say nothing of what was said in their homes. And then there were the 'bakery riots'. Until the outbreak of the Napoleonic wars the bread made by the Viennese bakers was famous for its quality and also for its cheapness. By 1805, with soaring prices, the quality had long since deteriorated, and in July a sudden outbreak of rioting started in the suburb of Wieden and spread across to Mariahilf. Officialdom panicked and over-reacted, the army fired on the crowds, killing ten and wounding 200. Several hundred people were arrested and most of the men were packed off to the army, though not before 1,800 strokes of the birch and 1,300 of the cane had been distributed among them. The affair gave the government a considerable shock, though in no very salutary sense as Franz was convinced that a Jacobin plot was the cause of it all. Later, however, he did take to having samples of bread sent up to him from the nearby Michaelerplatz.

It was hardly to be expected that the bakery riots in July would

[1] The pseudonym of Joseph Richter, writer of a popular news-sheet.

be forgotten by November, and nothing could have done more to pacify the Viennese population than the strict attention which Napoleon paid to the food markets and to smooth-running delivery of supplies to the capital. How many people realized that Talleyrand was lodging in the Empress's apartments and having a good read among the government's most secret papers, or cared that he used the imperial box at the theatre? Bonaparte himself kept very much in the background, and apart from the routine army parades at Schönbrunn, took great care not to let people know where he was and what he was doing. Not even his marshals and the palace guard could always say where he had spent the night. The lights of Schönbrunn might blaze out into the night and he was not there, or the first-floor rooms might be dark although he was. Chief of Police Franz Hager was certain that he sometimes wandered about the streets of the walled town at night in disguise, doing a Harun-al-Rashid act.

When things had settled down Dr. Henry Reeve made the obligatory trip to Schönbrunn to see the ogre and found his appearance—as people almost invariably did—disappointing; to make matters worse Napoleon had shaved his head. It was more rewarding to visit Haydn at his home in a suburb to which he had retired when he left the service of Prince Esterházy. 'He calls himself a very old man of 75, but he has not at all the look of so many years.' His head and chest were troubling him, and on account of weak nerves the physican had forbidden him to compose or write, which he took very hardly. But he was in good spirits and 'spoke with rapture of England, calling it the first and best country in the world'. He told Reeve that he had composed a great deal while he was in London 'amidst good eating and drinking'. He took a delight in working on Scottish songs, and as soon as he felt up to it, 'he should write music for some words Mr. Thomson sent to him lately.'

The French had been in Vienna for a week when Reeve went to the first night of *Fidelio* at the Theater an der Wien. There was no difficulty over tickets as the audience was sparse, consisting almost entirely of French officers. But the warmth of their applause and possibly too the complimentary verses which showered down from the gallery may have consoled the composer, 'a small, dark, young-looking man wearing spectacles' who presided at the pianoforte and

1. Baroque Vienna: Schönbrunn Palace

2. Baroque Vienna: The view from the Belvedere by Canaletto

3. The last coronation of a Holy Roman Emperor: Franz II at Frankfurt am Main in 1792

4 Meeting on 4th December 1805 after the Battle of Austerlitz between Napoleon I and Franz II (I of Austria)

directed the performance himself for the half-empty house, in which the prisoners' chorus was being heard for the first time.

Reeve pondered at some length on the curious effect on public opinion of false or misleading information or none at all, provided alternately by the home government and by the conqueror. When after some delay the news of the Battle of Austerlitz reached Vienna many people dismissed the story as a fabrication: the French had *not* won a great battle, there was *no* armistice, and the prisoners brought into their neighbourhood and even into their midst were, they insisted, French soldiers dressed up in Russian rags. The general scepticism was beyond belief.

New Year's Day came, bringing 'cards and presents and almanacks and emblematical figures' into every home, to many of which the evacuees were already streaming back, adding new confusion to the disorder caused by an army engaged in reluctant preparation for withdrawal from cushy billets. Countess Lulu Thürheim, now back from Budapest, hurried off to Schwertberg, the family estate on the River Aist in Upper Austria. She trembled at the thought of what she might find, but the moated castle had hardly suffered any damage. Strange, she thought: on the whole, 'hardly have the enemy forces left our country, and already prosperity and content-ment burgeon, soon effacing all the marks of war.' It had always been the same. 'The people live only for the moment, and bestow not one thought upon the French.' And in a rare moment of objec-tive analysis: 'I have always noticed that in Austria the consequences of war are a great deal more easily forgotten than those which follow upon bad internal administration. . . . For some countries the most terrible because unseen adversary is not the stranger attacking from without but the arbitrary manner in which it is ruled.' The com-ment is worthy of Gentz.

Archduke Karl sat down and composed a letter to the Emperor. He wrote: 'Your Majesty stands alone at the conclusion of a short but frightful war. With your country devastated, your treasury empty, the honour of your arms tarnished, your credit exhausted, your reputation diminished, the prosperity of your subjects de-stroyed for many a year to come, the suffering of your peoples has rendered their love for you inconstant. You are without allies—alone at the helm, without help, without counsel in the midst of the chaos of an administration shattered by the generally prevailing desolation.' They were hardly encouraging words. At various times Karl had already written long, formal state-of-the-nation memoranda (they were more constructive than this quotation might suggest) as well as personal letters to the Emperor which give such an appalling picture of the economy and of an overblown, practically inert administration that it seems almost incredible that the Habsburg Empire was somehow to survive two more campaigns against Napoleon, state bankruptcy, and the expense—to look no further ahead— of the Congress of Vienna.

The climax of 1805 was the resounding victory for Napoleon at the Battle of Austerlitz in which the allies engaged at the insistence of the Czar before the arrival of reinforcements. For Austria this marked the climax of a series of defeats. The peace treaty of Pressburg confirmed the loss of Austria's Italian possessions, cut off the Vorarlberg and Tyrol from the rest of Austria, relinquished Salzburg to Bavaria and imposed 40 million gulden in war damages. Such a treaty, striking directly into the heart of Austria, was not—as Talleyrand well knew—likely to be taken lying down.

On 16th January, 1806, Austria's lawful ruler returned to his capital. The crowds greeted him with demonstrations of enthusiasm and many tears were shed, whether by the paid cheer- and tear-leaders as well as by those they led no one could quite say for certain. The object of so much emotion was himself much affected and Mass was ordered to be said annually in St. Stephen's Cathedral in commemoration of the occasion. Of Archduke Karl's warning, 'Be not misled by demonstrations of joy at Your entry on the part of the inhabitants of Vienna, demonstrations purchased, besought and compelled by frivolous persons, and thus overlook the prevailing mourning, the misery and distress of Your provinces,' he took no notice. Once home Franz sacked all his ministers, doing it in a way that was peculiarly his own. Colloredo was simply dismissed in a note containing a few ill-chosen words; the Emperor's mentor and friend for 33 years commented with some justice that his treatment by the Emperor was 'unexampled'. Cobenzl was put through a different process, one of exclusion from the imperial presence to the accompaniment of all those little cruelties which all-powerful personages know how to dispense, until even the Empress protested.

Napoleon at the Gates

Now at last a man came on the scene who was worthy of high office: Count Philipp Stadion. Latterly Ambassador to St. Petersburg, he had a well-stocked, liberal mind and an honest character. Although the Emperor had no sympathy for the wave of romantic patriotism which was now beginning to stream through the German lands, a movement of both intellectual and emotional power which would transform the resistance to Napoleon in central Europe, in choosing Stadion he had found the man of the hour. Unfortunately he made at the same time two other appointments: Baron Anton Baldacci and the singularly unsavoury Baron Johann Kutschera, both court toadies on the truly classical pattern. From now on they would form the nucleus of the anti-Karl faction and their influence would do much to widen the distance between the Emperor and his brother. And soon, they were able to confirm the Emperor's worst suspicions by carrying to him a rumour which must have sent a stab of fear through his heart: Napoleon, it was said, had offered the Austrian imperial crown to the Archduke Karl.

3

A New Will to Resist:
the Viennese under Siege

It is easy to spot a change of mood; much more difficult to discover its cause. Between 1806 and 1809 a fresh wind swept through Europe and it carried away the war-weariness, the apathy caused by a feeling of helplessness in the face of an apparently invincible conqueror at the summit of his power. The romantic movement spreading through all the German-speaking countries was a vital element, though it was not the whole story, in a new spirit of resistance to Napoleon, new in that this resistance now became a popular cause. No longer was liberation to be expected of armies, a large proportion of whose manpower consisted of the lowest social class—unemployed agricultural and the slowly developing industrial proletariat. The whole nation must rise against him. It would not be true to say that the Viennese, schooled in feudal-style loyalty, knew nothing of patriotism. In 1798, the French representative Count Bernadotte had hoisted his country's flag on his house in the Wallnerstrasse, and the near-riot which resulted surprised both him and the authorities who had not been informed of his intention. But since then there had been a great change in popular feeling. As for the Tyrolese with their traditional exemption from military service outside the Tyrol and its corollary, their duty to fight in defence of their home territory, their patriotic fervour had caused the Austrian government discomfort before now and would do again. But in the country as a whole, as well as in the capital, other factors played their part in developing the will to resist.

A New Will to Resist: the Viennese under Siege

The assumption by Franz of the title Emperor of Austria was perhaps a minor contributory factor, but social changes were decisive: the gradual, late, emergence of a middle class, and the general rise in literacy, so that the writings of Friedrich von Gentz, of Archduke Johann's friend Baron Josef von Hormayr, and of a Swabian recruit to the Austrian civil service named Johann Armbruster, to say nothing of the leader of the young romantic movement, Friedrich von Schlegel and his friends, now reached a greatly expanded readership. Not that the newspapers and periodicals were in any way adequate to their task. Since the middle of the last century newspapers had been founded in some of the main towns of the Empire—sixteen in all—which, where hard news and comments were concerned, simply printed what they were sent. In Vienna there was nothing but the *Wiener Zeitung* which still survives today, and the delightful '*Eipeldauer*', the pseudonym of a writer as talented as he was prolific called Josef Richter whose *Letters to his cousin in Kagran* (a village beyond the Danube) kept the Viennese amused for many years. '*Der Eipeldauer*' kept firmly to the parish pump, while the *Wiener Zeitung*, for lack of any leader-writer with the authority or courage to say what he thought, consisted for years together of extracts from foreign newspapers, even—and most of all—from Napoleon's own superb *Moniteur*. That such a futile and even harmful practice must yield to some more positive editorial policy was realized in government circles at least as early as 1804, but state control was all too clearly reflecting disunity at the heart of the state itself, and traces of this ambivalent attitude never quite left the pages of the *Wiener Zeitung* at any time during the Napoleonic wars. Even when constructive attempts were at last being made to counteract the *Moniteur*'s anti-Austrian propaganda, any really energetic language directed against France was suppressed by the censor. The comparatively liberal Stadion himself was contemptuous of the new fashion of reading periodicals, and he consequently found himself in the same dilemma as his over-anxious Emperor: how to arouse the patriotism of the public, how to prepare them for the next, perhaps decisive war against Napoleon, without allowing the idea to enter their minds that, since this was apparently not only the Emperor's war but theirs too, some constitutional rights might accrue to them as a result. For popular enthusiasm, Franz I never doubted for a moment, was of its essence revolutionary. And so before and after each campaign attempts were made—in every case much too late—to make hearts beat higher in the hope that some of this emotion would seep down into the class which, not necessarily illiterate but seldom reading, must bear the major burden of war both in money and in blood.

No fresh wind was blowing through the Hofburg—or, as the case might be, through Schönbrunn. Apocalyptic visions, doom-laden nightmares pursued the senior servants of the Emperor, in particular the Finance Ministers who followed one another in fairly rapid succession. Each one of them prophesied state bankruptcy and the end of the monarchy: in the summer of 1807 Baldacci saw the monarchy teetering on the edge of the bottomless pit, and ten years later he would say that the era from 1805 to 1810 was the worst that he had ever experienced; during those five years state expenditure rose by about 150 per cent. And yet, bottomless pit or no, the winter season of 1807–1808 was among the most brilliant that its participants ever remembered, not least because of the descent on Vienna of Germaine de Staël.

Considering the enormous effort which went into censorship of the written word, the trouble taken to protect the Austrians from any stimulus from outside which might make their pulses beat faster and to spare Napoleon undue provocation, the anti-Napoleon propaganda one-man-band Madame de Staël was a visitor whose presence made censorship ridiculous, whose talk no agent could place on record. She swamped the drawing-rooms with her *esprit*, with her torrential monologues, asking questions but never listening to the answers. Her triumph was unexampled: 'l'on s'écrasait pour la voir,' said Franz Graeffer, secretary to Louis Bonaparte, but she was liable to leave her listeners exhausted and nursing nervous headaches. Yet at lunch in a private house she could be quite different. Then, she would drop her noisy, aggressive and heavily flirtatious mannerisms and her hearers were held both by her rare intelligence and by the soft, musical tone of her voice. But every diarist in Vienna struggled to find words to describe Madame de Staël's singularly unfortunate dramatic performances. These she held in the town houses of aristocrats such as the Liechtensteins. In her renderings of 'Agar dans le désert' or 'Geneviève de Brabant' her style of acting did nothing to compensate for the monotony of the endless flow of mediocre verse. Her 'enormous contours' most scantily covered, she crawled about the stage on all fours, her scarlet face partly concealed by thick black tresses through which two piercing eyes were visible, not unlike those of a wild animal. Her audiences marvelled that so intelligent a woman should be so incapable of assessing her own talents and qualities at their true worth. Germaine de Staël was a rather heavily built woman at that time not in her first youth; her features were sensual and a trifle coarse. She dressed with the evident intention of displaying with generosity and to the best advantage a beauty which was not there and nowhere less so than in Vienna where standards were of the highest. With tears in her eyes she told Princess Liechtenstein of her horror at the thought of death. 'Ah, when I look upon these arms, these breasts at the sight of which every eye is suffused with lust, and when I consider that this splendour must one day serve as food for disgusting reptiles, a cold shudder passes through me, compounded of horror and pity.' Princess Liechtenstein, devout mother of a large family, felt sorry for her.

She continued to dazzle the drawing-rooms so long as she kept to her role of goddess of the mind, but Madame de Staël's eye now fell upon a Liechtenstein cousin, Prince Louis, and soon her feelings for him grew into a seething passion. Her blandishments embarrassed him dreadfully, not only because he was in love with a widowed baroness, but also because his French was inadequate—a surprising social disadvantage at a time when members of the aristocracy seldom spoke German except to their servants. Perhaps he was simply inarticulate. Determined to stake all, win or lose, Germaine sent Prince Louis, or Alois, a note which, as she appeared to wish to discuss something with him, he was obliged to answer in person. She received him in négligé with languishing looks but was gently told that he was in love with someone else. Wildly emotional in all things, poor Madame de Staël was overcome by an attack of the vapours of alarming proportions: tears, palpitations and symptoms of asphyxiation, culminating in a faint. The cause of her distress kept his head, placed her ample form carefully on the chaise-longue, rang for an attendant and left.

Before long, Germaine de Staël managed to transfer her affection to Count Moritz O'Donnell, and this astonished the drawing-rooms yet again: how hungry must she be for love to offer her heart to such a boring, materialistic old boot as O'Donnell? The helplessness of this *femme supérieure* of European reputation in her private affairs is rather touching, and it speaks for many of the leaders of Vienna society that they felt this; they respected and remained fascinated by her intellectual power, even while pouring oceans of sarcasm and ridicule over her dramatic efforts.

In the arousal of patriotic feeling and resistance to Napoleonic propaganda Germaine de Staël played her part; in the city which was then a magnet for foreigners she provided a season with its sensation. But another woman, equally an implacable enemy of Napoleon, had now come on the scene. She would become the leader of the war party and she would reign over the Congress of Vienna: Franz's third Empress.

Luigia d'Este had for her hostility towards Napoleon the best of personal reasons. Her parents, Archduke Ferdinand and Maria Beatrix d'Este, had been driven from Milan as the result of Bonaparte's sweep through northern Italy in 1796 and since then were living in Wiener-Neustadt. Brought up in obscurity as the youngest of a large family, the distance between Wiener-Neustadt and Vienna must, in a sense, have seemed so insuperable that the odds were not worth calculating. And yet only four months after the death of the Empress Marie-Thérèse Franz was engaged to her, and on 6th January, 1808, they were married. That he liked her there can be no doubt because no dynastic considerations were involved, and at first all went well between them.

There is a portrait of the Empress Maria Ludovica, as she was now called, which reminds one irresistibly of a tadpole. It is a rather waif-like figure, too small and slight to provide an adequate show-case for crown jewels, and no one tells us that she was beautiful. Describing the entry of the imperial family at a *Redoute*, Caroline Pichler tells how the Empress, on the arm of Archduke Karl, outshone her step-daughter the Archduchess Marie-Louise, but then this was no very impressive feat. The picture drawn by some historians of an implacable warmonger is also in its way unattractive, but this view is only possible if a one-sided impression of Archduke Karl is given also: the peace-loving martyr being hounded into war by a harridan with no thought for the misery that war brings with it or consideration for the economy and the security of the crown. Her contemporaries saw her quite differently.

Maria Ludovica may well have been one of the best-loved consorts ever to trundle to and fro between the Hofburg and Schönbrunn; loved, it should be added, not so much by her husband as by court and nobility, and if her education was no better or worse than was usual among the aristocracy at that time, she made good use of it. Her greatly superior intelligence put the Emperor out of countenance, as he objected not so much to clever women as to intellectual gifts as such. This well-known prejudice of his is perfectly summarized in an address which he made to the dons at the University of Ljubljana: 'I have no need of scholars, but of honest, upright citizens. It is incumbent upon you to educate youth towards this end. Whoever serves me, must teach what I command. If he be unable to do this or if he propagate new ideas, he shall go; if not, I shall remove him.' He soon came to feel that his new consort was a bit beyond him. Within the family she was in all other respects a blessing, as she was constantly preoccupied with her royal step-children, particularly with Ferdinand, the mentally retarded heir to the throne. If, however, she dabbled more freely in affairs of state than was good either for herself or them, this was largely the result of her dismay over the collection of irresolute weathercocks to whose advice Franz I listened by turn. Clemens Metternich, the man who, to the Austrian Establishment an outsider, would come to dominate the Emperor and with him the Empire, and whose will would sway events throughout the Continent, was already standing in the wings but his cue had not yet been spoken. In the meantime, 'Maria Ludovica and Stadion', wrote an observer in 1809, 'are the only people at the summit of the state who possess a clear will and a soul of fire. She is in despair because she is unable to bring her wavering husband and Archduke Karl, all these half-hearted creatures around her who yet hold the destiny of the Empire in their hands, to share her conviction . . . it grieves her to observe that her husband is not the Emperor but only so in name.' To Archduke Johann who would always be a close confidant, she wrote: 'Ah, would I were a man, to serve the State . . . I confess', she said, referring to Franz I, 'it pains me to observe the way he tarries forever behind the army like any baggage porter.'

Vienna was now standing on the brink of a major ordeal. Until now the sounds of battle had been remote, all the more so for the lack of news and the air of studied unconcern under which those in authority concealed their profound anxiety over the future. Seen from the Kahlenberg, or if it had been possible, from the air, the town looked very much as it had for well over a century and as it would continue to look until 1857. Vienna lay like a great starfish, its arrowhead-shaped bastions pointing out into the surrounding Glacis, the defensive ring, 1,900 feet across, as wide as the range of a late seventeenth-century cannon.

Now, when so few of those palaces are left which the great architects of the late seventeenth and early eighteenth centuries, Fischer von Erlach the elder and younger, Lukas von Hildebrandt and others, built along the outer rim of the Glacis, it is not easy to visualize the splendour in which the capital of the Empire lay, surrounded, as was the person of the monarch, by names which were the jewels in his crown: Schwarzenberg, Schönborn-Batthyány Trautsohn, Auersperg, Harrach, Kinsky, Liechtenstein. And the patch of grass which the survivors may still possess, what consolation is this for the gardens on which speculative building so soon encroached? The greater part of this defensive belt upon which nothing was allowed to be built consisted of meadows, lanes and poplar-lined avenues, while the noxious River Wien flowed between the Karlskirche and the city walls. Further down to the south-east a 'flea market' offered the poorest sector of the population all sorts of second-hand goods, particularly clothes, and the lowest prostitutes were to be found after sundown near the walls, but well clear of the gates. The impression given by contemporary artists, who, of course, always exaggerated distances, is of a kind of vast no-man's-land separating the walled city from the encircling palaces, and all the villages at their backs. The scene is often shown relatively empty of people, apart from a picturesque hay wagon or two. The truth must have been quite otherwise, and the traffic on the main roads—through the Kärntnertor (Carinthian Gate) and along the present Wiedner Hauptstrasse, or through Mariahilf to Schönbrunn, will have been heavy. Mostly on foot, there were thousands whose business brought them daily into the city; not only the hewers of wood and drawers of water—rising rents were consistently pushing people with fixed incomes out into the suburbs. And public transport was increasingly in demand. Only a few years later we read of a coach plying every hour and a half between the White Swan Inn on the Neue Markt where Germaine de Staël stayed, and Dornbach. On Sundays it left almost hourly from 8 a.m. to 10 p.m. A coach ran an hourly service to Hietzing from 7 a.m. to 7 p.m., and there were services to Meidling, Unter St. Veit, Hütteldorf and Schönbrunn, and further out to Mödling, Neu-waldegg or Baden.

Some 75 carriages arriving at the White Swan Inn every day and an equal number leaving, with all the loading and unloading, the bustle and shouting which this involved: that was what the Neue Markt was like in those days as opposed to the somnolent peace which many paintings suggest. All the same, the Glacis did form a psychological barrier which in winter became almost insuperable. Caroline Pichler whose quiet drawing-room, in spite of her restricted income (her husband served in the forestry department) and the very modest refreshments handed round, drew every writer and every visitor from abroad with intellectual interests across the Glacis to her suburban villa, remembered: 'We spent the winter almost without social life. For if even now most inhabitants of the inner town shun the way to the suburbs, and for many the Glacis is an untraversable ocean to whose tempests and perils they scarcely dare expose themselves in wintertime . . . it is not difficult to imagine how it was more than 40 years ago.'

On the circumference of Vienna, beyond the *Linie*, the outer town wall where the Gürtel now runs, little beauty was to be seen, as it was here that the new proletariat was struggling to gain a footing against all the efforts of the authorities to prevent it. Between the beginning of the Napoleonic era and 1805 the population of Vienna rose from 215,000 to about 240,000, but it dropped during the wars of 1805 and 1809 to 225,000, then drew ahead once more. The increase was entirely due to immigration, as there was a strong deficit in the birthrate which in its fluctuations reflected the Emperor's policy on housing and marriage. The French émigrés presented a problem for a time, but it was then decided to expel them all, beginning with the flocks of tutors and governesses. The working-class immigrants from Bohemia, Galicia or the Bukovina were a source of anxiety for a very similar reason: they palpably felt no loyalty towards the House of Habsburg or the country. At the same time, such traditions as they might have possessed they appeared to have lost on the road to Vienna, where they could hope for little better than a life on or below the subsistence level in a shack or hovel on the outskirts of Favoriten, Wieden, Mariahilf and the rest. The government, and Franz I himself, approved of industrial development, yet no one—here the Austrians were certainly not alone —had any understanding of the problems involved. For no less than thirty years the rise in the population of Vienna was accompanied by a running battle to prevent the construction of houses for them to live in. But this would not have been Vienna if there had been no loopholes. In 1790 Vienna counted 6,159 houses, but by 1820 there were 7,540 in spite of determined efforts to prevent building. Among the councillors there was, however, much difference of opinion, and Count Zinzendorf said that it was particularly cruel to prevent small flats and cottages being built. To allow speculation in housing to run riot, he added, was certainly one way of keeping the population down. Zinzendorf, Archduke Karl and Count Kolowrat considered Franz's prohibitions on marriage even more oppressive, in fact immoral, and they were able to persuade him—this was in the early years of his reign—gradually to relax them. Even then, ordinary working men had to apply to the local town hall for permission to marry, and even long after the end of the Napoleonic wars the only classes allowed to marry without permission were the nobility, civil servants, lawyers, landowners, householders, master craftsmen and manufacturers.

Within the walled town, overcrowding had been the normal state of affairs since the Middle Ages, and foreigners were always amazed at the crush in the streets, where on any normal day it seemed as though the entire population was on its way to or from some major public spectacle. The Kärntnerstrasse remained a notorious bottleneck until it was widened in 1894. 'At every hour,' a traveller noticed, 'indeed one might say at every minute of the day, this street is so filled with people and with carts and wagons, that one might believe all to be streaming home from a religious service.

We became truly dizzy at the sight of such a scene.' 'Good Catholics', wrote another visitor with rather heavy humour just before the widening took place, 'require themselves to be administered, either at St. Stephen's Cathedral or by the Augustinians, with the holy sacraments for the dying before attempting its passage. In order that the requisite density for a major town be maintained, a number of ironmongers' shops are accommodated in the street, in front of which freight wagons stand throughout the day, thus causing the desired disturbance to the vehicle traffic. Each year when the entry of the Mariazell pilgrims takes place, this important thoroughfare is closed entirely.' Strangers always wondered why it was that so many people were not going about their business but merely milling around or propping up the walls. 'Is it some great feast of the Catholic Church?' asked a German Protestant, noticing that thousands were standing about doing nothing, while upon every window-sill elbows were resting. What, it was an ordinary working day? 'In my country such a thing would not be possible.' In spite of the harsh working conditions of the time, and perhaps partly because of them, the Viennese were certainly a great race of spectators. But as we shall see later, on public holidays the town was caught up in a quite different momentum, and on such an occasion Princess Colloredo and some of her friends extracted themselves with difficulty and not before their delicate muslin dresses had been half torn from their backs.

This was a demoralizing time and it was to become more so. The immemorial contrast between the fabulous wealth of the ruling class and the poverty of the labourers, with a modestly prosperous artisan or trading class in between, was no longer characteristic. With constantly rising prices there was easy money about for traders, and yet destitution existed of a kind never experienced before. Napoleon's Continental embargo of 1806, which cut off the centre of Europe from British and French competition, brought prosperity to the Viennese manufacturers of luxury goods, and this was a factor in the development of the Viennese bourgeoisie. They were good times for butchers and millers, while—owing to a persistent shortage of horses—for anyone who could hire out transport a golden age had dawned. Millions were to be earned by men who were resourceful enough to supply the armies with what they needed. Horses, harness, boots, cloth, as well as arms, food and forage: when a new campaign loomed all these things and much else were needed, and yet not only the means of communication and transport, but the way in which it was organized, had altered very little for centuries. By road and water, over great distances and in all weathers, the necessary goods had to be drawn to the right place at the right time, often with no security for the supplier other than the reputation of the dealer. And considering the qualities called for—this was by no means simply a matter of cornering goods in short supply but involved immense energy, determination, precise knowledge of conditions in remote corners of the Continent and genius in discovering the right contacts—these 'profiteers' probably earned their money.

One of these men was Andreas von Fellner, 'Principal Supplier and Commissioner to the Army, Factotum of the Directory of Military Economy'. He built up a network, spread out with a dowser's instinct for future political developments, in which thousands of dealers, agents, corn brokers and so on between Northern Russia, Persia and Naples, in Poland, Bessarabia and Italy, sent convoys rumbling along the lanes which were often preferred to the main roads. (Remembering those sacks of 154,000 bills it is preferable not to ask how many primary producers and carters were left unpaid.) Fellner himself was given a barony in 1801 which will certainly have staved off, or at least reduced, a settlement of the government's debts to him. Now totally forgotten, for a brief period he was the most celebrated merchant in the Empire, owning castles, estates, factories and depots. He died bankrupt in 1819. Like his younger contemporary Josef Freiherr von Dietrich and the better-remembered Baron Braun, he lived on a royal scale at a distance infinitely removed from his beginnings as the son of a peasant in the district of Sopron. Transport was also the road to wealth of Josef von Dietrich. His wealth and his usefulness to the state reached its apex in 1809, when flood waters carried by the Danube and all its tributaries, by destroying bridges and making fords unusable, placed an unusually heavy burden on transport of supplies of every kind. They would also play a decisive part in the battles of Aspern and Wagram.

A New Will to Resist: the Viennese under Siege

How did the Austrians come to fight these two successive battles almost under the walls of Vienna?

During the winter of 1806–1807 Archduke Karl's reasons for wishing to avoid involvement in hostilities were those which he always put forward: the army was not ready, he saw no prospect of sufficiently strong forces being put into the field to bring about a decisive defeat of the French, and there was no money. To begin with the Archduke and the Chancellor Count Stadion were largely of one mind, and it was this factor which made possible such army reforms as did take place. But they came very near to quarrelling over whether Austria should come in on the side of Russia and Prussia. The next twelve months brought what appeared to be a shift in the fortunes of the enemy. The French army in Spain was seriously weakened by the forces of the Duke of Wellington and by constant harassment at the hands of the local population. In Napoleon's absence from Paris, the question of the succession in the event of his death in action or by assassination was under urgent consideration by the newly reconciled enemies, Talleyrand and Fouché, and a leak caused pandemonium among those who were on the inner information circuit, leading to Napoleon's break with Talleyrand. Finally, among the central European states a new mood was abroad which combined romantic patriotism with bellicosity. All these factors convinced the war party in Vienna that the time to reopen hostilities, if necessary alone, was at hand. Now even Karl agreed; he had in fact reached the conclusion as early as the summer of 1808 that war was inevitable. His change of mind at last put an end to the belief held in some quarters that he was pro-French at heart and that on his staff at least one senior officer was in the pay of Napoleon. So convinced was the Prussian Minister in Vienna, Finkenstein, of the truth of this, that he asked for 10,000 gulden to buy off the chief suspect; additional funds to be distributed among anti-war members of Karl's entourage would, he thought, be money well laid out.

Who was this alleged French agent at the heart of the War Council, who as Chief of Staff and as a personal friend was so close to the Generalissimo that Russian diplomats called him his 'evil genius' and the Empress Maria Ludovica never ceased to lament his influence over the Archduke?

A New Will to Resist: the Viennese under Siege

Lieutenant-Field-Marshal Count Philip Grünne's connection with the Archduke began, in the capacity of military instructor, as far back as the time when he went to live with his aunt and uncle in Brussels. Although at that time the association was brief, it was resumed later, and all efforts by the opposing camp in Vienna to shift Grünne were resisted adamantly by the Archduke. When Grünne retired after the Battle of Wagram, Karl appointed him to his own household where he remained as long as the Archduke lived. That Grünne was actually in the pay of the French has neither been proved nor disproved. The French Ambassador to the Hofburg, Comte Antoine Andréossy did not, so he wrote to Talleyrand, believe the story and nor, evidently, did Archduke Johann who held a very high opinion of Grünne's character. It is possible that more may yet come to be known about Grünne's influence over the thought and actions of Archduke Karl. That he dominated him is possible: the virulence of the hostility which his privileged status called up at Court is a measure of it. Worn down by the in-fighting among his senior staff officers Karl tried, twice, to press him upon the Emperor, who rejected the suggestion in terms which clearly shook the Archduke. Franz I could be very crude. But if the question of whether Grünne was actively working for the enemy and was using his influence over Archduke Karl to muzzle the Austrian resistance to Napoleon may be categorized as unproven and on the whole unlikely, the consensus of opinion is that there *were* men both in the Archduke's camp and at Court who were working for the French, and that a clue to their contacts can be deduced from the movements of Napoleon's celebrated spy, Schulmeister.

Grünne had a rival in Major-General Mayer von Heldensfeld. Mayer had access to the Emperor's ear through a Private Secretary, Jakob Szvetics, who is worth mentioning for the light that he throws on the Emperor's tendency to appoint men to his household who, as Archduke Johann said in this case, were 'repulsive to all decent-minded people'. At one time under suspicion of taking bribes, Szvetics spared no efforts to prove his loyalty through willingness to carry out any mission however delicate (a euphemism for spying on his superiors) and he soon found a promising field of research in Freemasonry. The country, he maintained, must be thoroughly cleansed not only of Freemasons and Illuminati—this

5. The Theater an der Wien. Here Beethoven conducted the first performance of *Fidelio*

6. Franz I, Emperor of Austria, his second wife Marie Therese and their children, at Laxenburg, 1807

7. Empress Maria Ludovica, third wife of Franz I, leader of the war party against Napoleon (before her marriage)

8. Archduke Johann

went without saying—but of foreigners. His idea that Austria of all countries should be purged of its foreign element ought to have aroused little attention apart from mild hilarity: Eugen of Savoy, Lacy, Browne, Wallenstein come to mind; nevertheless, Szvetics had hit on one of the most common of human emotions, and he capitalized on it. Worse, Szvetics poured suspicion of Archduke Karl into the Emperor's ear, and in this he was to be ably seconded by Franz's Adjutant-General Lieutenant-Field-Marshal Johann von Kutschera, who received special instructions to spy on the Archduke.

The enmity between Mayer and Grünne was now almost violent in its intensity and it coloured all the preparations for war, which, after a nocturnal meeting on 23rd December, 1808, at the bedside of the temporarily indisposed Stadion, advanced to an active stage. A major contribution to the debate must not be overlooked: it was made by Metternich. As Ambassador in Paris, his estimate of the French war potential and of the political situation inevitably carried great weight at the Hofburg. The great twentieth-century Austrian historian Heinrich Ritter von Srbik believed that Metternich seriously underestimated Napoleon's strength at that stage, and that there is no denying his responsibility for the war of 1809, which, said Srbik, was entered upon against the better judgement of Archduke Karl. Inconsistencies in accounts of the Archduke's state of mind are apparent: did he want war or did he not? Knowing as we do his ideas on the general situation, it is a reasonable assumption that from an earlier opinion that war was undesirable but inevitable, in view of Napoleon's difficulties against the British and Spanish forces in Spain, he had now swung round to the view that the moment was propitious. He never forgave Metternich for the part which he played at this crucial juncture, and it can be said with some safety that this—subsequent corrections of the record by Metternich himself notwithstanding—was the first major intervention in policy by the man who was to play such a dominant role in the shaping of Europe.

Even so, the decision to strike in the spring of 1809 was not easily arrived at. The Emperor's military advisers were in favour, while he himself was against it, and Archduke Karl was now for it but his advisers were not, with the exception of General Mayer von Heldensfeld. Here Archduke Karl was clearly not of one mind with

Grünne. Nothing could better illustrate the atmosphere of intrigue in which Archduke Karl had to live than this: at the Emperor's command, General Mayer had to write a deposition showing reasons why his own commanding officer, Archduke Karl, should be relieved of his post. Mayer's sense of loyalty may have been strained; this was a job which Count Grünne would never have accepted as he was certainly not disloyal to Karl—he never, for example, discussed the Archduke's physical disability with anyone. Mayer evidently did not relish his task, and whether it was that he suffered pangs of conscience which gnawed at his nerves, or whether the strain of his feud with Grünne was responsible, it was reported that he had been babbling about General Staff plans in his cups, and he was immediately posted to an obscure garrison at Brod on the River Save. It is quite possible that he had done nothing of the kind, but the struggle for power between the two men had now ended in a victory for Grünne. All the same, Mayer's disgrace created an unfavourable impression, and shares on the stock exchange dropped sharply in consequence.

The Emperor could hardly have it both ways. All the endless bickering, the intrigues, the incessant attempts to undermine Karl's position, to drive him even out of the War Council, had to be put on one side, at any rate for the moment. Franz I appointed him Supreme Commander of all the armies in Germany, Italy, and Poland, of all defensive localities and all branches of the military administration. He was now invested with powers such as no servant of the House of Habsburg had possessed since the days of Wallenstein, not even Prince Eugen of Savoy. And yet a counterweight was there: an opponent, Count Karl Zichy, was made Minister for War.

Mobilization was in full swing, and now, in complete contrast with 1805, the general public was in a state of mind bordering on elation. Men were flocking to the colours. In Vienna the bustle, the uniforms, the marching in, the marching out: 'You ought to have seen the consecration of the banners in St. Stephen's Cathedral on 9th March, when the Empress herself knocked in the nails and then accompanied the colours on foot. On such days mothers, wives, loved ones, sisters, from all classes of the population, lined the streets and walls of the town in showers of rain and snow, watching their menfolk march off with gay courage. . . . From the beautiful Empress who on these occasions appeared on foot on the city walls, to the least kitchenmaid, all were touched to the heart to see the territorials march away.'[1]

The regular troops had been set in motion on 25th February, and by 9th April the main army was standing in Upper Austria: on the banks of the River Inn, on the frontier with Bavaria not counting artillery and sappers, about 171,000 men. Archduke Karl left Vienna on 6th April after issuing his celebrated Order of the Day: 'The freedom of Europe has taken refuge beneath your banners . . .'

Napoleon founded his fortunes—the Rothschilds learnt from his example—on swift transmission of news. On 22nd January he had dashed back to Paris, both because wind of fresh speculation as to his successor had reached him and because he heard that the Austrians were mobilizing. At 8 p.m. on the evening of 12th April a signal, flashed stage by stage, reached the Tuileries. Napoleon had already gone to bed and had to be woken. Archduke Karl had crossed the Inn.

At this juncture the French forces were split into two sections, with Massena and Oudinot near Augsburg, and Davout near Nürnberg. If Karl had attacked at once he might have rolled up the two flanks one after the other, and the events to come would have taken a very different turn. Bad weather, inadequate victualling, overhasty mobilization—Karl hesitated, and now Napoleon himself was facing him, his generals' tactical errors corrected. The Archduke made up his mind, and the decision he made is surprising in that he had so often advised against an attack when insufficient resources were available to give a reasonable chance of a decisive victory. Detaching the units under Archduke Ludwig, the Emperor's youngest brother, and Lieutenant-Field-Marshal Hiller, he marched them off in a westerly direction to prevent a join-up between Davout and the Bavarian army, and in case Davout should move towards Abensberg and Rohr the remainder went off to the north.

The news that the Tyrolean peasant leader Andreas Hofer with his men and a regiment of the imperial troops had marched into Innsbruck reached Franz I and Stadion at the Emperor's head-

[1] J. F. Reichhardt.

quarters at Schärding,[1] but this historic victory was only of marginal significance for the main issue. Archduke Karl had divided his army, and on hearing this Napoleon was thunderstruck. 'Now they are in my hands!' he cried. 'That army is lost—in a month we are in Vienna!'

He was better than his word. The main Austrian army was thrown across the Danube near Regensburg; the remainder presented no serious problem. The non-commissioned officers were unused to the new methods of communication, the men were not physically fit and were exhausted by long marches.[2] The end of the pitiful story: seven generals killed, 44,700 officers and men killed and wounded—a quarter of the whole army. Stadion, when the news reached Schärding, fainted.

The reaction of the Supreme Commander shows up a side of his character which recurs throughout his career. Perhaps the shock of defeat, even more the shock at so much bloodshed, threw him into one of his moods of deep depression and led him to write an appeal for peace in terms of exaggerated respect and humility which were inappropriate coming from the Austrian Supreme Commander and brother of the Emperor. It was a letter which damaged him in the eyes of his contemporaries and of posterity. Napoleon was evidently struck by the contrast in tone between the Order of the Day and this letter, because he said: 'These people are as puffed up in good fortune as they are despicable in misfortune.' The letter was not answered. But at the same time Napoleon himself now made a great mistake: he failed to follow up his victory and allowed Archduke Karl's army to escape. While Hiller made a dash for Vienna along the southern route, his rear protected from the French who were on his heels by a series of brilliant skirmishes carried out by General Radetzky, Archduke Karl's army made its way down through Bohemia into Austria where it came logically to rest on the historic battlefield east of Vienna, on the left bank of the Danube.

Predictably, a storm of vituperation and calls for his dismissal broke around the Archduke's head. They were mostly from 'political' personalities: Stadion, the Empress, and Baldacci, with the odious Szvetics agitating in the background. His letter to the Emperor in

[1] On the River Inn opposite Passau.
[2] The extraordinary mobility of the French troops, in emergency up to 60 kilometres per day while the Austrians averaged 12 to 13, also played its part.

which he describes public opinion in Hungary where people are wondering how long His Majesty will tolerate that pair, Archduke Karl and Grünne, who will most certainly lose him his crown, is a most unsavoury document, and Franz I evidently saw nothing unbecoming in allowing his secretary to write in such a way about his brother. But only a madman would have dismissed Karl at this juncture.

This time Vienna was to be defended. The gates were being hastily barricaded with wooden beams and planks, and entry was only permitted by ladder at the eastern side near the Rothenturm; this was always looked upon as the Achilles heel of the defence system. The imperial family had left with the exception of Maximilian d'Este, and most of the nobility had gone too, unless they had responsibilities which kept them there. Very largely, the Viennese were now on their own. It was a long time since they had withstood a siege, all of 126 years, and many must have wondered, not only what they were in for, but what effect inevitable tribulation would have on the minds and characters of a people said to have 'no profound thoughts, no long griefs, but rather a jovial ease, sufficiently voluptuous to attract the joys of life, to prefer them even to ambition, to money, to that national vanity which is a caricature of patriotism'.

In spite of its walls, bastions, courtines and the rest of it, Vienna was no longer a fortress in any sense which had much meaning in 1809, and the thickly populated outer districts could not possibly be either defended or abandoned. The garrison of anything up to 50,000 men was now, of course, partly on active service, but there remained 16,000 infantry of the line, yeomanry, *Landsturm* (rather similar to a home guard), the *Bürgermiliz* (burghers' militia), and finally about one thousand enrolled students and members of the Academy of Fine Arts. Among the former was Franz Grillparzer. Amidst this assortment of semi-trained and wholly untrained men now scrambling into uniforms or, if they were of the humbler sort, sporting badges and armlets, the *Bürgermiliz* is worth a closer look. Comparable perhaps to the Honorary Artillery Company in the City of London, the Militia had a great tradition behind it extending back to the sixteenth century. It had fought in both the sieges of Vienna, in 1529 and 1683, and had taken over the duties of garrisoning the capital in 1741 when, at the outbreak of the War of the Spanish Succession, the regular units were sent abroad. Aware of their significance in the maintenance of order, Napoleon treated them in 1805 rather as a police force to guard hospitals, munition depots and food transports, and on his departure he thanked them, pointing out that he had done them the honour of leaving them in charge of their arms depot. They stood for middle-class Vienna, and they are interesting for that very reason. Sandwiched between a numerous aristocracy and a working class between which relationships, based on close personal interdependence since neither could live without the other, were often close and even intimate, the bourgeois was in a sense suspect to both. Educated but not emancipated, when it came to the point he might defend the town. And afterwards? Circles to which the War Council lent an ear asked whether it was altogether wise to pay too much honour to members of the bourgeoisie. What about their right to wear uniform? Was it right that their officers should be on an equal footing with regular officers? It was decided that the Treasury's contribution to costs of accoutrement of the *Bürgermiliz* should cease.

The Mayor of Vienna, Stephan von Wohlleben, was the man who, although Maximilian d'Este was in command, was in charge of administration and for the next few weeks he was hardly to take his clothes off. His relations with the Commanding Officer got off to an unpropitious start. How was the city to be provisioned? The deputation led by the mayor was told that what the Emperor required was not suggestions but obedience; as no orders had been given it was, however, hard to see what should be obeyed. Constant friction with Archduke Maximilian, who was not over-exerting himself in his own sphere, was now to be one of Wohlleben's problems as preparations were made to withstand a siege. By some oversight the artillery ammunition had been left outside the town, but 70,000 rifles were distributed. This was done entirely without method, some men having three or four pressed upon them, others having none; the number is certainly unreliable and one can be sure that not enough ammunition was available to turn all these rifles into a serious danger to the population. They were not to worry the invaders.

The advance of Napoleon's army upon Vienna was not unresisted. Apart from heavy fighting in the Tyrol and in the province of Salzburg, there was an action at Dürnstein, and the country was harshly treated in consequence: all the churches along or near the route from Enns to Vienna except Melk and St. Pölten were plundered by Saxon and Württemberg troops and the population suffered severely. On 10th May French units were first sighted on the outskirts, and a burst of activity began on the walls of Vienna. Until now the men on sentry duty had taken—no doubt quite appropriately—a wholly civilian view of their duties. They had brought chairs to sit on and sat there eating sausages, drinking beer and smoking, while at mealtimes they were likely to go off in a body to the nearest *Gasthaus*, leaving the look-out unmanned. The morale of the general public was not of the highest. Food shortages had begun to be felt very quickly. The Court and all the ministries had gone to Hungary and, as we saw, it was left to Wohlleben to enquire what arrangements the government had made. The conclusion can only be drawn that the authorities had not asked themselves what Vienna was to eat when traffic between Austria and Hungary—whence Vienna imported the greater part of all its food supplies—would cease as the result of enemy occupation. Soon food prices soared. Bread and flour trebled in price, beef rose by a third, veal too trebled. Much worse was to come: by July prices would again be three times what they were in May, and many people would go out of their minds and be led off to the Narrenturm, that strange circular asylum for the insane; others jumped into the Danube. But now, with the news that the enemy was pouring through the outer suburbs, down what is now the Mariahilferstrasse, this insatiably curious population or at any rate those with the leisure to do so, most of them women, rushed up on to the town walls, but not without putting on their best clothes for the occasion in spite of the early hour. At 9 a.m. a French officer with a trumpeter appeared at the town gate called the Stadttor, asked for admittance and was let in. Whereupon the crowd, joyful ease not being for the moment uppermost and never having heard of the sacrosanct nature of emissaries, dragged the two men from their horses and lynched them.

The watchers on the walls could see movement in front of the imperial stables (now the Messepalast) where howitzers were set up on the attic floor, but the Glacis was almost deserted, and the

A New Will to Resist: the Viennese under Siege

initial excitement gave way to inaction and suspense. All that day and night nothing much happened. Where, people asked, was Archduke Karl? Where was Archduke Johann? Ascension Day, too, was quiet. In the evening at nine the shelling began. Caroline Pichler, watching from her garden, noticed with characteristic precision that most of the firing from the French guns was following the same line as the shots from the Turkish cannon in 1683, from the Spittelberg towards the Hofburg. Following as it seemed an almost horizontal course, the shells from the French howitzers looked like gleaming white, quivering snakes, while the Viennese guns were answering with balls of fire lobbed high over the Glacis. In Gumpendorf, Joseph Haydn comforted his anxious household. 'Children, have no fear. Where Haydn is, nothing can happen.' In the early hours women in their best hats were still watching from the walls, but in the town the ordinary folk and perhaps the servants of the spectators were fighting for bread in front of the bakeries. The more far-seeing were performing all those ritualistic burials of household goods in the back garden which have been the invariable accompaniment to every hostile invasion from time immemorial, occasionally to the profit of the owner, often to that of the enemy, but far more often to the profit of the neighbour. Joseph Haydn was deeply distressed. During the next few days he would keep rushing to the piano and playing his national anthem. Several French officers went to pay their respects to him and he was treated almost with reverence, but he was inconsolable.

At three in the morning the shelling began to lessen in intensity, soon it ceased altogether. At eight, the Pichlers heard that the town had surrendered. It was reckoned that between 1,600 and 1,800 howitzer shells had landed in the city, causing the deaths of 23 civilians. This time the streets were not lined with people to watch the entry of the French. The spectators were gone from the walls, the streets were empty, the shutters up, the shops closed. The troops had to kick aside broken glass, bricks and rubble as they marched. Gradually, people emerged from their houses, overcoming their fear and perhaps even their hatred in the exasperating business of acting, yet again, as hosts for a ravenous army which, apart from Frenchmen, consisted of Portuguese, Poles and Italian dragoons, their helmets jauntily decorated with strips of tigerskin.

A New Will to Resist: the Viennese under Siege

The question which everyone was now asking was: why was any attempt made to defend the town? In what sense was a purely token resistance worth the candle? Houses burned to the ground, people killed and injured—all just for reasons of prestige? And this resistance called down the wrath of Napoleon upon the capital and was made an excuse for the bad behaviour of all who were not restrained by their personal standards. As such, the entire performance was more farcical than tragic; few sieges had ever taken place with such restraint. How different it would have been, people said, if it had been a matter of containing the enemy while 'our beloved Archduke Karl' crossed the Danube and came gloriously to raise the siege of Vienna! Why, then any sacrifice would have been worth making.

They were quite right: the position would have been very different. In fact, it was only on 16th and 17th May that the survivors of the Battle of Regensburg came within sight of the spire of St. Stephen's. They had been much held up on the way by uncertainty as to whether or not they were still being followed and further fighting could be expected. But civilian opinion that Archduke Karl might cross the Danube and induce Napoleon to retreat, while it was understandable but founded on lack of information, was strangely enough shared by the Supreme Commander himself.

It is beyond comprehension that Archduke Karl, almost on the eve of the battle which established his place in history, should have described as his 'favourite plan' a manœuvre which must inevitably place his army in acute jeopardy.

4

Sound of Battle: the Enemy Departs

So long as Karl stayed where he was, he was all right. Napoleon was once again in Schönbrunn, and the prestige involved was considerable, but he had done it before. He had acquired comfortable billets, and that was all. On the chessboard of war, Vienna meant little: a few pawns had been eliminated but the principal figures still possessed freedom of movement. And one might add, shifting the metaphor: Archduke Karl was on his home ground, Napoleon was not.

It was precisely this inestimable advantage, freedom of manœuvre, that Karl, in crossing the Danube, would have sacrificed. At the present time the Archduke had by far the greatest part of the Austro-Hungarian Empire at his back. It was this that he must defend, from there he would draw his reserves, even though they might be his last, of men and material. Depots, garrisons, stores of food and forage: all these things—there was no need to look to the farthest corners of the monarchy—were near to hand, all on the left bank of the Danube. Why cross the river, with the enemy waiting on the other side? Why risk total defeat, which might mean the break-up of the Empire, the end of the monarchy? Let the Danube defend the Empire. Fabius saved Rome, as Daun saved Austria, not through haste but through delay.[1] The Austrian army, or more accurately, the nations united under the Austrian flag, would wait. Napoleon must come and get them.

These were the arguments which were put to the Archduke by the

[1] Field-Marshal Count Leopold Daun defeated the Prussian army at the Battle of Kolin on 18th June, 1757, thus relieving Prague which was under siege.

newly appointed Quartermaster-General, Baron Maximilian Wimpffen. Wimpffen stands out as a most refreshing figure on the staff of the Archduke because his opinions were his own, not framed merely to out-manœuvre those of others, and he was prepared to put them into practice and carry responsibility for the consequences. There was no hurry: he was aware that the Austrians were holding a large section of the French armed forces and Napoleon himself in check, and with every day that passed Spain was being given a valuable breathing space.

But on both sides, particularly among the non-combatants, the hiatus was beginning to cause impatience and the Emperor Franz was beset by advisers who urged him to get the armies moving and 'start them scrapping'.

Napoleon had been carrying out surveys since the moment he arrived, and on 13th May, some days before the arrival of the main body of the army, he sent Marshal Lannes to attempt a crossing to the north of the town, at Nussdorf. Outposts of the army group under the command of Lieutenant-Field-Marshal Hiller were, however, in time to repel the attack and Napoleon was forced to look for another place, which he found below Vienna at Kaiser-Ebersdorf.

Archduke Karl was not in the same happy position as Prince Eugen at the Battle of Zenta: of being able to attack the enemy while he has one foot on each side of a river. For some time he was still expecting the main spearhead of the attack at Nussdorf, but late on the evening of 20th May light cavalry followed by infantry units of the corps commanded by Masséna and Lannes crossed over to the Lobau, an island in the Danube, and from there, during the night, they reached the northern shore and occupied the villages of Aspern and Essling. Units of the Austrian army advanced to the attack.

It was Whit Sunday, and soon the sound of firing brought the whole of Vienna to its feet. People rushed on to the ramparts—this time, of course, on the other side of the town—while men and boys fought their way up the narrow spiral staircases of every church tower for miles around, only to be dragged down again by the occupying forces. By evening Aspern village had been repeatedly lost and won but, though in ruins, it was now mainly in Austrian hands, while Essling (the French have always called the battle by this name) remained in theirs. For some of the troops the lull when darkness fell may have brought the chance of an hour or two's sleep, but at three o'clock in the morning the battle was resumed, the French having in the meantime received reinforcements. With these fresh troops Masséna now recaptured Aspern. This was little more than a skirmish, as the climax was yet to come. The sun was already high when Napoleon, from his look-out post in a tree, sent his order to Marshal Lannes: three divisions of foot and the entire cavalry to take the main Austrian positions.

Where, as Napoleon's cavalry thundered towards the opposing lines, was the Austrian Commander-in-Chief? Safe on some convenient promontory, on a tower, watching through a telescope while men died? It was the whole secret of this Habsburg Archduke, difficult, delicate, torn by indecision as he often was, that he never demanded anything of the most insignificant Ruthenian peasant that he would not do himself. Hating war as he did, his presence nevertheless electrified an army which Wimpffen, only days before, was describing as partly trained, partly equipped and overtired. Seeing the Austrian lines sag under the impetus of the cavalry charge Karl galloped forward, seized the colours of the 15th Regiment of Foot Baron Zach, and stormed into the battle. His Adjutant-General Count Colloredo was killed beside him, but the troops gained heart and stood their ground.

(This is how the Archduke is immortalized in stone: his equestrian statue on the Heldenplatz in Vienna shows him with a raised arm, holding the flag high. Many years later a young man asked him to tell the story: how did it all happen when he stormed into the thick of the fighting, seized the flag and all that? Archduke Karl laughed and said, 'Do you know how heavy regimental colours are? Do you suppose a little chap like me could go off with them? I simply grasped the staff.')

Marshal Lannes, withdrawing and regrouping, sent for reinforcements, and having, as he thought, seen to their despatch Napoleon ordered Lannes to resume the attack. Suddenly, there was a dramatic intervention from an entirely different quarter. Upstream at Lang-Enzersdorf, unobserved by the French, a young staff captain called Magdeburg and a small detachment of soldiers had been filling a number of small rowing boats with stones, and on

Archduke Karl's orders these were now sent on their way down the swollen river. At the very moment when Marshal Davout with the relief force was about to cross by the pontoon bridge to come to the aid of Lannes, the stone-laden boats crashed into the bridge and tore it to pieces. Napoleon had no alternative but to order Lannes to retreat to Lobau Island. Having done so—the time was about one o'clock in the afternoon—Napoleon fell into a deep sleep which lasted for thirty hours. It was more like unconsciousness than normal sleep, 'death-like' his generals thought, and they began tentatively to discuss that perennially fascinating subject: the succession if Napoleon were to die. It was fortunate for them that he never learnt of it.

The state of mind of the Viennese who can have had no way of judging which way the battle was going can be imagined. The guns were now silent, and the first wounded men were coming into the town, brought on horseback or in farm carts. Then they hobbled into Vienna on foot, the Landstrasse was crowded with them, men from both armies making their way to the various hospitals and emergency sick bays. Now the people showed themselves at their best: they rushed to support the wounded, carrying their rifles, and in spite of the food shortage they shared with them food and wine; above all, they succoured both their own men and the enemy, the victors and the vanquished.

It was an Austrian victory. Only on points, perhaps, but Napoleon himself had withdrawn from a battlefield, and this news flashed across conquered Europe and brought fresh hope—particularly to Andreas Hofer and his men in the Tyrol, who won a battle at Berg Isel a week later.

Franz I wrote to Karl a letter of such profuse thanks for his services, expressed in such baroque terms of affection, that no one could have believed that so much as a shadow lay between them.

Archduke Karl did not overestimate his victory. There had been heavy losses on both sides. Napoleon left 7,000 dead on the battlefield, Marshal Lannes among them, and including the wounded and prisoners of war, he had lost nearly half of the approximately 90,000 men engaged. Karl considered that his own advantage was just sufficient to provide a basis for a negotiated peace. 'The Battle of Aspern', he wrote to Duke Albert of Sachsen-Teschen, 'has brought Napoleon to a more temperate frame of mind. We should extract profit from this good fortune which we shall scarcely experience a second time.'

It would have been truer to say that Napoleon could hardly credit his good luck. This was approximately his position: he was stranded on the Lobau with a beaten and exhausted army, short of food, water and munitions. The high water carried by the Danube which had helped Captain Magdeburg's operation had turned most of the island into a swamp and the men, standing in water up to their ankles, were tortured by mosquitoes. Why, then, did Archduke Karl sit back and do nothing? Hardly had the applause for his victory and his personal gallantry at Aspern died down, before he was again the subject of passionate controversy.

The floods, the partly-destroyed bridge across to the Lobau, the exhaustion of the men, the losses in troops and materials, the lack of timber to repair the bridge: these reasons have been put forward as sufficient explanation for the Archduke's inaction. But it was being said in government circles that 25,000 men, with a supply of pontoons, were standing in reserve upstream—men who had not fired a shot throughout the battle. And of those who had fought, some 100,000 were still on their feet. During the days that followed the French army could have been encircled and compelled to surrender. Napoleon's retrospective contributions to this controversy always varied according to the mood of the moment. In his memoirs written on St. Helena he said that both during and after the Battle of Aspern Archduke Karl had done everything that he ought to do and could do, but much earlier, while still in power, he said 'You cannot imagine the state of my army at that time and what a misfortune would have befallen us if we had been faced by an enterprising enemy.' In the meantime, violent differences of opinion had broken out among Karl's senior staff officers. Hiller was for storming the bridge at once, in other words for continuing the battle without a pause. Wimpffen and a Baron Stutterheim disagreed, and in an altercation which followed some days later mortal insults were exchanged.

During those weeks after Aspern, while nothing was being done to hinder the free movement of the French on the right bank and the arrival of reinforcements, while Karl was evidently losing control over his generals—Wimpffen was preening himself as the hero of Aspern and being arrogant and condescending to all around him—the Archduke's line of thought was not confined to military considerations. It almost seemed as though these played no part at all. What other motive could he have had, other than a wish to fill them with revulsion, for taking Franz I, Stadion, the Minister for War Count Zichy, and others on a tour of the battlefield over which there still lay the stench of corruption? He could not, he believed, take the responsibility of embarking on another battle. 'Napoleon and I', he wrote to Duke Albert on 1st June, 'are watching one another to see who will make the first mistake.' And a week later: 'I shall take no risks, because the forces at my disposal are the country's last, but I shall seize with great energy every opportunity which presents itself to me, to carry through a decisive blow.' How did the Archduke suppose that such an opportunity was to present itself when fresh troops were streaming towards the French positions?

Philipp Stadion saw the question from a different angle. The time for a concerted effort to defeat Napoleon was approaching. Already, the news of his defeat at Aspern had begun to have its effect, and it was only because of inadequate support by the regular armed forces that the popular risings in the Tyrol, North Germany and Italy were abortive. 'Hatred of the oppressive political system of the French, the longing for liberation, are so great that they presently hold the scales against mistrust of Austria's active assistance.' The Emperor should decide. But Franz I knew that Napoleon had repeatedly said that he would be willing to make peace at once without unduly repressive conditions—later he would say, without any conditions whatever—if Franz would abdicate, leaving the succession to his brother Archduke Ferdinand, now Grand Duke of Würzburg[1]—or to Karl. The Emperor had always suspected that Napoleon raised the subject with Karl on the occasion of their first meeting at Stammersdorf, though Karl had said nothing. Now it was Karl who rejected the suggestion of abdication and told Franz what he thought in passionate terms. He would, he said, sooner fight to the end.

Archduke Karl fought the Battle of Wagram against his own

[1] Ferdinand III of Habsburg-Tuscany, having lost his realm to Napoleon, was consoled with Würzburg.

convictions to save his brother's crown. His chances of success, he thought, were meagre.

The Austrian army, about 120,000 men, lay with its northern tip, the right flank, at Nussdorf and beyond, and extended southwards past the Bisamberg, Stammersdorf and Wagram to Markgraf-Neusiedl. All through the rest of May, all through June, the army had stayed almost exactly where it found itself after the Battle of Aspern, only slightly withdrawn and with the command at Wagram. It was an exceedingly hot and dry summer and the troops were fully exposed to the burning sun and to clouds of fine dust which, if a light wind rose, could even cause exercises to be broken off. Training went on all day, because there were many raw recruits in every regiment, and three times daily a bugle blew the assembly for prayers. There were no tents except one to each regiment which served the dual purpose of a chapel and shelter for the colonel in command. Otherwise, all, officers and men, slept on the ground, usually in shallow trenches lined with brushwood and dry grass; everywhere the grass was burnt up by sun and drought, and along the banks of the Russbach, the stream which was to be fought for with such desperation, the leaves had dropped from the willows. From positions nearer to the Danube, the troops, men from all parts of the Empire, and no doubt the generals too in their stone-blue coats and scarlet breeches, watched the French sappers as they busied themselves at repairing the bridges across the river and laid new ones between one island and another and the shore, 'the continued labour of carpenters and shipwrights,' says Varnhagen von Ense, 'the arrival of artillery and powder waggons—none of this escaped our notice.' What purpose it served that these things were noticed if nothing was done about it he does not explain. They also gazed across towards the spire of St. Stephen's, which they could certainly see when haze and dust were not concealing it: the landmark of an occupied city.

The temper of the Viennese was not at its best. A town where overcrowding—even in the districts *extra muros*—was endemic, now had for the second time to endure occupation by soldiers whose demands were hard to satisfy, although discipline was strict and excesses of any kind were instantly clamped down upon. Rationing was unknown, and the result was an unending series of scenes and pitched battles in front of butchers' shops and bakeries. Shortages there were and queueing in the hours before dawn, but the fear of famine which gripped so many people was probably much exaggerated; the Viennese were normally speaking vast eaters, particularly of meat, and easily panicked at the prospect of pulling in their belts. The very severe decline in moral standards which is widely mentioned in contemporary chronicles reflects the terrifying effect of severe inflation on people with fixed incomes. Even middle-class women and girls took to prostitution; in the circumstances it was the simplest solution to their problems. The soldiers will often have paid for these services in kind, in other words with the more easily portable souvenirs which they had accumulated about their persons en route, or perhaps in the course of a change of billet. One way and another a great quantity of plunder was in circulation, and a need clearly existed for an exchange and mart where, by free confrontation, the value of these goods might be established and where they might even be converted into rapidly devaluing paper money. The women, after all, could not pay for their groceries in brooches, bracelets and earrings, and in any case it would have been a depressing thought that half the town was yielding up its virtue, to be rewarded with bric-à-brac lifted from the other half. Accordingly, a black market exchange sprang into life by St. Stephen's Cathedral. At first it consisted of nothing more than small groups of soldiers and civilians, but as the news began to spread that on the Stephansplatz there was often jewellery to be had at a fraction of its normal value, the circle of buyers and sellers widened daily, gold and silver came into circulation and the market became too conspicuous to be overlooked. One day, the former French Ambassador, now Governor, Comte Antoine Andréossy threw a cordon round the whole group and buyers and sellers were led off to the police stations. On 7th August an order was issued forbidding the sale or purchase by soldiers in public places of anything whatsoever. The natural assumption is that after that the traffic removed itself from the streets to the inns.

Those regiments which were not quartered on the Viennese lived in a large camp near the Tabor Bridge which the French laid out with such loving care that, when the time came to break camp, they could hardly bear to go. On either side of four long, dead-straight

F

lanes stood rows of little wooden cabins just large enough to accommodate between 10 and 20 men. Each one was numbered, brightly painted and tastefully decorated inside and out; the predominant colours, red, blue, white and green distinguished one lane from another. After dark the whole camp was lit up by lanterns. The non-commissioned officers' cabins were fitted out with curtains and comfortable furniture, and the senior officers' houses, built of stone for better protection from the heat, were even more comfortably equipped, all of this, of course, having been requisitioned— that good old military euphemism—from houses in the nearby villages whose owners had to watch their doors and windows, sometimes even the roofs, being carried away. Trees by the hundred, all cut off above the roots, formed avenues to lend a little welcome shade to the immaculate, sand-strewn lanes, and behind the huts, on the grass, the troops practised jumping, fencing, putting the weight and so on, watched by their officers from beneath yet more drooping but still shady trees. And here, in the comparative cool of the evening, to the strains of military bands, Vienna society—not the best, perhaps—wandered about, admired the fine uniforms and the fine men inside them, resting after a while in front of an *estaminet* where a cooling drink of lemonade was to be had. As for the occupiers, they felt cosier with every day that passed, and they declared that no conquered territory had ever provided, let alone offered, such comforts.

A number of people of the more sensitive type were unable to make up their minds whether or not to go and join the crowds during the parades at Schönbrunn. Caroline Pichler confided her scruples to her diary: did one indulge one's vulgar curiosity, bearing in mind that Napoleon was the most prominent man of the age, or was it more dignified to remain quietly at home? In her case, one went. Lulu Thürheim kept on about it until it was too late, as he had gone. And the dramatist, Franz Grillparzer: 'With hatred in my heart, and being at no time a lover of military pomp and display, I nevertheless missed not one of Napoleon's inspections at Schönbrunn and on the Schmelz. I can still see him, running rather than walking down the open staircase, his adjutants the two crown princes of Bavaria and Württemberg behind him, now standing alone, his hands joined at his back, surveying the march past of his martial hordes . . . he fascinates me as the snake does the bird. Watching him at the theatre, also with hatred in her heart and longing for a sharpshooter to pick him off in his box, Frau Pichler considered that taken singly he possessed good, even noble, features, but that his all too broad, fleshy face and his undistinguished figure left a general impression which to her mind was rather vulgar.

Napoleon was indeed capable of fascinating women but he never attracted the Viennese. He was not, as a man, their type. 'They like', said a contemporary in explanation, 'flatterers, people who make them laugh, who dance with them, who tell stories and turn gallant couplets. Frederick the Great at least played the flute.' Nor did they care for his harsh voice. Napoleon was not, however, dependent on the favours of the ladies of Vienna. He had long ago settled the Polish patriot, Countess Marie Walewska, into a pleasant house close to Schönbrunn; it was there that she conceived the son who was born in May of the following year. At this time, and throughout his residence in Vienna, he was constantly on the move. Nothing escaped his attention. He inspected schools, munition factories and workshops, monasteries and hospitals. He would turn up unexpectedly, terrifying all concerned, give a hasty look round and depart as suddenly as he came. He was not as unimpressed as he appeared to be. Andréossy said later that Napoleon would like to have taken three things with him: the tomb of the Archduchess Marie-Christine in the Augustinerkirche, Klosterneuburg, and Schönbrunn. He might have added that this greatest plunderer of all time did not leave Vienna empty-handed: he gave expression to his admiration for other treasures which were not fixtures—in the Hofbibliothek for example—by having them transferred to Paris.

On 5th June the Austrian Ambassador to Paris, Count Metternich, arrived in Vienna under police escort, accompanied by Prince Paul Esterházy, his secretary, and a young man called Philip Neumann, variously believed to be the illegitimate son either of the Elector Maximilian Franz, the youngest son of the Empress Maria Theresa, or of the Ambassador's father. Napoleon who disliked all diplomats nursed a particular distaste for 'le beau Clément' because of his presumption in having an affair with his sister Caroline Murat, Queen of Naples. Clemens Wenzel Lothar, Count Metternich-Winneburg-Beilstein now spent three boring weeks as a prisoner of state in a villa near Hetzendorf. He was soon exchanged for a number of prisoners of war and on 2nd July he joined the Emperor at his headquarters at Wolkersdorf, a village to the northeast of Vienna on the main road to Bohemia.

During the night of 4th to 5th of July a thunderstorm of extraordinary violence burst over the Marchfeld. The crackling, the thunderclaps, the hissing rain obscured all other sights and sounds while the crash of thunderbolts shook the earth. The storm's ferocity was maintained for two or three hours, and when it abated, Napoleon stood with his army of 160,000 men on the left bank of the Danube.

Once again, Napoleon could hardly credit his good fortune: for the second time he had brought an entire army almost unscathed across the Danube. It was not so much the success of the crossing during the storm which amazed and delighted him, as the fact that the whole build-up had been greeted with no more than token resistance. The news that the French were on the move reached Archduke Karl's headquarters on 2nd July, but he himself was by no means sure in his mind that the main attack was again to come from the Lobau. It might be a diversion, and Archduke Johann facing Marshal Davout[1] at Pressburg might have to bear the brunt to begin with. In either case, the main weight of the army was with Napoleon and a crossing was inevitable, so that for the lack of opposition only one explanation is possible: that they were intended to come across. All along, Wimpffen, and almost certainly Grünne as well, wanted this decisive battle to take place, and it is the opinion of military historians today that the man whose will dominated the strategy of the Battle of Wagram on the Austrian side was not the Archduke, but General Wimpffen.

By about midday on the 5th, the French lines were advancing to the attack, and the sun was dipping towards the horizon when Napoleon gave the order to charge. As successive waves were beaten off, for the last time in his life Archduke Karl was in the thick of a battle. The Vogelsang Regiment faltered and began to give way, and seeing this he galloped into their midst and turned them round to face the French. It was now that an adjutant noticed that he was

---

[1] Marshal Davout, stationed on the opposite bank of the Danube at Hainburg, had his lunch sent daily from the palais Schwarzenberg where he was billeted.

wounded in the shoulder. 'This is not', was the reply, 'the moment to discuss it.'

From the Bisamberg, a hill to the north, the Emperor Franz was watching whatever was to be seen, which at a distance of several kilometres from the main scene of action was not much, but Metternich, eye glued to telescope, provided an ecstatic running commentary: 'Incomparable! Superb! Now our cavalry is hurling itself forward! *Now* they're getting a move on!'

Napoleon sat motionless on his horse. He had issued orders that he would retain sole command in his own hands, so that a continual stream of staff officers came and went, taking with them precise instructions given to them by Napoleon in a quiet, unruffled tone of voice. Towards evening, a heavy attack on the Austrian central positions was made in an attempt to force a break-through, but to the men in Napoleon's entourage the failure of the attack soon became evident. Now, for the first time, Napoleon was seized by a kind of restlessness. Dismounting, he wandered off and began, calmly and with close attention, to pick wild flowers and ears of corn which he made into a bunch. Apparently satisfied, he then abruptly tore the bunch apart and threw it away, only to begin again on another. He went through this process half a dozen times, before, with a face of stone, he remounted and rejoined his staff officers, not one of whom dared say a word. The night was spent on the battlefield, and there was little hope of food or much rest for man or beast. At the Archduke's headquarters at midnight, dispositions were being made for the next day: at four o'clock in the morning the enemy was to be attacked simultaneously on all fronts.

It was while these events were engaging the minds of several hundred thousand people, including the Viennese who were again having to succour innumerable wounded (the Pichlers somehow managed to care for 17 men in their villa) that a tragically lonely drama was coming to a climax elsewhere. On the second day of the Battle of Wagram, 6th July, Pope Pius VII issued an apostolic letter, informing all who cared to listen that he could only be torn from the Eternal City by force. Less than a month beforehand, on 10th June, he had proclaimed Napoleon's excommunication 'by the authority of Almighty God, the Holy Saints Peter and Paul and by Our Own'. Napoleon treated the Bull with contempt, but he kept its contents strictly secret all the same. His Apostolic Majesty, however, the Emperor Franz I, sent Napoleon a message of sympathy. During the night that followed on 6th July, General Radet carried out the abduction of the Pope. Tied to a chair, he was let down by ropes through a smashed-in window on the garden side of the palace, where a carriage was waiting. Often fainting from exhaustion, the poor old man was now swept off to Grenoble and thence after a while to Fontainebleau.

Seen from the Austrian side of the fence the outstanding factors in the second and final stage of the Battle of Wagram are these: the unco-ordinated start—only Prince Rosenberg on the left flank advanced at the agreed time—the desperate resistance of the Austrians at Markgraf-Neusiedl, and the failure of Archduke Johann to arrive in time.

The violent impact of Rosenberg's advance caused Napoleon, who feared, too, that Archduke Johann's division might already have arrived, to throw in his regiment of Footguards in support of Davout, thus forcing the Corps Rosenberg back to its point of departure. Although the battle in the centre and on the Austrian right wing was soon in progress, the main focus of events was the area embracing Markgraf-Neusiedl and Aderklaa. The second of these two villages was contested for some hours and the Austrians' advance at this point, forcing the Saxons to withdraw, was met by Napoleon in two ways. Bringing forward a hundred pieces of artillery, he halted the Austrian advance, and, hearing that no reinforcements were in sight, he ordered Davout to make a circuitous movement with the Third Corps, to outflank Markgraf-Neusiedl and roll up the Austrian left wing.

Archduke Karl was now in trouble. In the belief that reinforcements must come at any moment the men of the Corps Rosenberg who were defending the Russbach stream and the tower hill at Markgraf-Neusiedl were holding on, and it was midday before the French were able to take the hill by assault. At about 2 p.m. the Supreme Commander received news that his brother would not enter the area of operations for another three hours. Having relied absolutely on these 12,000 men he had no further reserves. It was checkmate, and Karl ordered the retreat which, after nightfall, was so skilfully carried out that on the following morning the Austrian army seemed to have melted away and Napoleon's scouts were unable to say where it had gone. Karl had in fact withdrawn across the Kreuzenstein heights north of Korneuburg on the road to Znaim.

Can the blame be placed squarely upon Archduke Johann?

To the Austrians, Archduke Johann is a most revered and beloved figure. Occasionally subject to fits of accidie though he was, few Habsburgs have been his equal in intelligence and mental stamina as well as in physical vigour. The fact that he failed to turn up when and where he should have done is therefore one of the curiosities of Austrian history, but at the same time, if nineteenth-century academic historians found the whole subject difficult to handle, this is hardly surprising. Even so, the amount of selective quotation indulged in by historians both professional and amateur down to the present day is as striking as the heat with which they present it.

If the opinion of the men most immediately concerned were to be taken as final, no clarity would emerge at all. Hiller and the military genius Radetzky both said that the Archduke could not have saved the day even if he had arrived in time; the turning of the flank could not have been fought off. Karl, however, disagreed. This much is generally agreed upon today: Until about 1 or 2 o'clock in the afternoon of the 6th the battle was still undecided. If, therefore, even a token force had turned up, the battle might have been won. This assessment gains weight from the fact that a mere rumour of outriders having been sighted was enough to cause a panic among a section of the French Third Corps which spread to the artillery train and to the camp followers. The extraordinary scene of chaos as grooms wearing the French imperial livery galloped past shouting 'sauve qui peut' and soldiers fell to plundering the coaches of their own generals and the stalls of the sutler-women, is vividly described in the memoirs of two men who witnessed it, General Waldemar Baron Löwenstern, a Russian officer on Napoleon's staff, and General, later Marshal, Boniface Comte de Castellane.

The reason for Archduke Johann's continued presence at Pressburg (Bratislava) in command of 12,000 men was that his brother was not sure at which point the main attack would begin, and in the meantime Johann, with his relatively small contingent, was holding down a sizeable portion of the French forces. To this end, too, a number of small sorties were carried out. As 4th July wore on, all uncertainty ceased. The troop movements in the region of the Lobau and the left bank of the Danube could no longer be a diversion; this was clearly the real thing. Meanwhile, Davout had already left the bridgehead at Pressburg and was about to link up with the French forces on the Danube. At 7 p.m. on 4th July a courier left Archduke Karl's headquarters, and at 6 o'clock the next morning Archduke Johann held his marching orders in his hands. The ground to be covered amounted to 50 kilometres, and the Austrian army of those days, which as we have noticed was not celebrated for its speed, could be expected to cover such a distance in the time required. The calculation went like this: 16 hours of unbroken marching time, plus 15 hours for assembly and rests, equals 31 in all. Time enough to come to the relief of the men who were holding on at Markgraf-Neusiedl, watching and waiting for reinforcements.

What was the younger Archduke's point of view?

He always argued that he should have received earlier warning. Why was he not given orders on 2nd July to break camp? The answer to this we know: Napoleon's intentions were not yet clear. He could only withdraw his troops from their positions, he went on, including the artillery, under cover of darkness, for fear that Davout would storm the bridgehead. He added that the troops had to eat and rest before they began the long march and that they were wet through. But had he not watched the enemy forces as they got under way? 'All day', he recorded, 'the movement of troops has continued through Fischamend in the direction of Schwechat and from Bruck on the Leitha towards the same. It is Marshal Davout and the Viceroy [of Italy, Eugène Beauharnais].' And still he dawdled, as one paralysed, even though the Supreme Commander, the brother to whom he had been devoted since childhood—no hostile undercurrent can possibly have been at work—sent a further despatch urging him to lose no time.

Admittedly, a wide gap yawns between theory and reality, and it is not possible, for instance, to assess exactly to what extent sluggishness in carrying out his orders held up the preparations of the Archduke's troops. Undoubtedly, however, in view of the preceding actions Davout's troops were equally in need of rest, and the rain had not fallen upon the Austrians alone.

Did it never occur to him to send an advance detachment ahead of the rest? Clearly, no one could have foreseen that a couple of shots fired from an unexpected direction would cause such an extraordinary outbreak of panic in the very vicinity of Napoleon himself that, disturbed while resting (it was soon after three o'clock in the afternoon), he was obliged to leap on his horse before he had finished buttoning up his jacket and breeches. Nor could Archduke Johann know of the desperate efforts of the heavily outnumbered Austrian left flank. But that his brother had no other reserves he must have known. And yet, so far from his mind was it to reach the battlefield with some of his forces rather than none, that he dallied yet again. At 10 a.m. Archduke Johann halted at Marchegg, where he was met by his brother's A.D.C., Prince Reuss, with orders to go straight on without stopping. This order he simply disregarded: because, as he wrote to the Emperor at a later date, the artillery had not arrived and he had to wait for it to catch up.

Recently, a clue to the Archduke's actions has been seen[1] in an out-of-date attitude of mind which still saw the Austrian soldier as a mercenary—which he no longer was. The conditions of service of mercenaries laid down that no exceptional feats of endurance could be demanded of them, and they could not be ordered to march unless they had slept and eaten, even though the fate of 'their' country might hang in the balance. Archduke Karl knew this, it was what his army reform was largely all about. Commanding officers in the Austrian army, this argument continues, belonged for the most part to the senior nobility, who, after a lost battle, could go home to their estates and sun themselves in the admiration of their peers. This is perhaps going a little too far: those times were changing, though slowly, and neither Hiller nor Mayer were aristocrats by birth. But the underlying principle is true: Austria could be defeated in war again and again; and if not sooner, then later, it would fight again. Napoleon, on the other hand, could not afford to look upon war as though it were country house tennis, and the fate of his generals was intimately bound up with his. Once his star faded, they would disappear, unless possessed of remarkable agility, into the obscurity from whence they came. Meanwhile even his comrades in arms, the Marshals and Generals—Löwenstern noticed this—would repeat

[1] Helmut Hertenberger, *Die Schlacht bei Wagram.*

their orders just like any junior staff officer, leap into their saddles and gallop back to their units at full stretch. These were men who had fought their way up, while it was Archduke Johann's misfortune to be a brother of the Emperor, obliged to carry a responsibility for which his nature and temperament, his education and training, had not fitted him. Other talents he had in plenty.

Archduke Karl has the right to the last word. 'With regret, I am obliged to state that your earlier arrival by a few hours, with even a few thousand men, would have decided the fate of the battle.'

Immediately, Archduke Karl now came up against the war party. The question to what extent, in his fear of precipitate action by Napoleon against the Habsburg crown, in his customary anxiety to end hostilities, he overstepped his authority to secure a cease-fire, is now academic. He has often been accused of agreeing to peace terms independently, but in view of the commotion prevailing at the time it is equally justifiable to hold to the version that Franz I authorized the terms but immediately withdrew his word under pressure from the war party, leaving his brother dangling in mid air.

It was inevitable that the Supreme Commander should now come under general fire. It was being rumoured that he had panicked during the battle, that during the night he had had one of his 'attacks of nerves', and had lain in a deep sleep for many hours—an odd parallel to Napoleon's 'deathlike sleep' after Aspern. This alleged epileptic attack may have taken place, but it is by no means a proven fact. It may have been an invention put abroad in some quarters to save his reputation and place all responsibility for the latter course of the battle on Wimpffen and others. It would certainly have been a most uncharacteristic moment for one of his attacks. Inaction combined with stress—these were typical conditions. In a crisis, Karl was always at his best both physically and mentally. In this case, admittedly, there had been some loss of blood to increase his exhaustion.

Imperial disapproval was soon given expression in a letter which demoted the Archduke from his rank of Supreme Commander, confined his authority to the troops under his direct command and ordered the removal of his old friend Count Grünne and his entire War Ministry staff. At this, Karl, who had already fought for

Count Grünne's retention in an earlier letter, resigned—as he was intended to do. To his foster-father, the Duke of Sachsen-Teschen, the Archduke commented that Franz I was now in the hands not only of Stadion, Baldacci and Gentz, but of Metternich. He felt later on that he should have managed things more skilfully: he should have gone straight to the Emperor and tried to straighten out the misunderstanding. Unhappily, he said, he was still so exhausted at the time that he could hardly climb on to his horse, and he allowed his better judgement to be clouded by ill-temper and bitterness. We might add: there was in fact just a chance that he might have talked Franz I round, but only if he had got there before the letter was on its way. After that, no other course was open to him.

Stadion's head was the next to fall: he was sacked in October.

Between the Emperor's headquarters in Hungary and Schönbrunn the principal negotiators, Field-Marshal Prince Johannes Liechtenstein and Count Ferdinand Bubna, shuttled to and fro. Well might Napoleon say that the talks were a farce: his appalling territorial claims, the crushing reparations which he demanded, were repeatedly accompanied by the almost mocking assurance that if Franz would only abdicate, he, Napoleon Bonaparte, would simply walk away leaving the Empire unscathed. The fate of the Spanish Bourbons can hardly have left the thoughts of Franz and his wife for an instant. For, far from being minded to abdicate, the question in the forefront of the councils was simply whether or not to resume the war. Metternich, his assessments of Austria's remaining war potential wholly off-beam, was urging war; echoed, of course, by the Empress. Prince Liechtenstein, who like all the senior officers wanted peace, and complained to Gentz that he found it difficult even to get the Emperor to listen to him, thought that Maria Ludovica's obsession with war was a form of compensation for what she might feel to be her lack of success in other fields. She was childless, she was tubercular, owing to her thinness she was no longer attractive to her husband (who a few months later had a mistress found for him on the advice of his father confessor). Therefore, Prince Liechtenstein believed, she appeared to have made up her mind to excel at something. She would be a goddess of war—better perhaps than victory, she might die a glorious death. Her hold over Franz was made up of various components which were noticed earlier, but he now had a bad conscience as well, and this made him more shifty, more resentful, more vacillating than ever.

Liechtenstein's views on the main issue were shared by almost the entire General Staff. That they should be urging a peace settlement is understandable after a loss of 15 generals, 772 officers and 37,608 other ranks dead and wounded (French losses were on a similar scale), while in addition the army was carrying a sick list of 70,000 to 90,000 men. Metternich was now talking of the 'inexhaustible' resources of the Austrian army, of there still being 250,000 troops of the line at the Emperor's disposal—'the finest army in the world!'—while the very idea of having to conjure up an army capable of taking the offensive, let alone conquering Bonaparte, filled the minds of the General Staff with consternation.

And yet—were the warmongers right after all? Napoleon never had any doubt whatever but that the Austrians abandoned their war effort too soon. Metternich, to men such as Liechtenstein exasperatingly unrealistic and bombastic, was to be told by Napoleon himself, that, in principle, he had been thinking on the right lines, and if the war party had gone through with its intentions (but with Archduke Karl as Supreme Commander) he, Bonaparte, would have been a lost man. And to Prince Karl Schwarzenberg when he was Ambassador in Paris, Napoleon painted a graphic picture of the situation in which he would have been placed. He alone would have been able to keep order, while his generals, surrounded by a hostile population, would all have lost their heads. In other words he would have had to remain permanently at hand 'because I was living in the midst of a people determined upon resistance'. Napoleon knew that when all was said and done what he had achieved on Austrian soil was not very impressive. A law of diminishing returns seemed to be operating of which not only he was aware. The French losses, at Aspern and more so at Wagram, were extremely heavy, an ever-larger proportion of his troops consisted of young and inexperienced men, among whom, and also among the old hands, a distinct disinclination to die was becoming noticeable. At Wagram, the vanquished had captured more flags than the victors, the French had amassed less booty than ever before. This time, the death of so many comrades in arms (to use an empty phrase, as anything approaching friendship with his marshals was quite foreign to him) oppressed his spirits.

The peace talks meandered on, which is to say that dissension at Court raged, while Liechtenstein and Bubna were on several occasions kept by the Emperor of the French as a captive audience whom, for as much as five or six hours together, he treated to monologues on the art of war. Where the conditions of a peace treaty were concerned, what was the point of fussing about 'bits and scraps of land which will one day come back to you'? All this, he argued, 'can only endure as long as I am alive. France cannot wage war beyond the Rhine. Bonaparte was able to do it. Yet this will end with me.' He gave himself another 10 or 15 years, so Bubna told Friedrich Gentz who made a note of it in his diary, before he 'croaked', whereupon 'you can have everything again the way you want it.'

Perhaps such an intensely personal view of the destiny of nations has never been so baldly stated.

The 'von' before the surname of Friedrich Gentz is not reliably documented. Historians have usually allowed it although Jean de Bourgoing's peremptory footnote '*not* "von" ' seems to rebuke professional laxity among his colleagues. Gentz would have said that the title of nobility procured him a seat at the tables of the aristocracy, in whose hands lay the power in the state, and thus was not a vain adornment but a basic requirement. Had it not existed he would have been compelled to invent it; Gentz possessed an inventive mind and, for much of his working life, little else. In his youth a passionate admirer of the thought of Edmund Burke, Gentz acquired influence in two ways. As a publicist, he informed and moulded the opinion of the literate classes, and as a political analyst his glittering intelligence enabled him both to bombard all the influential men of his time with an unfaltering stream of informed comment and to draft for the government he came to serve texts designed to support or destroy any policy or theory whatsoever, either alternatively or successively. His capacity for sustained mental effort was exceptional, in the circles in which he moved unheard of, and all the talents of this one-time Prussian civil servant came ideally into play in the political overthrow of Napoleon, and in the subsequent rearrangement of Europe. In Metternich Gentz found his destiny, in Gentz Metternich found an ideal instrument.

Suddenly the wind shifted, and it was Gentz who caused it to do so by using all his powers of persuasion on one of the Empress's advisers. Count Ferdinand Palffy was a patron of the arts who two years later was placed in charge of the court theatres. His ownership of the Theater an der Wien all but ruined him, but he may be encountered in mid-century memoirs living in undiminished style and comfort at his country seat as though nothing had happened. Coached by Gentz, he now set to work on the Empress, and was able to convince her that there was a very real danger of the Hungarians responding to Napoleon's call to rise in rebellion against the House of Habsburg. The possibility that Napoleon might whisk the crown from the head of Franz I with no more ceremony than he had shown in the case of the Spanish Bourbons in 1808 was no mere spectre. Yet it seemed unreal, blasphemous, a tempting of Providence, a threat which, surely, the man who had conquered Revolution, who had placed a crown upon his own head, would hesitate to carry out in earnest? Gentz thought—whereupon Palffy told the Empress Maria Ludovica that she should think and advise Franz I to do the same—it was all too likely, given one more unsuccessful attack which would instantly be labelled 'treachery', that the man whom Archduke Karl called the 'first principle of evil, all that is most exceptional in power, in mind and in infamy' would indeed carry out the threats which at this very time he was uttering in public so that all the world could hear.

On 12th October, during an inspection of troops at Schönbrunn, an attempt was made on Napoleon's life by the seventeen-year-old Friedrich Stapps from Naumburg. On the 14th the Peace of Vienna was signed and on 16th October Napoleon left Vienna. Once again, Napoleon had imposed crushing conditions. It was not only the loss of the so recently acquired Salzburg and areas in Upper Austria, the restriction of the army to 150,000 men: for the monarchy to lose its access to the sea on the Adriatic coast was a blow which made a resumption of hostilities at some future opportunity inevitable.

The terms of the peace were not yet known to the general public, but at 4 p.m. on the day of Napoleon's departure the Viennese were obliged to witness the start of a noisy, unskilled and to them profoundly humiliating symbol of defeat: the demolition of the city's defences. 'These venerable walls', wrote a private citizen,[1] 'to whom Vienna and all Austria twice owed deliverance from the Turkish yoke, which had e'er shown a bold front to the foe, by reason of their construction impregnable and had they been skilfully defended would not have been conquered in this recent war, were now transformed into a mound of rubble and the materials presently fill the moat. Thus, through wickedness and tyranny . . .' etc. etc. The poor old gentleman was allowing his feelings to warp his judgement: even in 1683 the Turkish sappers succeeded in undermining the walls in one or two places and skirmishes took place within the labyrinthine underground passages of Vienna; in 1809 defence was pointless.

To demolish the walls of conquered cities was a purely spiteful gesture in which Napoleon frequently indulged, and the Viennese felt, as they were meant to, humiliated and furious. Did some people see the finger of fate making frantic signs to them to seize this chance, to clear away the whole medieval clutter and let in air and light, as Lady Mary Wortley Montague would have had them do in 1740? If they did, I have failed to find the evidence. Nearly half a century had to pass before the walls finally went, and even then the public hated it.

The first detonations on 16th October were carefully timed to allow Napoleon to leave beforehand. He left Schönbrunn at 2 p.m., and it was not until four o'clock that the engineer officer in charge received the message that he had gone, and lit the fuse.

First the Schottentor was blown up, then the Kärntnertor, finally the Burgtor, and now the inefficiency of the French sappers aroused in many people pent-up feelings of exasperation, particularly if they owned or lived in houses in the vicinity of the detonations. Clearly, the engineers were not bothering to drill to a sufficient depth, as at each explosion the neighbouring houses were shattered as by an earthquake, showers of bricks and debris were flung into the air and landed in the streets and narrow lanes or, on the perimeter, halfway across the Glacis. The violence of the explosions was so great that in the government offices where councillors were

[1] Johannes N. Schrail whose papers came to light towards the end of the century.

95

drafting the ratification document of the peace treaty the conference table leapt and quivered under their hands. Fires broke out among the stacks of firewood in the yards of houses, hardly a pane of glass remained intact, but it seems that the only casualties were suffered by the French: one officer was killed and at each detonation several men were wounded.

The French clung to Vienna as though this defeated capital of the Empire, with all its languorous *joie de vivre*, offered not only the cosiest billets in all Europe but also some hint of permanence, of timelessness and therefore of reassurance which France, for a whole lifetime, had not offered. The endless hot, dry summer tailed off into an autumn which gave little promise of anything but a dreary winter: the crops had been trampled into the ground, the fruit shaken from the trees by the occupiers and eaten before it was ripe; the pantry shelves were bare of preserves and the cellars were empty. The battlefields had been tidied up, or where they had not, nature, as usual, was dealing with matters in her own way—apart from burned-out villages there was not much now to be seen and the Sunday excursions to the scenes of past grandeur and horror on the fields of Aspern and Wagram run by a few enterprising owners of transport had been discontinued. And inevitably it was a bad winter. Not only money troubles plagued the Viennese but all sorts of illnesses, caused, people thought, by the exceptionally rainy and foggy weather which continued for three months from 21st September until Christmas, as well as all the strain and hardship which that historical year 1809 brought with it. Worst of all was a disease called 'putrefying nerve fever' which attacked young, healthy adults in particular, and many died after a week's illness, while the elderly were more resistant. Croup raged among the small children. Nevertheless, on 29th October in the Apollosaal a Grand Ball was given which Eugène de Beauharnais, the Prince de Neuchâtel, Marshals Davout and Oudinot were pleased to attend.

To create the splendour of the Apollosaal on the Schottenfeld, nature at its most artificial had been wonderfully blended with all the plushy luxury which the imagination of early nineteenth-century man could conjure up. On entering, the visitor found himself in an entrance hall surrounded by small drawing-rooms, and already the sensation of being in an odd combination of park and salon had begun. Reaching the far end of this large antechamber he now stood at the top of a broad flight of stairs carpeted (then a rarity calling for comment) with green cloth and bordered by a golden balustrade overlaid by a cascade of climbing plants in flower, their colours thrown into relief by artfully placed lights. Extending from the base of the staircase lay an enormous hall with three circles of parqueted floor for dancing, while down the sides between avenues of cedar growing out of the ground and interspersed with statues, ran acres of the same green cloth, simulating grass. At the far end, taking up the whole width, stood a massive cliff, covered and surrounded by trees, bushes and flowering shrubs, at its foot a grotto, upon its summit Apollo driving his steeds, while coloured lights played upon him and his attendant muses. The dance orchestra was concealed behind the cliff. Apart from the grotto with its caves, galleries and fountains, there was a 'quiet room' extending the whole length of the hall. Here, away from the noise and glare of the dance hall, was a living garden where in the cool half-light people could wander between flower beds, beneath the spreading branches of trees, and through shrubberies, and the loudest sound was the whispering of fountains. In the centre stood a golden tent containing—rather an anti-climax—a billiard-table, and three other tents offered refreshments. But this was by no means all. Three dining-rooms with staggering fittings rounded off the amenities of a place of public entertainment (the Vauxhall Gardens are said to have been copied from it) of which the gross takings might be anything between 20,000 and 40,000 gulden in one evening. Unfortunately, the upkeep of the Apollosaal, combined with the high rate of interest at which it had been financed, ruined the owner. A too large proportion of the hothouse paraphernalia had constantly to be replaced, there were the thousands of wax candles, and all the luxury and general chi-chi which assumed the presence of a large reservoir of wealthy patrons who existed only to a limited extent.

And so, at last, the officers carrying with them the memory of this farewell ball, the French pulled out, leaving Vienna to cope with itself as best it might: flooded with beggars who continually streamed in from the stricken countryside with its burned-out villages, with the unemployed and the disabled, with refugees from as far off as the Tyrol who presented a social problem of their own;

Sound of Battle: the Enemy Departs

Vienna, when Franz I crept incognito but recognized and duly cheered into his capital on 26th November, was not a happy place. Material want, or some of its worst aspects, was gradually overcome as unemployment declined and all the channels through which charity and the rudimentary social services filtered came into operation. But for the educated public, as well as for all those people throughout the country who had been caught up in the flush of popular enthusiasm for the war against Napoleon, shocks of a different kind lay ahead.

The first of these concerned the fate of the people of the Tyrol. Led by the innkeeper from the Passeier valley, Andreas Hofer, inadequately supported by units of the regular army under the Marquis de Chasteler, they fought the French and Bavarian armies in a series of actions which ran parallel in time with events in the east of Austria. They won resounding victories at the two battles of Mount Isel, and threw the already installed invaders out of Innsbruck. It was not until after the Battle of Wagram when Napoleon had troops to spare that a pincer movement—French from the south, Bavarians from the north—was able to break the Tyrolese resistance. The Treaty of Vienna which handed over the Tyrol to Bavaria left the patriots hanging in the air: it was a situation which 'did the Court of Vienna no honour'.[1] Not that the Austrian government could have prevented the cession of the Tyrol. Napoleon was determined to sever the province from the rest of Austria so as to secure that direct passage between western Germany and Italy which from time immemorial until today traders have used and strategists have coveted for its value as a short cut. The *Landlibell* granted to the Tyrol in 1511 exempted the population from military service outside their frontiers but made them responsible for the defence of their province. Every man had the right to bear arms. Archduke Johann and his friend Josef von Hormayr were deeply involved in the Tyrolese resistance, and while this fact was a cause of displeasure to the Emperor, Hofer was personally known to Franz I, having reported to him at Schärding on the situation in the Tyrol, and latterly he held the rank of *Landeskommandant*. Andreas Hofer and his followers were therefore no mere guerrillas. Leaving aside

[1] Erich Zöllner, *Österreich, sein Werden in der Geschichte.*

the controversy over the legality or otherwise of Hofer's execution by order of Napoleon, it is however clear that if he had wanted to, Franz could have demanded that the Tyrolese patriots be treated as regular prisoners of war, and it is equally clear that when the time came not a finger was raised to save the lives of Hofer and his friends.

Prussia had collapsed on the fields of Jena and Auerstädt. Throughout 1809, borne up and swept along by the writings of the Schlegels, of Friedrich von Gentz, Adam Müller and many others, the hopes of central Europe had come to be focused on Austria. But from the beginning the Emperor Franz profoundly disliked the *Volksbewegung*, the people's movement. In all forms of popular enthusiasm, not without reason, he saw the seeds of social change if not of revolution itself. At the end of 1805 after the Treaty of Pressburg, he had promised the peoples of the Empire that their intellectual fetters would be loosened. But the positive results were negligible. During the French occupation the censorship was raised, but as no criticism of the French was allowed little improvement in the supply of reliable news and comment in the press resulted, since one form of bias was simply replaced by another. The effect on the supply of books, however, was sensational, and the reading public rushed to the bookshops to lay in the collected works of Goethe, Schiller and other standard authors. Once back in his capital, Franz I rounded on the popular movement. Suddenly, from members of the imperial family to writers of patriotic songs, those who had led it were personae non gratae watched by agents of the secret police, their correspondence censored. The main targets of the Emperor's suspicions were, of course, his brothers Karl and Johann. At moments he even fell to wondering whether he ought to see Karl's defeat in battle in a new light. Was it, perhaps, intentional? Baron Kutschera was instructed to keep an eye on Archduke Karl, a task in which success evaded him, presumably because Karl seldom invited him to his table. A man of painfully undistinguished appearance with the unattractive habit of sorrowfully referring to himself in such terms as 'poor swine', Kutschera is at least to be thanked for eliciting a touch of humour from Franz I. He had been, he told his master, to a 'naked ball'—one assumes in a brothel. 'Oh?' said the Emperor, unmoved, 'You must have been quite a sight.' Many years after the death of Kutschera, 'Kutsch' was the slang equivalent of the English 'cad' or 'bounder'.

If, as has been made out, the influence of the unspeakable Kutschera over the Emperor was 'daemonic', then not only in the sense that he fed the monarch's appetite for the gossip of the town, but in that he, and Baron Baldacci with him, consistently fought to counteract the influence of the royal brothers. Metternich, too, was already making himself indispensable to the Emperor, but the magnitude of the challenge which he now faced placed him in a different dimension from the concerns of Kutschera and Baldacci. As winter descended, this was nothing less than how to continue the fight against Napoleon by other means. Such a vulgar sentiment as 'If you can't beat 'em, join 'em' would greatly have offended Metternich's susceptibilities: this, nonetheless, is what he had in mind. To put this policy into practice it would be necessary to clamp down on the whole patriotic movement, to put it, in fact, into reverse. Patriots were now unfashionable—worse, they were subversive, a view with which the Emperor had no difficulty in agreeing since he had thought so all along. His cold enquiry to Castelli, writer of innumerable patriotic songs who now mentioned his services in the hope of preferment, is still a byword in Austria: 'Who told you to do so?'[1] The shock of this volte-face, the bitterness it aroused particularly among the educated middle classes, would be felt for a long time to come. Among the general population, interest in matters above their station would be more severely discouraged than ever, with an effect which the author of a memoir, *Meditations on the Peace in Vienna*, described as follows: 'As the path towards education of the mind and pleasures of a higher sort are being more and more restricted, people are becoming ever more sensual, at the same time more witless, thus sinking into a state of oafish ease in which it would be inadvisable to disturb them.'

Advisable or not, the whole of society, from courtier to lamplighter, was now dumbfounded by a piece of news which turned their whole world upside down. What did it mean? Was this the ultimate dishonour? Did it proclaim, as though with trumpets of silver, the salvation of the Empire, of the crown, of home and hearth?

[1] 'Wer hat's Ihnen angeschafft?'

5
'An amazing marriage':
Metternich in the Saddle

The Archduchess Marie Louise, eldest daughter of the Emperor Franz I, was to marry Napoleon Bonaparte. As the news of this forthcoming event, in its way perhaps the most unexpected in the whole era of the Napoleonic wars, travelled across Europe, few people can have been able immediately to grasp all its implications. To many, the marriage looked like a particularly shameless bit of barter. At the Court of St. James the feeling was that the proposed 'amazing marriage' was 'disgusting to every sentiment of honour and delicacy', a new humiliation for the House of Austria at the hands of Bonaparte. The hubbub in Vienna was indescribable, and opinions differed from one class to another and altered as the days passed. In the inns and coffee houses bewildered disapproval was at first almost universal, but soon, prompted by the newspapers and in particular by the ecstatic '*Eipeldauer*', doubt and resentment melted away and rejoicing took over. People began to see the whole thing from its sentimental angle: the loving father making an almost intolerable sacrifice so that his country might have peace, or at any rate, time to recover, to heal its wounds. 'They see', wrote Lulu Thürheim, 'our power re-established, peace secured and our finances placed in order. And yet there are those who are dismayed at the prospect that a daughter of the House of Austria should marry a parvenu, a man without principles, the enemy of our Fatherland and of humanity; that she should wish to ascend a throne from which the stench of her aunt's blood has scarcely departed.' Others again, she went on, saw Austria harnessed to France's chariot, its youth bleeding not to save home and country, but in the service of a tyrannical ambition. Was it not an act of despair like jumping out of the window of a burning house rather than be consumed by the flames? There was a risk of breaking one's neck. No one, she wrote in retrospect, thought of the real motive— no one, with the exception of one man, Metternich: Marie Louise was to avenge Austria.

There are many accounts of what people were thinking at the time, and they show that the sense of outrage was strongest and most lasting among the aristocracy and at Court. It was one of the things which they were always to hold against Metternich. But Lulu's words 'that she should *wish* to ascend a throne' must have been a slip of the pen, or possibly a touch of hindsight, as the Archduchess clearly wished nothing of the kind.

Marie Louise had been brought up to think of Napoleon as the devil incarnate. Twice, she and her family had been driven from Vienna, he was the enemy who had laid waste her father's dominions and brought the state to the edge of bankruptcy, and she took her cue from her stepmother's implacable hostility. Her political views apart, the Empress Maria Ludovica was fond of Marie Louise, and the thought of the girl being thrown to the wolves in this unworthy manner enraged her. Many years later, Marie Louise said that at that time her uncle Ludwig was in love with her and she with him, although the man she really wanted to marry was her cousin Franz of Modena, a brother of the Empress. At some time during the winter of 1809 and 1810 she began to sense what was in the wind and the prospect terrified her while at the same time she could hardly credit it, 'for Papa is too kind', she wrote to her close friend Victoria Colloredo, 'to use compulsion towards me in a matter of such magnitude.'

Napoleon's marriage to Josephine had brought forth no heir: was this her 'fault', or his? The pregnancy of Marie Walewska confirmed what he may indeed have known before, and the attempt on his life by young Stapps played its part in his decision to divorce Josephine and found a dynasty. First, he considered the Czar's youngest sister, the 15-year-old Grand Duchess Anna, and it is one of those fascinating 'ifs' of history to speculate on the likely consequences of such an alliance. But the idea of marrying the daughter of the last Emperor of the Holy Roman Empire fired his imagination even more. For a Bonaparte, the watchword must be legitimacy, and the unchallengeable prestige of the Habsburgs would cast a mantle of respectability about the throne of his future heir which would make of the Bourbons feeble spectres, devoid of substance, casting no shadow.

The Austrian Ambassador in Paris, Prince Karl Schwarzenberg, was told by Napoleon to probe the climate of opinion in the Hofburg, and on 4th December he wrote to Metternich in tones of robust commonsense: 'The great question is, what to do now? Do not be startled if I say that she must be sacrificed. . . . There would otherwise be no hope of gaining a few years of peace and quiet. Our downfall would soon follow upon a refusal. Can one hesitate when one has the choice between the ruin of the monarchy and the unhappiness of a princess? Millions of people have been sacrificed, and would it not bring glory to a princess to save her fatherland, even if she herself were lost? . . . That is my opinion, and if the marriage with the Grand Duchess Anna does not take place, there remains only this means to save ourselves. . . . Only thus shall we be able to stifle mistrust and to gain the time we need to reoccupy that place in European politics which is our due.'

Napoleon was not accustomed to having to wait for anything. The diplomatic feelers extended towards St. Petersburg and Vienna consequently bore a load both of urgency and of a need for extreme discretion; the Emperor of the French must not be seen to have been refused, and whichever prospective bride rejected his advances would be astonished to learn that a marriage contract had already been signed by the other.

This diplomatic juggling act accounts for the appalling situation in which Prince Schwarzenberg found himself on 7th February, 1810. A report from the French Ambassador in St. Petersburg, Caulaincourt, had arrived saying that consent seemed extremely unlikely. This was enough. At 4 o'clock in the afternoon the Bonaparte family council met in the Tuileries, and as far as Napoleon was concerned everything which followed may have seemed a mere formality. For Schwarzenberg this was far from being the case. At six o'clock he was asked to go to the Ministry of Foreign Affairs and sign the formal engagement contract in the name of his Emperor, while Champagny did the same on behalf of Napoleon. But Schwarzenberg had received no instructions from Vienna to undertake this binding commitment. How indeed could he have? Not only had such impetuosity on the part of the bridegroom not been foreseen in Vienna, but Napoleon had not yet made his formal request for the hand of the Archduchess, and according to etiquette, such a contract would always be signed at the place of residence of the bride, not of the bridegroom. For this brusque treatment the Emperor Franz never forgave Napoleon.

A considerable degree of mutual sympathy not far short of friendship existed between Napoleon and Schwarzenberg. Not long afterwards Napoleon's appreciation of his soldierly qualities was increased by admiration for the Austrian's conduct during the terrible fire at the Embassy reception for the Emperor and Marie Louise when Princess Schwarzenberg, among many others, lost her life. He took Schwarzenberg with him on journeys of inspection and out shooting, and he even went so far as to take him into his confidence over appointments to public office in France. In 1812 he would ask that Schwarzenberg be given the command of the Austrian auxiliary force. But for the moment the Ambassador was completely alone with a crushing responsibility. And he signed. With what anxiety he wrote his report to Metternich can be imagined: 'If it is truly the case that this objective has been taken by storm, yet Napoleon never acts in any other manner, and I thought it to be my duty not to let the favourable moment slip. That I have served my Lord and Master well I am fully convinced; should it be my misfortune to have aroused His displeasure by the action which I have taken, His Majesty can quite simply disavow me, but in that event I must request my immediate recall.'

The contract was now signed, but not only had the father of the bride not been asked for her hand in marriage, she herself had not been asked either. Franz I was by no means a stranger to the idea of marrying off Marie Louise to the arch-enemy, as the subject had first been mooted in 1804, curiously enough well before the two occupations of Vienna, when she was only 13 years old. According to the Comptroller of the imperial household, Johann Skall, who as such accompanied the family on all its peregrinations, in January

1806 there was much talk on the same lines. And now, all unawares, with everything signed and sealed behind her back, Marie Louise sat down and wrote to her father, asking for his consent to her marriage to the man she loved, Franz of Modena. The Empress also intervened on her behalf, to be told testily, 'You've got nothing, I've got nothing either and the girl has nothing; what sort of a marriage would that make?' Marie Louise's innocence of what was going on may have been due to the fact that she was staying in Budapest at the time. Now the news was broken to her, and after she had wept over the loss of a short-lived illusion that a royal princess could possibly be allowed to follow the call of her own feelings, she produced the following gallant statement: 'I desire only that which it is my duty to desire; where the interest of the state is concerned it is this interest which must be consulted and not my will. Ask my Father to take counsel of his sovereign duties and then to subordinate not one of these to considerations affecting my Person.'

Metternich, said Gentz, was *ivre de joie*, and he lost no time in drafting the instructions which Franz I was to give him: 'My consent to the marriage will secure the monarchy a few years of political peace which I shall be able to employ in healing its wounds. All My powers are devoted to the welfare of My peoples, therefore I cannot falter in My decision. Send a courier to Paris and declare that I shall accept the solicitation for the hand of my daughter, but with the express proviso that no conditions be affixed to it either on the one side or on the other; there are sacrifices which may not be sullied by anything which may smack of a transaction.' As to this, the business world had its own opinion, and at the news of the engagement shares in Vienna dropped by several points and only recovered as the result of hasty buying by the government. And the pessimists were to be proved right. No tangible advantage accrued to Austria from the marriage, either at the time or later. Metternich was hoping for a loan, and also for the return of provinces, but nothing came of either, while a trade agreement which at last took shape after long delay was most disadvantageous to Austria and Metternich was finally obliged to accept the opinion of the Finance Presidium to this effect and advise the Emperor not to ratify the treaty.

In the midst of the negotiations, on 20th February, Andreas Hofer was executed in Mantua.

'An amazing marriage': Metternich in the Saddle

It appears that to begin with, very little time and effort were expended on the question of the impediments to the marriage, and it came as something of a surprise when the Archbishop of Vienna, Count Hohenwart, sharply asked whether he was expected to compound in a bigamy? Sympathy for the Empress Josephine was general. Had she not been a loyal wife and companion to Napoleon throughout his rise to glory? Had she not been crowned Empress of the French? And now came the most serious impediment: had the civil marriage not been subsequently blessed by Cardinal Fesch? Reports, messages, memoranda were now flying backwards and forwards between Vienna and Paris. Cardinal Consalvi assured Metternich that according to Pope Pius VII, Fesch had deceived him over this benediction, and the marriage was unquestionably invalid. Archbishop Hohenwart, however, was dissatisfied with this assurance and he demanded clear answers to the following questions:

In obedience to what laws and under what form of marriage was the union between Napoleon and Josephine Beauharnais contracted? Was it a purely civil contract, or was there an intervention on the part of the Church? Had the civil contract, if such it was, an indissoluble union in view or one which, under certain conditions, would be set aside? If only a civil contract had been signed, was it renewed and conformed by the coronation performed by the Holy Father? Upon what grounds was the civil marriage dissolved, and what procedure was adopted by the spiritual authority in pronouncing the marriage to be null and void?

The Archbishop evidently meant to be awkward, at any rate until he could be relieved of the onus of consecrating a marriage which must make any Catholic's hair stand on end. Napoleon's excommunication, and although the Bull did not mention him by name it was a fact, was not mentioned at all, but there can be no doubt whatever that it had made a deep impact, not perhaps as much on the Viennese as on people up and down the country.

The Archbishop of Vienna was waiting for an answer.

An extraordinary diplomatic feat of sleight of hand now took place, a kind of 'now you see them, now you don't', carried out by Napoleon's emissary in Vienna, Comte Otto, with documents of pre-eminent legal importance; and for what happened we only have the word of the participants.

Papers containing all the evidence required by the Archbishop, and for that matter by the father of the bride who all this time was deeply offended by Napoleon's offhand manner, left Paris and were delivered into the hands of Comte Otto in Vienna. After a careful perusal of their contents he sent them—back to Paris. It was a very strange thing to do. Comte Otto was not a skilled diplomat. This conclusion may be drawn because he was generally disliked in Vienna, and good diplomats do not permit themselves behaviour which makes them unpopular in the country to which they are accredited. And yet he can hardly have sent the documents back to Paris out of sheer stupidity, carelessness or frivolity. It was always suspected that Metternich was behind their disappearance, either because he had read them and knew that they did not hold water, or because he knew that they could only consist, in equal proportions, of perjury and idle chatter. Be this as it may, the mystery of the vanished papers was a master-stroke because of the pressure of events. With Napoleon going ahead with preparations in his usual elemental style, there was no chance whatever that the papers might be recovered and handed over to the Archbishop or to the government for scrutiny. Otto, full of explanations and excuses for the unfortunate misunderstanding, did come up with an argument which was convincing as far as it went: no one had a greater interest in the legality of his second marriage than Napoleon, as it was upon this that the rights of succession of his heirs would rest. Any deception, he implied, would be entirely gratuitous. Count Hohenwart suggested that a *collegium* of lawyers be set up, but he allowed himself to be talked out of this, and at last agreed to accept a sworn statement by Count Otto about the content of the papers, to the effect that 'the original documents containing both judgments of the Diocesan and Metropolitan Law Offices of Paris, he having handled and perused the same, are essentially based upon the absence of all formalities prescribed by the Laws of the Church, and that herein lie the grounds whereby seven venerable Princes of the Church have pronounced the first marriage of His Majesty the Emperor Napoleon to be null and void in Canon Law and in the light of convincing original documents.'

These assurances got the Archbishop off the hook, and if it is tempting to feel that he allowed himself to be hoodwinked, then he must in all fairness be sharing in the humiliation of the Catholic Church as a whole. Cardinal Fesch had thought nothing of declaring the benediction which he had pronounced on Napoleon's marriage to Josephine to be invalid, and he subscribed to the desired view that the clerical court which had confirmed that marriage was not competent to decide, this being the prerogative of the Pope. And in effect, the Pope was now in captivity. But had he not crowned Josephine Empress of the French? True, he was tricked into doing so, but he had done it, and had the Pope crowned a mere concubine?

What of the rest of the Sacred College of Cardinals? It is perhaps pleasant to remember that not all of them went down like skittles. 29 cardinals were in Paris, 13 of whom found themselves unable to quieten their consciences. Led by one of the most brilliant minds in the Catholic Church, Cardinal Consalvi, the 13 rebels stayed away from the wedding, and if their choir stalls were conspicuously empty, their absence from the reception, where their crimson robes (symbolizing preparedness for martyrdom) would have lent an almost garish splash of colour to the scene, was equally noticeable. Napoleon was in such a benevolent mood that he took no action for the moment, but at a *levée* on 3rd April he dismissed them angrily from his presence, and the unfortunate baker's dozen had to squeeze their way out against the incoming tide and had great difficulty in finding their carriages. They can have had no doubt of the sequel. Dismissed from their posts and robbed of their emoluments, they were banned to the provinces where they lived as ordinary priests until, at last, the survivors were able to be reinstated.

Waggons full of wedding presents were arriving in Vienna, and on 8th March, at long last, the Grand Ambassador, the Duke of Neuchâtel, drove in state to Court to ask for the hand of the Archduchess Marie Louise. On Sunday, 11th March, Count Hohenwart consecrated her marriage to Napoleon by proxy, Archduke Karl standing in for the absent bridegroom. For these services Napoleon sent his recent enemy the Grand Cross of the Legion of Honour and the plain cross of the same order, with the citation: 'The one in homage to your genius as a General, the other for your exceptional courage in battle.'

Marie Louise was 19 years old. With a rather over-long face and the characteristic Habsburg lip, she was no great beauty but redeemed by a well-proportioned figure, shapely hands and feet, a good complexion and fine, plentiful chestnut hair. Napoleon must have known this and more, because he sent instructions for her to have her teeth cleaned. On 13th March, that extraordinarily doom-laden date in Austrian history, her state coach, in a procession of seven carriages each drawn by six greys, moved across the Michaeler-platz, down the Kohlmarkt and Graben, turned right up the Kärntnerstrasse, out through the Kärntner Gate and across the Glacis, along the Mariahilferstrasse to the outer line of defence, the *Linie*. There were flags, and crowds, and cheers, the bells of Vienna were ringing and guns were firing; Marie Louise, her old friend Countess Lazansky beside her, was in tears. Little girls dressed all in white, without whom no celebrations could ever have taken place in Austria nor ever will, popped up in small groups here and there, notably under the wing of a celebrated heroine of the Napoleonic wars, the locksmith's wife Franziska Klähr, who made a short speech, though what she was thinking she kept to herself. An odder scene took place on what used to be called the Braunhirschengrund at the end of the Mariahilferstrasse, not far from the house and grounds of the great hostess of the age of Jewish emancipation, Fanny von Arnstein. A more humble establishment was owned by one Friedrich Halderlein, licensed brewer of coffee, who set up a *tableau vivant* at his door. A draped table representing an altar was flanked on either side by 14 maidens, who, on their knees, raised their arms in supplication to the deity. Flames rose up from the altar behind which stood Halderlein, in his arms a small child which also, on the approach of the state coach, put its hands together and held them up in prayer.

And so the Emperor's eldest daughter left Vienna. At St. Pölten her father and stepmother were waiting, incognito, to cheer her on her way. On to Enns and Wels, and Lambach: this was the road which Marie Antoinette had followed before her, and here on 23rd April, 1770, at Lambach, on her way to her wedding in Paris, Maria

'An amazing marriage': Metternich in the Saddle

Theresa's daughter had paused to open the Abbey theatre. Forty years had passed between the one royal progress and the other, and if by chance some elderly courtier was present at both series of ceremonies and felt as though time had stood still, he was not dreaming: Metternich had sent for the files, showing, it was thought, a striking lack of tact. But as Marie Louise, titular Empress of the French, changed at Braunau into clothes and jewels from Paris and set off again for Munich, Augsburg, Nancy, Reims and that dramatic encounter at Courcelles which cast all protocol to the winds and left innumerable dignitaries along the road to Paris with speeches unread and presentations unpresented, she was moving not only towards pomp and brief glory, but towards a term of happiness as well. In spite of all the mutually denigrating comments that both were one day to make, the marriage was a success from the outset. Here, for the moment, we must leave her.

The extent of Metternich's influence and his responsibility for events has always been disputed. But there can be no doubt that by this time his personal influence over the Emperor was already such as to arouse the intense hostility of the nobility, and it is one of the more curious aspects of the long 'reign' of this statesman that the hostility was as general as it was implacable; with the exception of his family, his loves and a few immediate associates in subordinate positions, Metternich aroused little affection. This might appear to point to a surprising lack of skill in public relations, but his career rested on the solid foundations of his relationship with two people, Franz I and, in spite of all his love affairs, with his wife. It was as the grand-daughter of Prince Kaunitz that Eleonore (Lorel) was able to pave the way to a career in diplomacy in the service of Austria, she herself having the entrée to every drawing-room in Europe while she was also drawn into those inner circles where affairs of state were discussed rather than fashion or the latest play. She was tubercular and she passed on that scourge of the times to her seven children. Owing to her belief that the air on the banks of the Seine suited her better than the mists which rose from the Danube, soon after Metternich's appointment to office she return to Paris. There she played her part, quietly but effectively, in cementing the new alliance with France. It was not an easy task because of Napoleon's annoyance over le beau Clément's *lèse-*

majesté in philandering with his sister, Caroline Murat, any more than he had enjoyed the uproar created in Paris society on identical grounds by Laure Duchess of Abrantès and Madame Récamier, in their agonies of fully justified mutual jealousy. But Napoleon always liked Countess Metternich, rude though he could sometimes be: 'Well, Madame! We are growing old; we are getting thin; we are growing ugly!' It must have stung, but she only laughed, and was rewarded with an approving 'You have far more intelligence than all the rest of these salon coteries put together.'

It was after Metternich's return to Vienna at the end of the protracted talks in Paris that she made herself indispensable as a commentator and informant on the political scene. Moreover she was disinterested, frank and completely loyal, and he repaid her in the manner of a *grand seigneur*: with gratitude, sincere friendship and all manner of attentions, he wrote to her constantly and visited her when he could. After many years of married life which can have been anything but easy, she said that she could not imagine how any woman could resist him. It was a generous remark, characteristic of Lorel Metternich who tacitly acknowledged and was kind to the daughter of Princess Bagration, born early in 1802 and defiantly christened Clémentine, who was undoubtedly Metternich's daughter.

After the initial stepping-stone of his marriage the chief secret of Metternich's rise to power lay in the ventriloquist's art with which, while disclaiming personal authority and authorship, he converted Franz I into an instrument of government. With infinite delicacy he told him what to think, he guided his mind and his actions, and how carefully this had to be done will become clear when the Emperor's deep distrust of men with brains is remembered. Basically, they were of one mind, and it was only that Metternich was infinitely more subtle, more articulate, than his master, so that he could play on the Emperor's fears and yet give him confidence. Metternich may have been speaking the truth when, as a much older man, he told the Russian Ambassador for the information of Czar Nicholas that if ever he had attempted to force an action upon Franz I against the Emperor's will he would have been dismissed from office immediately. To be out of a job, to be relieved of perhaps the one post in all the courts of Europe which it amused him to occupy, was not however a predicament which was likely to overtake Metternich; he would not have been so careless.

But in proportion to the growth of his influence over Franz I, so hostility within the imperial family, the Court and senior nobility towards Metternich spread and deepened. There were several reasons for this. Initially, of course, he was an outsider, a Rhinelander, and he had ousted Stadion, a man who belonged to the innermost circle of Austrian society. But to educated men and women who had grown up in the eighteenth century, the first handicap was not insurmountable, while a man possessing such exceptional physical advantages added to charm and powers of persuasion might have won over part of the enemy camp in time. This, in all his years of office, he never did. His involvement in the marriage of the Archduchess brought him a tapestry, a bust of Napoleon and a set of Sèvres china ('a service for a service' remarked the Prince de Ligne) for 150 people, worth altogether about 12,000 francs, but odium as well: many people in Austria, beginning with the Empress Maria Ludovica, could not forgive him for it. His critics saw the humiliation, but they overlooked the fact that this marriage alliance drove a wedge between France and Russia, or, to the extent that they did realize it, they disapproved.

When Metternich came to power the stark facts of the situation were that Austria now lay open to attack by Napoleon or his successors all the way from Bohemia to Northern Italy. The Tyrol had gone; Salzburg and Berchtesgaden with their salt mines had gone; access to the sea and the trade routes of the world was cut off; Galicia, prosperous and by the standards of those days relatively densely populated, was lost as well; and the Empire was crushed by war indemnities and stood within an inch of bankruptcy—which in fact followed only a year later. Where Metternich differed from the Empress's following was in the conclusions to be drawn from this appalling state of affairs. In their view, to stay with England and Russia against Napoleon until he should at last be defeated was from every point of view the only desirable policy, not least because it was the only honourable course. Metternich disagreed entirely. This was not the moment for bellicose gestures but for infinitely delicate diplomacy and for cautious reinsurance. To his mind a Franco-Russian marriage alliance would have been an unmitigated disaster. This had been fended off, but at the present moment Austria could not afford any compromising alliances whatever which would cause offence to other powers.

And yet total disagreement over foreign policy was not the only reason why the imperial family had begun to loathe—the term is not too strong—the Minister for Foreign Affairs. The German proverb is apt: a man's shirt lies closer to his skin than his jacket, and Metternich now presented a tangible threat to those near to the throne because he had insinuated his person between them and the Emperor. Along the road to power Metternich never had any other choice: he must dominate the Emperor, and to do so he must not merely serve him as his adviser on foreign affairs, he must learn to tread on the thin ice of his neurotic fear and suspicion of his brothers. There was never to be an open breach between Franz I and the Archdukes Karl and Johann, not even when the imperial displeasure was a matter of common knowledge and may today seem not unjustified, but Metternich would always know how to make the most of these occasions in his own interests and he would very soon feel sufficiently sure of himself to increase the estrangement between the Emperor and his wife. For the moment, the dominant preoccupation was the economic situation.

This potentially so infinitely wealthy Empire was forever tottering on the brink of financial disaster. It had never been otherwise, particularly throughout the long struggle against Islam when the commander in the field had to maintain extensive military campaigns on a hand to mouth basis; the wails about the Emperor's empty coffers were never silenced. The Napoleonic wars saw a new development, or one never used on this scale before: economic warfare. For twelve years the monarchy was menaced by a flood of forged currency manufactured with the approval of the authorities in Verona, Brescia, Ancona and other towns within the area of Napoleonic conquest in Italy. There were also printing presses in France where banknotes were forged for circulation in the Austrian territories, and as late as 1809 Napoleon caused Austrian currency printed in Paris to be handed over to his generals with orders to say that they were war booty, and he himself referred to these supplies of money in the presence of Viennese town councillors, though without mentioning their true origin. The councillors were not deceived, as they knew that for years past the government had been fighting to ward off this threat to the economy by all diplomatic means and also by bribery. The marriage of Marie Louise to Napoleon brought this evil to an end, but the misery of people such as civil servants and soldiers' families who had to exist on fixed incomes was mocked by the conspicuous wealth of all those who were able to float on the inflationary situation, and neither sector was encouraged by the evident helplessness of the government. After a rapid turnover in Presidents of the Hofkammer, or Ministers of Finance, the man in office in 1810 was Count O'Donnell, a man, at last, with a grasp of the principles of economics. But he died of what Gentz called 'anxiety and distress' since he failed to win the full support of the Emperor Franz, who, being 'quite incapable of comprehending the system of O'Donnell or of anyone else' now bestowed the office upon Count Josef Wallis, the Governor of Bohemia. Horrified, Wallis protested that he knew not the first thing about finance, but the Emperor reassured him. 'No matter! Such a man is the one for me. You were a loyal Governor in Prague, therefore you will be a trustworthy President of the Hofkammer.'

Count Wallis was certainly not slow to act. His name is remembered for the *Finanzpatent* promulgated on 20th February, 1811, a currency reform introducing *Einlösungsscheine*, redemption notes as the only legal tender at one-fifth of the face value of the paper money in circulation. If he had hoped to stabilize the economy by this measure alone he was soon to be disillusioned, not only because Metternich was demanding munitions and would not be denied them, nor even because no adequate steps were taken to control prices. Unhappily, the vital element of secrecy was absent. Days beforehand, the news of what was to happen must have become almost common knowledge, as a great many members of the aristocracy and a number of leading financiers and industrialists were able to bring their fortunes to safety. Baron Thugut and some of his friends bought up old government stocks which were not affected by the devaluation. Prince Liechtenstein, the Emperor's mother-in-law, the Archduchess Maria Beatrix, and even the Empress herself used one of the court lawyers, Dr. Neubauer, as their agent with the bankers Arnstein and Eskeles and managed to convert all their available old currency in good time, while everyone else in the know naturally followed suit. What Wallis himself did is not altogether certain. The rumour went the rounds that he secretly paid all his debts in old currency before he announced his *Finanzpatent*; conversely, in this tricky game of paying your creditors and dodging your debtors he is known to have refused a payment of 10,000 florins in old currency but to have demanded it in new redemption notes after 20th February.

Count Wallis's policy did arrest inflation to some extent for a short interval. But in the chancelleries of Europe the *Patent* was looked upon as an extremely crude financial manœuvre which would certainly have the political effect of preventing Austria from lending active support to Napoleon when he attacked Russia. The publicist Adam Müller, a protégé of Friedrich von Gentz who worked in the State Chancellery in Vienna, wrote in August 1811 to the Prussian Minister of State, Count Hardenberg: 'It can be assumed with certainty that no active participation by Austria is to be expected.' This was 'the sole favourable result' of Wallis's currency reform: Austria would be kept from marching with France against Russia for at any rate the next eight or ten months.

These prophets had not yet learned to reckon with Metternich, whose view it was that the national economy must be the servant of foreign affairs, never the reverse. He accordingly disregarded it and embarked with infinite care on one of the most delicate balancing acts of his life. In pulling it off he was extremely fortunate, but as Baron Wessenberg, a diplomat who watched his rise at close quarters, said, 'Metternich's luck was phenomenal.'

In this case his good fortune consisted in the fact that his diplomacy was based on an altogether false premise. For Metternich believed that Napoleon would conquer Russia.

Throughout that year the diplomatic scene was overshadowed by the forthcoming campaign. Napoleon was determined to have the active assistance of Austria, to the extent, at least, of an army of 40,000 to 50,000 men preferably under the command of Archduke Karl, and as the Emperor's son-in-law, he was in a position to override all opposition. Empress Maria Ludovica was up in arms at the very idea. How could anyone with a sense of honour, dignity or loyalty, contemplate asking an army which for a generation had fought and bled in the struggle against Napoleon, to turn round and fight at his side against an ally? Had the House of Habsburg not sufficiently lost face in the marriage of Marie Louise that it must now humiliate itself totally? This was the general opinion at Court, and in course of time it was to spread with perhaps even greater bitterness to the army. The Archduke was infuriated to find that, as near as no matter, he had been committed to taking over the command of an auxiliary corps without being consulted. What would the Czar think of him? Had he not wished to marry Alexander's sister Catherine—a plan which Napoleon had ditched? Metternich, of course, was not deterred by personal links between Romanov and Habsburg; Archduke Joseph, Palatine of Hungary, was Alexander's brother-in-law by his marriage to the Grand Duchess Alexandra Pavlovna, since whose death in 1802 the Archduke had remained in close contact with St. Petersburg because of his affectionate relationship with the Czarina Mother.

Archduke Karl refused the command, saying that to accept it would place him in a false position. A general who was not a member of the imperial family might plead that he was under orders, but this would not do for a brother of the Emperor. Nor could he publicly support an alliance 'which runs counter to the true interests of the state, as well as to the sentiments of the Sovereign and the mood of all the peoples of Austria.'

This left Schwarzenberg. Napoleon would have preferred to have the Archduke for the very reasons that caused him to decline: because his status as the Emperor's brother offered the guarantee he sought that the corps would not suddenly defect. Failing this he had perfect confidence in Schwarzenberg, 'a man of honour upon whom I can rely.' The Prince accepted the command, but with a heavy heart.

At Napoleon's wish the two Emperors were to meet—they had never done so before—at Dresden, accompanied by their consorts and a considerable retinue. If the Empress Maria Ludovica could have stayed behind in Vienna she would certainly have done so to avoid an encounter which she felt to be profoundly disagreeable. On the other hand she and her ladies were not incurious to see what changes might have come about in Marie Louise, who for her part would undoubtedly be happy to see the father whom in her way she adored and to whom she still wrote in terms of anxious submissiveness as well as loving concern, even though she had been a married woman for two years.

Napoleon and Marie Louise arrived in Dresden on 17th May, the Austrian party a day later—that much honour at least was paid to them. Marie Louise's public manner was always chilly, and even in private she gave off little warmth, but Maria Ludovica's description is in marked contrast to the impressions gained by members of the Court in Paris who found her friendly and unassuming, her general approach unaffected and girlish. 'She is still just the same as she always was. Amiable, not lacking in spirit but cold and very childish, she is fond of making silly remarks, like the whole illustrious family. In this they are all alike. No souls, no interests: automatons, well educated perhaps, but incapable of arousing the least affection in the people around them. For my own part I can say that she was most kind because she cannot be other than she was; others would call her cool and most rough in her manner. Well, she was thus with her Father and her Father with her. So are they all, they are made of a most strange material, such as must dry out souls and cause all hearts to die of thirst.'

Franz I quite fell for Napoleon and exasperated his suite by muttering at frequent intervals, 'That's some fellow, that is!' Archduke Johann left Dresden after two days because to watch the Emperor being dazzled by Napoleon and showing it in all sorts of servile little ways he found quite intolerable. Metternich was not so much annoyed as alarmed, fearing that at any moment Napoleon might win some fatal concession from the Emperor: that, for instance, he might be talked into accompanying Napoleon on to the field of battle. His anxiety is understandable, for Napoleon could cast a spell over men and women if he wished to, and at the moment he did wish it: no need now to try to draw Franz over to his side through his wife's letters to her father; the parvenu could fascinate the Austrian Emperor in person and try to neutralize the aura of implacable hatred spread by Maria Ludovica. For the moment he succeeded, and yet it was not Franz I alone who was fascinated. Napoleon, who had always understood perfectly the difference between his personal position and that of the legitimate scion of an ancient dynasty, was more than a little impressed by the Habsburg glamour. And not only that but he found there was more to Franz than he had supposed: common sense, and good judgement in practical matters. After 20 years on the throne Franz I had accumulated so much experience that he was able, his son-in-law found, to reduce him to silence again and again.

The encounter was dramatic; it was news, but it was not as epoch-making as any of the participants thought at the time. No irredeemable gaffes were perpetrated on either side. All the same, Dresden too was chalked up against Metternich by his enemies in the Hofburg.

The Empress Marie Louise left on 4th June, but not for home, as she was allowed to spend a further three weeks, most enjoyably, with her family in Prague. Here too she did nothing to endear herself to the crowds whose short-lived enthusiasm she quenched with a stiff nod of acknowledgement. She left Prague on 1st July and was back in St. Cloud on the 18th.

During these leisurely days in Prague a most striking document was drafted and signed. It was addressed to the Chief of Police in Vienna by the Emperor Franz and dated 16th June, 1812.

The friendship between the Empress Maria Ludovica and her brother-in-law Joseph, the Palatine of Hungary—at no time was it more than that—provided an outlet for them both in times of stress and irritation and it consoled her a little in her increasing feeling of isolation. To a woman of her temperament this loneliness was not without its perils. The fact that she was no longer sexually attractive to her husband affected her position, if the comparison is at all permissible, in a way that Eleonore Metternich was spared. Metternich's love life was no business of his wife's, but never would he have dreamed of being anything less than solicitous and considerate towards her; he remained her friend to the end. Franz I—it is difficult to escape this impression—looked upon the ill health of his consort as a nuisance, and he was put out by it. As she no longer pleased him, she was falling short on that service to the crown, to himself, which was her sole function. Ill health was a form of disloyalty. And as he had always resented the fact that she was too clever for him, now he took his revenge in small ways. Maria Ludovica never shirked her duties, but she found it a bit unnecessary to be taken for long drives in the heat of the day and to be bounced up and down on roads full of potholes. Metternich was watching her and she knew it. There was that day two years ago when she had to stand for hours receiving 94 ladies of the nobility, and the exquisite figure of the Foreign Minister hove in view. Exhausted and irritated she rapped out: 'Count Metternich, what is your rank as a peeress, and with whose permission have you come here unannounced?' Scarlet with mortification, Metternich bowed and retired. The snub, the smiles of the peeresses, smarted.

He not only watched her, he also caused her to be watched. Her letters to her great friend Countess Esterházy were perhaps a trifle indiscreet, and in a different way so were those that she wrote to the Crown Prince Ferdinand, a mentally retarded youth for whom she felt deep compassion and concern, because of the criticism they contained of life at Court. But her correspondence with Archduke Joseph presented by far the most promising target because, by means of selective quotation, the impression of an embryo love affair could be presented, while in view of Franz's suspicious nature he could be relied upon to detect a slight flavour of high treason by association. In the case of this Archduke it was not Napoleon, but Alexander I of Russia, who would like to have seen him wearing the imperial crown. The fact that, like his brothers, he too would have rejected, or did reject, the very idea with horror, made little difference. It is surprising, since she must have known that her letters were censored, that the Empress failed to think of all this, or perhaps she did but didn't care. Metternich decided that the time had come, and he wrote a memorandum to the Emperor warning him about Maria Ludovica's association with the Palatine. Metternich has often been accused of hypocrisy, not always with justice, but on this occasion he surpassed himself, or—since these were early days— it could be said that he set up a record which he would find it hard to exceed. In tones of sanctimonious concern he advised moderation, counselling the Emperor to adopt towards his consort an attitude of 'paternal mildness', to the end that mutual trust and a sense of security be restored to the imperial marriage. How this highly desirable state was to be regained when, if any element of it had still existed, he himself had now destroyed it for ever, Metternich did not explain. The instruction to the Chief of Police, drafted by Metternich and signed by the Emperor, runs: 'Dear Baron Hager, You are to submit to me in brief and without delay all details concerning the correspondence between my Consort and the Arch-duke Palatine, the intermediaries of this correspondence, the means and channels used for its furtherance and the maintenance of secrecy regarding it, together with all other available information pertaining to the alleged connection between the above persons.'

The Emperor was not altogether a stranger to his wife's corre-spondence, but from now on this material figured more promi-nently in what Hormayr referred to as his *Morgenplaisir*: together with a close scrutiny of anonymous letters from all over the Empire, reading the personal mail of his closest relations was now taking up several hours of his time every day.

Baron Hager, like his predecessor Count Pergen, was not at all a sinister figure. A first cousin of Lulu Thürheim and a close friend of Caroline Pichler and her circle, he was all that a civil servant should be: a man of undoubted integrity, hard-working, discreet, unassuming and loyal. Metternich gave a bad report of him to the Emperor: Hager was 'nervous' and 'of weak character'—comments which simply reflect the consternation of a respectable senior civil servant at being ordered to spy on his Empress. Metternich's attack upon her was well-aimed and well-timed. He was right in supposing that his opponents would give a year's rent to unsaddle him, he had now anticipated any attack from that quarter and he had strengthened his position still further, while from the point of view of foreign policy it was a blow against the anti-French, pro-Russian *camarilla*.

From Prague, Maria Ludovica went to Teplitz to take the baths. Goethe was there, in attendance on the Duke of Weimar, a dis-covery which delighted her. 'I see him every day, his company is highly instructive. To listen to him while he reads delights my heart.' Goethe said that in the 26 days which he and the Empress spent in Teplitz she invited him to her table no less than 11 times, an honour which, his patron apart, no other royal personage ever bestowed on him.

Winter came, and with it, almost unremarked by history in the shadow of the disaster of the Grande Armée in the retreat from Moscow, the fate of the Austrian auxiliary corps. It was a force of about 20,000 combatants, 29,000 in all, of whom 7,000 fell in battle while another 4,000 died of disease or exposure. The survivors, not much better off than their French allies, were stranded in Poland without money. As Prince Schwarzenberg described the situation in letters to his wife, there was no money to pay the troops, officers were living on credit and in Warsaw the wounded were having to sell whatever possessions they had about them to pay their hospital expenses. Bread was soon in such short supply that the men had to make one loaf last anything up to a fortnight. 'The commissariat', he wrote, 'has turned my hair grey.' And at the end of November: 'Man and beast are approaching complete disintegration.' The army's predicament was partly a result of the obstinacy, or the tenacity, of Count Wallis in clinging to his currency reform. To give his point of view, the failure of his efforts to restore the economy must be put down to Metternich's insistence on involving the country in yet another military adventure beyond its means.

The traumatic fate of the Grande Armée in Russia fundamentally altered Austria's position in Europe. Napoleon was in mortal danger. The moment had now arrived when Austria, drawing to its side Russia, Prussia, all of Germany, and Italy, could have called upon Europe to awaken and overthrow the usurper. Metternich might well have achieved this. Never mind that he had believed Napoleon could conquer Russia: it had been his policy to align Austria with France only to the extent that was vital for survival and for as long as he must for the salvation of the monarchy, and without calling down the wrath of Alexander—after all, the auxiliary corps was a mere token force. The Commander-in-Chief, Count Radetzky, had no doubts at all: this was the opportunity. But Metternich hesitated, his political instinct warned him that the consequences of unleashing such popular emotions were incalculable. And the Emperor was by no means ready to fall upon his son-in-law and destroy him. Not yet.

But there were other men, one of them close to the throne, who believed that the time to act had come, and if the Emperor and his Foreign Minister would not move, they would do so themselves. A plot was born, filled with the elements of Greek tragedy, which yet leaves one feeling irritated with all the participants. In some ways it is a very Austrian story.

The nineteenth century was to produce ample proof that the lot of a Habsburg archduke was seldom a happy one. Archduke

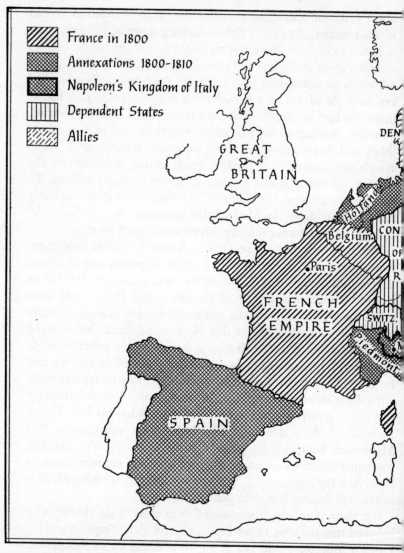

2. The Napoleonic conquests

Johann was now in his early thirties and his two appearances on the world's stage had been honourable but undistinguished. That celebrated romance for which the general public remembers him today, his courtship of the postmaster's daughter from Bad Aussee,[1] the interminable wait until at last the Emperor's heart softened, but also his unique services to industry and technology in Styria, all these things still lay in the future. He was a man who stood with one foot in the Age of Reason, with the other in the industrial revolution; soldiering was not his métier and he had no interest in the social life of Vienna. In 1804 his brother Franz had the inspired idea of sending him round the country to report on and reorganize the defence system. As a result, he learned more about the topography of the Tyrol, Carinthia, Styria and Inner Austria than any Habsburg before him, not even excepting Maximilian I. And, of course, while he was doing so he was getting to know the local civil servants, the game-wardens, farmers and cottagers. He felt a particular affinity with the people of the Tyrol, Europe's first democrats since Ancient Greece,[2] and he was in close touch with Andreas Hofer throughout the campaign of 1809.

Another leading actor in this drama was Baron Josef Hormayr, a senior civil servant and holder of one of the highest orders, the Order of St. Leopold, who at this time was Director of the State Archives. His friendship with Archduke Johann's former tutor the Swiss historian Johannes von Müller (not to be confused with the publicist Adam Müller) brought him into contact with the Archduke. The two men, as it chanced, were born on the same day. A most fruitful association developed, and Hormayr became the Archduke's chief assistant and adviser in all his projects. Two other participants were a Court of Appeal councillor, Anton Schneider, and a provincial civil servant, Anton von Roschmann. Together, these men designed a plan of staggering dimensions.

On Easter Monday, 19th April, 1813, a popular rising led by Archduke Johann was to start in the Tyrol and Southern Germany and spread across the whole alpine region of central Europe: Switzerland, Vorarlberg, Styria, Carinthia and Illyria. The purpose of the operation was to force the government's hand and compel it

---

[1] See *Austria, People and Landscape*, by the same author, 1971, pp. 143–49.
[2] Charter dated 28th January, 1342.

to form an alliance with Russia and Prussia so that together they would all fall upon Napoleon at this crucial moment. The word was to go round that the Emperor knew of the plan and was secretly on their side.

The *Alpenbund*, or Alpine Union, was not without allies. John Harcourt King, the British agent in Vienna, was in touch with London, and the leaders of the movement were told that they could depend on receiving arms, ammunition and subsidies. A down payment of £20,000 to £30,000 was expected any day. By February the Archduke's plans were complete. In the first stage he and his men would secure all the passes and defiles in Salzburg and the Tyrol as well as the chief towns. What happened after that would depend on the response in the neighbouring provinces and on the speed of events. If the southern flank followed the Austrians' lead, ships of the Royal Navy were to land arms and men at Fiume— King was keeping the Naval Command in the Adriatic informed as well as G.O.C. Sicily—and the British were to seize the Arsenal at Venice and land an expeditionary force at Genoa. In the meantime a friend of the Archduke, Lieutenant-Field-Marshal Wallmoden, was calling together volunteers in North Germany, funds being supplied by King. A Swedish task force of 20,000 was to be landed at Hamburg, while the Pasha of Bosnia was to invade Illyria. There can be no doubt that the Czar was kept informed. The rumour which, when he heard of it, particularly wounded Franz I, that Alexander meant to set up Johann as King of Rhaetia giving him the hand of the Grand Duchess Maria Pavlovna in marriage, was certainly untrue, but a Russian plan did exist to assassinate Metternich.

The whole affair was a glorious conspiracy on the grand scale, worthy to be placed beside the boldest of all time. And who knows? It might have succeeded. What seems so astonishing now is not so much the speed at which the plotters worked—the seeds of the plan must have been ripening in the minds of Johann and Hormayr before the invasion of Russia—as the fact that the highly expert censorship and the secret police of Franz's régime appear to have fallen down on the job. All those meetings, letters, couriers—and yet the authorities were completely unaware of what was going on. Suddenly, the plot was torn wide open. Roschmann lost his nerve and reported the whole story, adding that a courier would be leaving in a few days' time bearing highly compromising correspondence from John Harcourt King to Viscount Cathcart, the British Ambassador in St. Petersburg, for further transmission to Viscount Castlereagh.

During the early hours of 26th February, the courier, whose name was Danelon, was fallen upon by 'highwaymen' near Weisskirchen in Moravia and robbed of his papers and 300 ducats. The captured documents, eagerly examined in Vienna, fully confirmed all that Roschmann had said, and he was at once put back into circulation with orders to find out all that he could about the conspiracy's international network. Clearly, it was essential to work at great speed, making the fullest use of the time lag before King heard what had happened to the courier. Danelon, meanwhile, was lucky to escape with his life, as he had been lying in the snow, bound with cords, for three hours before he was found. Roschmann, a half-willing, timorous Judas, was soon able to report that some leaders of the conspiracy, Gagern and Schneider, were to leave Vienna on 8th and 9th March, while the Archduke would be staying on until between the 10th and 16th.

The time had come to pull them in. On 7th March Baron Hormayr had an evening engagement with a Baroness Matt whose salon was much frequented by members of the 'second society' and the bourgeoisie with intellectual interests such as the great orientalist Hammer-Purgstall, the Schlegels, Adam Müller and Caroline Pichler. This evening the intention was to give a reading of 'The Bride of Messina'. Frau Pichler had been looking forward to this, but as she was prostrated with migraine she stayed at home and missed the whole thing. Accounts conflict, but Hormayr appears to have been arrested at the party, while Anton Schneider and (for the sake of appearances) Roschmann were arrested in Hormayr's house during the same night. Certainly the women of Hormayr's house made a tremendous scene. They shrieked and wept, they gave a display of 'cramps' and vapours, all of this fully understandable in view of the desperate plight of the men, but to some extent the uproar may have been deliberate. At all events the officers of the law, evidently unnerved, left the house with their prisoners, and no search was carried out, no seal placed on desks or cabinets, no one was left behind to guard the place. The ladies must have rapidly recovered their composure, because by the morning not a scrap of incriminating evidence was to be found. Metternich was furious with Hager for his 'weakness' in allowing such a thing to happen, with some justification because from the official point of view Hager's lapse, if it was intentional, amounted to making himself an accessory, or if not, to gross carelessness. The documents taken from the courier Danelon were not admissible as evidence,[1] and in any case, opinion in foreign capitals had been sufficiently shocked by this flagrant breach of diplomatic usage without its authorship being officially acknowledged. Metternich was therefore left with a vast conspiracy for which he had no evidence which would stand up in a court of law.

It was still winter and snow was falling, but Hormayr, in knee-breeches and tails, was swept off to Hungary in an open carriage, and it was not until they reached Budapest that he was transferred to a closed coach. He can have had no doubt of his destination: the fortress of Munkacs, but the ten-day journey was wasted effort as he was soon transferred to the equally notorious Spielberg near Brünn, where he remained, uncharged and untried, at His Majesty's pleasure. What the Emperor was to do about his erring brother was a rather more difficult problem. The Archduke's chief equerry, Count Niembsch, was instructed to prevent him from leaving Vienna without the Emperor's permission, but this was an unnecessary precaution. His friends' arrest sent him hurrying to the Chancellery on the Ballhausplatz where he made what Metternich called a kind of general confession. He still had no idea who had denounced them, as he asked for clemency for Roschmann and Schneider, but he incriminated Hormayr to the fullest extent—or so Metternich maintained. It had been his dream to liberate Austria's lost provinces, but he recognized his error, he begged the Emperor's pardon and promised to be of good behaviour in the future.

It is perhaps difficult to say what crime he had committed. Not high treason; he intended no disloyalty to the crown. But in the

---

[1] Throughout the reigns of Franz I and his son Ferdinand incriminating material obtained through censorship and surveillance was never used as evidence in the courts. There was a reluctance to disclose the methods used, but also a fear that the courts might not convict.

eyes of Franz and Metternich the consequences, if the affair had snowballed, would have been equally unpleasant, whether successful or not. Meanwhile Archduke Johann had undoubtedly been guilty of the very thing which Franz I always feared and tried to forestall in the case of his brother Karl: playing at foreign affairs. Forbidden to set foot in the Tyrol—it would be twenty years before he went there again—Archduke Johann turned his attention to Styria. No more was said of the matter but he remained under surveillance. Franz donated the 300 ducats to charity.

In France, after the tragedy of 1812 a yearning for peace was deepening, and this was at last something more than a reaction to the shock of defeat. People wanted an end to slaughter, and the Parisians showed their feelings by giving comforts to prisoners of war as they were led through the streets. Even the generals wanted peace, everyone except Napoleon who could think of nothing but the disgrace of the retreat from Moscow—amounting in his case to a headlong flight primarily to save his life but also, as an immediate corollary, to secure his political survival and that of his dynasty. Austria must help him to wipe out the stain, and to drag the monarchy into new campaigns was the purpose of his celebrated meeting with Clemens Metternich on 28th June at Dresden. For what was said and done during that marathon talk-in we only have the word of the two men, and their accounts conflict. But Metternich's story is well enough in character. Napoleon ranted at him for the better part of six hours, but he had many a far more trying experience behind him at the Tuileries and elsewhere, and at last he protested:

'Your Majesty has used up a whole generation and has kept Europe at war for twenty years.'

'Monsieur!' flared Napoleon. 'You are not a soldier. I grew up under arms and a man like myself cares not a whit for the lives of a million men!'

Metternich was exceptionally insensitive to the feelings of the general public. Nevertheless his shocked indignation is credible:

'Why does Your Majesty use these words to *me* between four walls? Let us throw open windows and doors so that all Europe may hear you! The cause which I represent in your presence is not the one which stands to lose by it.'

9. The army banquet in the Prater after the Battle of Leipzig, October 1814

10. Napoleon and the Empress Marie Louise, with the infant King of Rome

11. Prince Clemens Metternich at the height of his power (by Sir Thomas Lawrence)

'An amazing marriage': Metternich in the Saddle

In a moment of impatience Napoleon threw his hat into a corner, and Metternich always liked to tell how he had left him to pick it up himself.

'You only confirm my conviction,' said Bonaparte, 'that I have miscalculated. In marrying an Archduchess of Austria I meant to enliven the Gothic prejudices with the innovations of my century. I was mistaken and I feel today the enormity of my error. It may cost me my throne, but I shall bury the world in its ruins.'

With the traumatic year of 1812 behind it, Europe was moving towards the Wars of Liberation and Archduke Johann would have no part in them. What of Archduke Karl, still in the eyes of millions the 'Saviour of Germany'? This 'personality with a character and mind of positively classical grandeur'[1] was devoting his mental energies to writing, and in that same year his first book *Principles of Strategy* was published anonymously. It is a work which some present-day military historians consider has more than held its own beside the writings of Clausewitz. Since his refusal to march with the French against Russia he was of course again in disgrace with Franz I, and in the natural order of things, with Metternich. Czar Alexander I, however, was not merely in favour of the Archduke being sent to lead the Austrian army, he now suggested that he be nominated Supreme Commander of the armies of Russia, Prussia, England and Austria in an effort to throw Napoleon back across the Rhine. This was not wholly out of respect for Karl's ability, his power of leadership or the magic of his name; he had a more frivolous motive: at this time the Grand Duchess Catherine, widow of George, Duke of Oldenbourg, had it in mind to marry the Archduke, and the Czar felt that this appointment would raise the status and prospects of his imperious sister's future *partie*. Metternich was wholly against Karl being raised to such dizzy heights of military—and, inevitably, political—power, and to the accompaniment of much disparaging talk of the Archduke's errors in 1809 the appointment was given to Schwarzenberg; the fact that the Prince had ridden, only months before, with France against Russia, was no hindrance. Nor was it in the world of diplomacy in which other values and more subtle distinctions obtained than the crude military

---

[1] Adam Wandruszka, *Das Haus Habsburg*.

chessboard could express, and in the bitter hostility between Alexander and Metternich which played such a part during the Congress of Vienna the issue of the auxiliary corps was not a component.

The peoples of Austria entered the war of 1813 in an entirely different mood again from that which had inspired them in 1809. This was not a people's war but one, to quote Heinrich von Srbik, 'to be fought with all the devices of cabinet policy and by dynastic armies'. Metternich sent the Austrian troops into the field in the interests 'not of a new, but of an ancient state system under the traditional legitimate powers, not for an idea of national unity but in the interests of a balance of the historically established powers.'

Immediately after the defeat of Napoleon at the Battle of Leipzig Franz I raised Count Metternich to the rank of Prince (Fürst), to the annoyance of the Empress, of Stadion and the rest. Had he not believed in Napoleon's victory over Russia? Had he not held off from joining the alliance against Napoleon until he was talked into it by the Duchess of Sagan? Never mind; there was no stopping him now. Metternich's new coat of arms incorporated the Austrian double eagle.

The Viennese remembered the spring of 1813 as a succession of golden mornings. They talked of the scent of violets rising warm from the grass of 10,000 gardens and from the banks of country lanes between Grinzing, Sievering and Pötzleinsdorf. New life pulsed through their veins and there was new hope in their hearts. The violets may well have smelled all the sweeter because the housewife had more money in her purse than for a long time past. The factories were working to capacity, on the whole there was full employment and in some sectors even a shortage of manpower. Trade too was looking up, and the ladies and gentlemen of the better classes were replenishing their wardrobes, more numerous and more ample courses marched across the tables of even the less well to do, and in spite of heavy rains and floods during the summer this happy state of affairs continued well into the following year. The government, however, always parsimonious towards its servants, made no measurable effort to better their condition. A postal employee earning 400 florins (new gulden)[1] per annum would pay 215 florins

---

[1] 1 gulden, or florin = 60 Kreuzer, about 2 shillings.
4½ gulden   = 1 ducat (used throughout Europe), about 9 shillings.

for his flat on the Laurenzer Bastei near the central Post Office, consisting of one room and a cubby hole. In the outer suburbs a most modest, even scruffy, apartment cost 150 florins to 200 florins. Graduates looking for jobs were hardly better off, if at all. A junior lecturer at Vienna University earned 400 florins a year, although a school-teacher might rise to 900 florins. The junior doctors on the staff of the main hospital, the Allgemeines Krankenhaus, made do with 120 to 240 florins, the salary scale of a primary school teacher. All would have to pay 11 gulden for a pair of boots,[1] and if they had the temerity to marry they could hardly buy their wives a new dress for less than 42 florins. There were rent allowances, but they lagged far behind the rise in rents. An aspirant to the civil administration, moreover, could expect to earn nothing whatever for as much as seven or eight years, which meant that only a man with a private income could afford to take up an employment which, otherwise, would keep him dependent on his father or father-in-law until he was perhaps 30 years old. It was in this golden year, 1813, that Austria's great dramatist Franz Grillparzer applied for a post in the Hofbibliothek but was warned that he had no hope at all of receiving a salary. The proverbially distressing situation of all except senior civil servants was naturally aggravated by the fact that a disproportionate amount of the family income had to go on father's back.

Contemporary accounts of the manner of life of the Viennese sometimes seem to conflict with later memoirs as well as with the records: they seem to be living so well when, by rights, they should be half-starved and miserable. To some extent this is due to the rapid fluctuations in the standard of living of the labouring classes. The moment that work was to be had a lower-class family could recover very quickly because women did the same work as men: they were bricklayer's labourers, carrying bricks and mortar on their backs or wheeling away loads of rubbish, or they might saw up and chop the wood which the timber dealer, regardless of the inconvenience to passers by, threw down in front of the houses. Equally, it was an attitude of mind. 'The Viennese are a very sensual people,' Dr. Reeve had said only a few years earlier. 'They take

---

[1] In 1810 Beethoven wrote to his publishers, Breitkopf & Härtel, that he had to pay 30 florins for boots and 160–170 florins for a coat.

snuff and smoke and delight in music, and go continually to sights'
(he meant spectacles such as bear-baiting) 'and game, and intrigue,
and eat and drink . . .' The young physician was rather shocked:
'No city can present such scenes of affected sanctity and real
licentiousness. Persons of loose character are received into what is
considered the best company, many women of quality have their
lovers, and many a man keeps a mistress and goes to the play and
walks in the streets with her, such things are talked of publicly.' He
found the same freedom of conversation, not of course where politics were concerned, but in connection with illness: 'Even at meals
the symptoms of dysentery, diarrhœa and the like are often discussed.' And if conversation at meals was apt to be 'dull, languid
and uninteresting', in ' "la bonne compagnie" ' it was 'often indecent and licentious. The married women are always expecting to
be in love, and to have young men *faire la cour* to them, and the
young misses are corrupted by what they hear, and are left to
amuse themselves.' What a prig he was.

Not one word of this would apply to the Pichlers' salon, all too
brav though it may have been, nor to most households of the middle-
class intelligentsia about which something is known, least of all to
the ménage of Schönholz's[1] grandmother who 'looked upon existence as a lifelong period of office, to be administered along lines
laid down by tradition, neither tolerating variety nor admitting exceptions to the rule'. In her house the clock was master, and
nothing whatever was permitted to disturb the routine of the day.
There was no noise, ideally there was hardly a sound to be heard:
the whole of life was subjected to self-discipline, self-control and
quiet. There was strict economy in all things, not only in the ways
which are dictated by lack of money, but in expenditure of energy
on movement and emotion. Children addressed their parents as
'Your Grace' and it was considered very lax, when sitting, to allow
one's back to touch the back of the chair. The men wore a permanent look of earnest purposefulness, and if this expression were
lacking as they approached the house they would adopt it before
they walked through the doorway.

It is hard to believe that Reeve and Schönholz are talking about
the same town. And yet, at that time, under-cover prostitution was

[1] Friedrich Anton von Schönholz, wrote memoirs of the reign of Franz I.

becoming very prevalent among those very families which were scraping by on fixed incomes, who were feeling the pressure of inflation more than any other class but whose womenfolk were for the most part doomed to inactivity. In pre-Congress Vienna, in a population of 240,000, about 20,000 women were thought to be living wholly or partly on prostitution, a figure which was no higher during the last years of the monarchy when the population had multiplied six times. At the time no German-speaking town could emulate it. After the Empress Maria Theresa's fruitless efforts to reform the morals of her capital—her 'chastity commission' does not count among her more glorious innovations—her son Joseph II went a step further, and tarts, their heads forcibly shaven, were put to work in gangs to sweep the streets. This measure was not a success either, because the women's language was frightful and if employed in the more respectable streets they were liable to hail their former clients as they hurried by, while in obscure districts the passers-by were sorry for them and were apt to hurl abuse at their guards. Franz I also tried the head-shaving tactic, but to no effect, and the police confined their own efforts mainly to preventing what they called 'the public display of vice'; procurers were put in the stocks on the Hohe Markt. An inordinate amount of work and public money was spent on compiling records about prostitutes of all classes and categories and their clientèle, and the sheer quantity is surprising until one remembers that many of the women were themselves, willingly or no, agents of the police, and that the whole system of surveillance in a police state rests on the assumption that if a man is kept long enough under observation he will say or do something of interest to the authorities.

Johanna Köppe, born probably in Linz in about 1790, unwittingly filled volumes of files during the course of her career because of the prominence of her lovers, though she evidently refused to prattle about them to the police. Some time during 1810 she brought off the remarkable feat of marrying a count, and the fact that he was an army officer was an additional advantage. She was now Countess Desfours-Walderode, and a year later she was the mistress of Count Heinrich Starhemberg who spent a great deal of money on her. The authorities were worried about this, and they minuted one another to the effect that there was no point in trying to detach her from him, or vice versa, as she would only set about ruining another member of the nobility. She was often expelled from Vienna but was always brought back through the intervention of some powerful protector such as the banker Baron Geymüller. By 1813 her husband had evidently left her as she was living on the Tuchlauben, that survival of a mediaeval village just behind the Graben, and she seems to have been going through a bad patch because she had descended to using the premises of a woman, Anna Heller, who though the widow of a wholesale dealer was a procuress and her flat a brothel. Perhaps Johanna was simply very bad at holding on to money when she had it, or perhaps she did not always put it first: she could have found a wealthier lover than Gentz who said of her 'elle m'a procuré des jouissances que je n'avais pas goutées depuis des années.' He enjoyed this bliss from January 1815 until 1823. Meanwhile boom times were coming, for Johanna Descours-Walderode and for her many equals and her innumerable more humble sisters.

This boom was ushered in by distant events. After Leipzig, Napoleon broke away to the West and was pursued into France. In the spring of 1814 a series of allied victories ended with the march on Paris (31st March), his abdication and internment on the island of Elba. Marie Louise, Empress and since the 30th of March 1813 Regent, had done her dynastic duty and apparently fulfilled her destiny in giving birth to the King of Rome—it had been a long and difficult delivery—but now that Napoleon had fallen she was suddenly as dispensable as she was undisposable, a diplomatic nuisance, though essentially less of a problem than her son. Marie Louise has been accused of disloyalty to Napoleon, of lack of character, over-submissiveness to the will of her father and of Metternich. Not all of this can be sustained. By nature she was sub-missive and nothing in her upbringing had taught her independence, but this quality made her in Napoleon's eyes a satisfactory wife and also a consort who, as Regent, meticulously carried out his orders or followed the advice of the men whom he had appointed for this purpose. At the time when she was separated from her husband and her own physical safety was not certain, she had only one idea, to rejoin him. Once Napoleon was on Elba, his aura paled and the bonds which held her to him slackened, while the childlike reverence for her father which had never left her surged up again and led her to place herself once again under his protection.

It is evidently this conflict, the feeling of being torn between Napoleon and her father, which led to a number of contradictory statements by her. During the dramas of 1814 she probably often hardly knew what her true feelings were and she began to long for a private life somewhere; the quiet, undemanding routine of a little court. On 8th September she wrote from Switzerland to her friend the Duchess of Montebello telling her that Napoleon had sent her one message after another begging her to leave the child in Vienna and come to Elba, but she had let him know that she was unable to do so. 'I shall give you my most sacred word of honour that neither now nor later do I intend to go to Elba. You, dear Friend, know better than anyone that I have no desire to do so.' She said once that in Napoleon she had loved only his 'grandeur, c'est à dire l'éclat du trône.' And yet only a few months earlier she was putting up a stubborn resistance to the efforts of Franz and Metternich to persuade her to return to Vienna. She was already titular Duchess of Parma—her full style and title was 'Her Majesty the Archduchess Marie Louise, Duchess of Parma'—and it was there that she wished to go as she would be within comparatively easy reach of Elba. Her resistance continued although members of the Habsburg Court in Paris were trying to drive a wedge between her and Napoleon by talking to her about Marie Walewska and whispering that he was suffering from venereal disease. But, in fresh contrast, her reaction to the news of Napoleon's attempted suicide hardly gives the impression of a deep love. Her Gentleman of the Bedchamber, Comte Sainte-Aulaire, brought the news to her at Blois, and she received him in her peignoir, bare feet hastily thrust into slippers, as she had just leaped out of bed. It was a written message, and having read it she asked for further details: was the Emperor still alive? 'It is more than probable', was the grave reply, 'that at this hour the Emperor is no longer among the living.' In the dead silence that followed, Sainte-Aulaire, his heart wrung with compassion for the Empress, bowed his head and waited. 'Oh!' exclaimed Marie Louise, 'don't look at my feet! My slippers are horribly large, I had no time to put on shoes.'

Metternich could hardly wait to remove the Empress Marie

Louise and her child from her politically inflammable surroundings, and he finally persuaded her to leave by saying that the French were sure to make trouble over her claims to the Duchy of Parma and that these would best be staked in conjunction with other claims to be made by the Austrian government in Vienna.

And so Marie Louise went home. 'As my daughter', Franz I told her, 'everything within my power is yours, my blood and my life not excepted; as Empress of France I no longer know you.' To Schönbrunn she brought with her a small household consisting of members of the French nobility who inevitably formed the nucleus of a foreign court. In spite of all her filial piety and her emotional dependence on him, Her Majesty the Duchess was very angry with her father for his attitude towards Napoleon, which the defeated son-in-law on Elba commented on in these bitter words: 'Ah, yes! But at the time of the marriage, how they did debase themselves! Vienna gave me the impression of a petit bourgeois who is marrying off his daughter to a Grand Duke.' She was writing whenever there was a chance to get a letter through to him—Franz I never in fact forbade her to do so—but for the most part her letters were impounded and Metternich simply put them on the files without telling the Emperor; he even opened Marie Louise's letters to her father, while Franz's letters to her were drafted by him. She was naturally not unaware of all this and up to the very end she was never wholly out of touch with Napoleon: she used, now and later, intermediaries who were either too skilful to be easily apprehended, such as the son of her chief Lady in Waiting, Anatole de Montesquiou and Napoleon's secret agent Charles Schulmeister, or too prominent, like Prince Eugène de Beauharnais who sent her mail via his wife in Munich. Her papers she kept in a locked cupboard, and although the key was large and heavy she always carried it on her person.

Marie Louise was altogether in bad humour and totally out of sympathy with her surroundings; the contrast with Paris was most marked. The respect and admiration with which, there, she had come to be surrounded, were partly the result of Napoleon's determination to keep from her the faintest breath of scandal, a matter of primary importance in a country where so many notorious women had been far too close to the throne. He once reproved her on hearing that she had received a man, innocent bearer of official documents though he was, while she was in bed. He, Bonaparte, had bought the very best quality, and the article must retain its full symbolic value. The will of Napoleon, his power, bore her up, they made her feel safe, and within the walls of the Tuileries and other royal residences she was able to be 'simple et naturelle'. Not so in Vienna. Four years in Paris had made her so French that now nothing pleased her. The crowds, cheering and waving ecstatically as she entered the capital, were offended by the same curt, frosty nods that she had distributed in Dresden and Prague, but the Court was irritated by the completely French way in which she now ran her household. If she preferred it that way, and considering that some leading members of her household were French, her lack of tact and the touchiness of her critics probably cancel one another out. But there were people from whom she had once parted in floods of tears, Countess Lazansky for example and Prince Trautt-mansdorff, who found her coolness towards them very hurting, and the 'extrême hauteur' of this girl, still only 23 years old, ridiculous. Did she really say, as posterity has not forgotten, 'die Deutschen stinken'? and again, that German women smell nasty? It is not impossible, as Napoleon is credited with saying 'German women smell of freshly slaughtered meat.'

'The Duchess is found too proud,' wrote Baron Braun, Minister of Hesse-Darmstadt, 'and she will not forget the throne of France. She has preserved affection for Napoleon, and she has just spent an hour sitting upon a bench which the Emperor Napoleon occupied in 1809.' The bench may merely have been conveniently situated where she wished to rest. But whatever the strength of her heart's allegiance, it was ebbing fast. It took much persuasion on her part to gain permission to take the waters at Aix, but at last it was granted. Among the party, in the function of a *chevalier d'honneur*, was the one-eyed Count Neipperg, whose international reputation as a lover of beautiful women drew Metternich's attention to him as a man who might help him to cope with the moping and irritable Duchess. Neipperg hardly needed to have his patriotic duty spelled out to him, and he told his mistress: 'I shall have her in bed within six months.'

On 16th June the Emperor Franz returned from Paris after the allied talks which culminated in the Treaty of Fontainebleau. It

was as though his furtive re-entry in 1809 had never been, and all
the sad memories of those times were wiped out. Stands were put
up wherever there was room for them to accommodate crowds of
people, who seemed, all of them, to be wearing new suits, new
dresses and bonnets. The *Bürgergarde* were wearing new uniforms
and every house was decorated. And as the long procession moved
in state through the grass and flower-strewn streets, checking every
now and again so that the obligatory little girls in white might recite
the usual verses of welcome, some of the onlookers thought that
Vienna had never seemed so beautiful or so lovable. Next day the
rejoicing continued with illuminations and fireworks, which, so
Friedrich von Gentz wrote to Rahel von Varnhagen, cost the unprecedented sum of between one and a half and two million gulden.
It was a wholly Viennese occasion and it marked the close of an era.
The capital of the Habsburg Empire was about to lay on the one
performance for which, if all else in its history were forgotten, it
would be remembered: by the time that the leaves in the Vienna
Woods were beginning to turn colour the first of the visiting
sovereigns were arriving, and though no one at the time would have
dreamed of such a thing, for nearly six months Vienna was to be the
epicentrum of Europe.

6
The Congress of Vienna

The Empress Maria Ludovica said that the Congress of Vienna cost her ten years of her life; to Goethe it was a tale so formless that it could not be told. There were many who saw it as no more nor less than a gigantic fun fair with a brisk slave market at the centre of it: they included the President of the United States, Thomas Jefferson, and the immensely influential bookseller and librarian Baron Cotta of Tübingen; this opinion was heard in the House of Commons, and it would be shared in his time by Prince Bismarck. Out of all the splendid band of eccentrics, 2 emperors and 3 kings, 11 sovereign or mediatized princes, 90 ambassadors and plenipotentiaries, to say nothing of 53 uninvited representatives of European powers, not one, with the arguable exception of Talleyrand, was satisfied with the outcome. The Congress was formless in the sense that it was never convened, and that it only truly existed when, at its conclusion and thanks to the labours of Friedrich von Gentz, the final Act with its 121 articles was put into writing. It separated populations which should have been united, and, in the case of Belgium and Holland, vice versa. And yet the Europe which emerged from this attempt to shake itself out after the Napoleonic wars had a certain stability: it was maintained unaltered for a generation, and a hundred years were to pass before the continent went up in flames; the mart in souls after the two great wars of this century was of a different dimension altogether.

Politically speaking the Viennese lived a sheltered existence, they had not been assailed by any of the more raffish ailments besetting other major cities of Europe, and the general population both in the capital and in other parts of the country had been exposed for too short a time to Napoleonic ideas on social reform for these to have had much effect. The emergent bourgeoisie was concerned with its own material advancement, while the intelligentsia had suffered a series of shocks the result of which would be seen in the years which followed. In spite of these things Vienna was, as it were, predestined to be host to the Congress if only for the one reason that in no other town in Europe outside France did the entire educated sector of the population speak the obligatory language of diplomacy, French. In the upper ranks of the civil service and diplomacy an endless store of knowledge concerning the peoples of the Empire and their neighbours was also there to be called upon when needed.

The walls of the city had been repaired, though they were still not quite finished, and there was now nothing to prevent people from taking that stroll along the ramparts lasting at an easy pace roughly an hour, which must have been one of the most enchanting walks that any city in Europe had to offer. Looking towards the Kahlenberg and Leopoldsberg the distant view from some points of vantage is not very different today, but the immediate surroundings have changed utterly. Beyond the Glacis with its trees and meadows, with its farm carts and carriages and its strollers, behind the palaces of the grandees of the Habsburg Empire surrounding the monarch as at a *lévée*, the Karlskirche and the Imperial Stables on whose roof only five years earlier the French siege guns had stood, lay the *Vorstädte* Wieden, Mariahilf and the rest. Here many of the houses were still reminiscent of the four-square farms of Lower and Upper Austria, each one a small world of its own, and some in fact were still farms, or partly so, owning a few cows and a small vineyard, but in their courtyards cobblers, locksmiths, bookbinders, all those trades which are still a distinctive feature of Vienna's daily life today, carried on their business. If there was poverty here it was still rural in character, and despite the presence of sleazy hovels on the outskirts there was nothing here, yet, to compare with the stews of London.

It all began immediately after the Battle of Leipzig when the Emperor Franz, prompted by Metternich, invited the Czar and the King of Prussia to come to Vienna as soon as they should find it convenient to do so. None of them dreamed that this meeting would snowball into a gathering which would raise the population of Vienna by one-third. As the time approached, the aristocracy began to have an inkling of what lay ahead, and now a hectic jockeying for position began, in which the leading families and those with a hot line to Court elbowed those with less influence out of their path in the hunt for jobs as ladies in waiting, chamberlains, adjutants and pages. In a city as crowded as Vienna, where families of the humbler sort were constantly seeking to increase their cramped accommodation, it was surprising to learn that an almost unlimited amount of space was suddenly available. Whether research has ever disclosed where and how the Viennese slept during the Congress is doubtful, but with the memory of two military occupations still fresh in their minds there was little hardship in doubling up and much to be gained. It was not only a question of bringing into the house or apartment a welcome addition to the housekeeping money: how else but with a diplomat for a lodger could one get a hold on the gossip? Lower down in the social scale even a housemaid or footman was effusively welcomed; they might have more to tell, of a sort, than their masters.

Lulu Thürheim was not going to be left out. 'When I returned to Vienna in the middle of September 1814', she wrote, 'I found the town greatly excited at the imminent arrival of the Emperor Alexander of Russia and the other sovereigns. People were talking of nothing but balls and banquets. A few days later and there they were: the Czar and King Frederick William of Prussia followed by the Kings of Württemberg, Bavaria and Denmark, the Grand Dukes of Oldenburg, Weimar and Baden, the Prussian princes, brothers and uncles of the King together with a crowd of other sovereign princes and ministers. Only Charles of Sweden preferred to absent himself, doubtless on account of his origins.'

Now all Europe was on the move, and the man who had twice been chased from his capital was host to this multitude. J. G. Eynard of the Swiss delegation found Franz's appearance sadly disappointing. 'The Emperor of Austria', he wrote home after their audience, 'possesses the most puny figure imaginable. He looks quite broken and old' (he was 46) 'he is small, lean of figure, round-shouldered and knock-kneed. His festive clothing is always the same: a white jacket, red leggings and black boots. During our converse the impression he gave of shyness and embarrassment was most marked. To look less like a sovereign and more like a petit bourgeois from a provincial town than he does would be impossible.' 'And yet', Eynard marvelled, 'this ruler is loved by all his people and by the Court.'

Franz I had made a wise decision: there was to be no skimping. 300 brand new carriages, all alike in shape and colour, stood at the disposal of the royalties and their suites so that they would always have their own means of transport, and the entire costs of the Congress were to be borne by the Austrian exchequer.

Gradually, to the accompaniment of much grumbling, the monarchs and diplomats settled down in the rooms provided for them. Lord Castlereagh was dissatisfied with his accommodation in the hotel 'Zum Auge Gottes' but Lady Castlereagh was quite won over by the beauty around her. 'I am near to dislocating my neck looking around me,' she told the Chancellor at their first meeting. After a brief interval they moved to Minoritenplatz 50 where 22 rooms were placed at their disposal. (The rent was a record—£500 a month.)

In the hope of seeing something to talk about at home, crowds of people stood wedged in the Burghof from morning till late at night looking up at the windows which concealed the kings and emperors. The watchers could often hardly lift their elbows and they hampered the movements of the troops on guard at each entrance who were constantly presenting arms to the roll of drums as the carriages rumbled in and out. Nowhere did they stand so patiently as below the state apartment of King Frederick of Württemberg, to catch a glimpse of whose monstrous physique it was worth waiting for hours together. Everyone knew that he could only eat at a table out of which a deep crescent had been cut to fit round his belly, and then there was that extraordinary chaise in the form of a shell in which, there being no room for another passenger, he rode out alone, drawn by four chestnuts, two of them ridden by lackeys in scarlet waistcoats with yellow sleeves. He was not, the craning crowd thought, a nice man, and it was pleasant to know that when the King, irritated by all this rapt attention, sent a message to the captain of the palace guard to send 'these gaping apes' packing forthwith, the reply came back that, with respect, the captain regretted he could do nothing: 'It is the custom here.'

The whole extent of the Burghof, leading into the Schweizerhof and beyond that on to the Josefsplatz where the carriages and their attendants waited on call, was the centre of attention and hardly ever free from a milling throng of people getting in the way of those whose work kept them there. In other parts of the town, within the wall and beyond the Glacis, knots of people stood at the entrance of every palais and many a more modest residence, waiting for someone with a name known throughout Europe, or, more piquant still, one of their famous mistresses, to drive out. At the other end, where the Amalienhof faces the 'House on the Ballhausplatz', the State Chancellery, the crowds thinned out and only a few people gazed up at the windows of this historic building, wondering perhaps what profound talks were being held there between the great powers or their plenipotentiaries who were now supposedly remaking the map of Europe. But little of importance was going on in the Chancellery and the crowds in other parts of the town were certainly on to a better thing. As the social life of the Congress began to gather momentum, impromptu confidential discussions in back rooms during balls and other entertainments were of greater value than committee meetings. A number of senior diplomats were to find a most convenient refuge in an uncomfortable attic bedroom, and the reason why this was so raises an aspect of the Congress which affected every single actor in it: the work of the censorship department of the *Polizeihofstelle* and the police spy system.

The machinery at Baron Hager's disposal was comprehensive and on the whole it functioned excellently, very much better, in fact, than any of the other departments of state although its value was enormously overrated.

Austria was of course very far from being the only country in which there was a postal censorship. Louis XIV had his *commissions inquisitoriales des postes*, a system which began under Louis XI, and Napoleon was immensely proud of his own organization. The Austrian censorship network extended far beyond the frontiers of the Austro-Hungarian Empire because, owing to postal rights accruing to the only recently discarded crown of the Holy Roman Empire of the German 'nation', and to Austria's rule over the

Netherlands, it functioned in most of the German states as well. After the Napoleonic wars a free-for-all broke out with everyone trying to get hold of everyone else's mail: Bavaria, for example, had postal 'lodges' in Augsburg and Munich, and the battle over codes and ciphers was intense. But it is safe to say that in this sphere no one could hold a candle to the Austrians. All the principal post offices had censorship departments, called *Logen*, attached to them, where the mail of persons of interest was secretly opened, copied and re-sealed in such a way that the recipient would not know that the letter had been tampered with.

In the capital, the routine of censorship inevitably became the object of unwelcome attention. At the Central Post Office which was then in the street called the Wollzeile, incoming mail had to be looked over in a large, damp ground-floor room under the eyes of the inquisitive postal clerks, but this arrangement was altered in 1818. Security was just as rudimentary at the Stallburg, in part of which the Cipher Chancery had its offices. 'Neither the side entrance nor the secret stairway nor the covered hampers [containing intercepts] escaped the notice of the postal clerks and the public.'[1] The *Geheime Ziffernkanzlei*, the Secret Cipher Chancery, dealt with about 80 or 100 items per day. More so even than the *postlogistes*, the men attached to this department were a race apart; it was said of many *déchiffreurs* that they read letters in code or cipher as readily as any normal text, and it was generally recognized that the department was able to break any code which came its way—with one notable exception, to be dealt with later. These civil servants were not listed in the State Calendar, they were denied—unthinkable deprivation in Austria—official ranks and titles and they were expected to keep completely in the background, appearing neither in society nor in places of public entertainment. For any man who set little store by these things the compensations were ample: salaries were free of taxation and other deductions, they could have loans and many other privileges for the asking, including the cherished right of direct access to the Emperor, and they had higher pensions on retirement.

Archduke Karl had once recommended as Chief of Police a man 'whom the people believe to be incapable of stooping to low

[1] Josef Karl Mayr, *Metternichs geheimer Briefdienst, Postlogen und Postkurse*.

12. Emperor Franz I, in 1832, three years before his death

13. The Congress. Left, in profile: Duke of Wellington. Seated: Prince Hardenberg. Prince Metternich is pointing to Lord Castlereagh. Seated with arm on table: Prince Talleyrand. (The painting by Jean-Baptiste Isabey)

methods, of slanderous spying and of prying into the secrets of families, thus acquiring in the eyes of his Monarch the appearance of loyal watchfulness, but at the expense of his honour.' And Hager really was such a man. He obeyed the orders of an inquisitive Emperor and his Chancellor in the interests of security and he made a brave attempt to achieve a relaxation of the regulations on censorship of printed words, but without success. He was now faced by a task which was altogether beyond the scope of his essentially efficient organization. It amounted to this: every single mission must be penetrated, all persons of consequence watched round the clock, their memoranda filched, their correspondence intercepted. Every major household in Vienna already harboured spies whose job it was to rifle waste-paper baskets and snatch crumpled or half-burned letters out of drawing-room and bedroom stoves. (Such stoves were often stoked from a back passage.) This organization must now be vastly expanded. Information would be required on the talk at dinners and receptions, more particularly at exclusive parties where foreign guests would be more likely to speak openly. For work of this kind, only members of the first families were of any use and they must be intellectually—and one might well add, physically—up to the job of going out night after night and filing a daily report.

It was a delicate recruitment problem. Among those who rendered sterling service were Count Benzel-Sternau, Herr von Leurs, Count K. Majláth and a Count Káráczay whose special task was to watch the Duchess of Parma. But there were many others, and just who they were will never be known as in order not to reveal their identity they declined to sign receipts. Alternatively, of course, they were acting from purely patriotic motives and took no payment. Prince Ludwig Starhemberg, a leader of the *fronde* against Metternich, was pained by the whole spectacle. Very soon he was saying that he objected not so much to the way that the foreign courts and missions were spying on each other, or each and all of them on the Austrians—'They will know enough about us by the time they leave'—as to the whispering and general intrigue within Austrian society itself which was rapidly becoming intolerable. 'Ferdinand Palffy is working for the secret police, Countess Esterházy-Roisin and Mlle Chapuis are the spies of old Princess Metternich . . .

Prince Kaunitz, Franz Palffy, Fritz Fürstenberg, Ferdinand Palffy offered their services to the foreign monarchs, but they were turned down.' Behind this mouth-watering list of grandees lurks a certain confusion. Oddly enough there exists not one single written report among the records of the secret police signed by a woman. If, as we must therefore suppose, the Princess was collecting information to satisfy her own avid curiosity, she was not the only one; at the afternoon parties where the dowagers congregated—Pergen, Schönborn, Colloredo, Fürstenberg, Groschlag, Chotek, Hoyos, Cobenzl, Callenberg and Batthyány—every scrap of news was assembled and sifted. We can, however, be reasonably certain that the peers named by Starhemberg were not intending to spy for the visiting royalties, but if anything to keep a watch on them for Hager. And here Hager's great difficulty was that for the most part the visiting royalties were not so innocent as to take young Austrian noblemen into their households; Alexander I lost no time in sending away the A.D.C.s who reported to him on his arrival.

Franz I was obliged to accommodate his fellow monarchs in the Hofburg, but by doing so he was making things very difficult for Hager. The royal palaces were out of bounds to the police, which meant that while it was left to them to suborn imperial servants, they had no legal right of entry. The large number of entrances and exits added to the difficulty by making it almost impossible to keep a check on the movements of individuals—particularly if they were deliberately trying to evade observation. The main focus of attention was the Russian household: together with the noble and elegant adjutants, Alexander I had also thrown out the entire domestic staff which had partly been engaged for him, partly seconded from the imperial household, and had taken on others. Hager anxiously conferred with the Lord Chamberlain, Count Trauttmansdorff, about the possibility of gaining the co-operation of these servants. The principal foreign missions were if possible even more careful. Lord Castlereagh, in a mood of what an agent with the pseudonym Siber quaintly describes as excessive caution, engaged his own housemaids. Before, said Siber, an attempt could be made to have torn up papers removed from desks and waste-paper baskets, he must get in touch with these women and see whether they might be relied upon. But Castlereagh was admirably security-minded. All despatches were sent by Foreign Office couriers, and his secretaries collected and burnt or locked away all papers.

Talleyrand baffled Hager's men at every level and on all counts. He arrived on 23rd September and took up residence in the palais Kaunitz in the Johannesgasse which, agents were soon complaining, possessed all the essential characteristics of a fortress. His very small staff he had brought with him, in his initial isolation he received few visitors and they were men preoccupied with their own interests or working for other powers; they were not of much use to Hager. Finally, an elderly servant who had worked for three French ambassadors in Vienna was persuaded to co-operate, and he smuggled out a few scraps of paper taken from his new master's desk. It was all rather ridiculous in the light of the fact that after the celebrated scene on 28th January, 1809, when Napoleon bellowed insults at Talleyrand in front of the entire French Court ('What a pity', was the cool reply, 'that such a great man should be so *mal élevé*'), Talleyrand became Metternich's principal source of information and handed him, among other things, the complete order of battle of the French armies.

Talleyrand apart, as one sifts through the 'material reports' made by ordinary agents who observed the movements of their quarry, it all seems a sorry waste of effort. Thousands record nothing more significant than visits to a mistress: 'Arrived at 6, left at 11.' And yet they form part of the *histoire galante* of the Congress and they have been happily studied by every writer in this field.

The celebrated painting by Isabey shows all the leading delegates to the Congress. In the left hand half of the picture, Metternich, more dancing master than statesman, dominates the scene. Otherwise the entire cast is grouped in such a way as to lead the eye to Castlereagh. He leans back in his chair, centre front, left arm hanging carelessly over the chair back, left leg (with Garter) crossed over the right, his whole attitude one of cheerful detachment. Even Metternich's gesture draws attention to the significance of this lackadaisical figure. On the right-hand side there must be a counterweight to Metternich: the eye demands it and here it is—we know that face so well, fleshy and pale, the cold, indifferent eyes and the mouth with downturned corners speaking of cynical distaste.

The Congress of Vienna

It is Talleyrand, that miracle of political survival, not peeping over the shoulder of some minor delegate as would befit a representative of the defeated aggressor nation (who, in any case, ever invited him to Vienna?) but firmly seated in the foreground, his right arm laid possessively on the conference table. How he got there is one of the central themes of the Congress of Vienna.

If this group of men had ever met as the picture shows them, probably not one of them would have failed to echo the retort of the Prince de Ligne while he was talking to Talleyrand shortly after the statesman's arrival. (The story was reported by the agent 'Nota' on 30th September.) 'You are playing a very great role,' said the Prince, 'you are King of France, and Louis XVIII can dance to your tune, if not he will find himself in bad case.' 'Prince,' said Talleyrand, 'seven years have passed since Bonaparte trusted me.' 'What?' exclaimed de Ligne, 'only seven years? Why, I've been suspicious of you for twenty!'

The scene in the painting is an imaginary one. The chief delegates never met all at one time in this manner, and Gentz would always say that it was a mercy they did not, as the protocol involved in holding such meetings would have absorbed weeks of valuable time. Prince Charles Maurice de Talleyrand-Périgord was not the only representative of his country as he was accompanied by the Duc de Dalberg, Comte Gouvernet de la Tour du Pin and Comte Alexis de Noailles. But it could not be said that he particularly needed them. Sometimes he would not speak to them for days, and it was the task of his protégé Sigismond Neukomm to play the piano for hour upon hour while the French statesman sat thinking and writing, self-absorbed and totally uncommunicative. Neukomm never knew whether or not he was listening to his playing. Talleyrand seemed to think little of Vienna: to a hostess who in greeting him remarked that now he, too, had arrived in Vienna, his reply was, 'Madame, I am making every effort to forget it.' When his niece the Princesse de Périgord took over the running of his household—she was a sister of the Duchess of Sagan and thus one of that startling batch of women nastily called the Courland whores—she may have helped him to forget his surroundings. There was nothing to prove it but a thin stream of enjoyable innuendo went the rounds.

Talleyrand never sought popularity and he would probably not have considered it a factor in diplomacy. He brought to the Congress something the importance of which every single other delegate, to say nothing of the monarchs, had overlooked: knowledge of the matters on the agenda. Alone among the negotiators Talleyrand had made a close study not only of the political issues but of the geographical realities. It was Lord Castlereagh's great weakness that he came to Vienna insufficiently briefed, and it was a disadvantage which some believed he never entirely overcame. Weakness in geography, this so frequent characteristic of British statesmen, was his Achilles heel and there was no deceiving Talleyrand. 'He possesses such a slight knowledge of all things relating to the military topography and also the simple geography of the continent—I might even say, no knowledge whatever—that, while the necessity to enlighten him upon the most elementary matters arises with great frequency, to achieve this presents difficulties of the highest degree.' Castlereagh was not unaware of this weakness, nor that, since he was powerless to diminish the exaggerated attachment and subservience of the King of Prussia towards Alexander I, his own sense of affinity with Humboldt and Hardenberg[1] did nothing to strengthen his resistance to the Prussian claims on Saxony. In the end it was Talleyrand who, by passing the message to London, contributed to the decision to recall Castlereagh and to send out the Duke of Wellington.

In the picture of which the centre and focus is Castlereagh, the Duke is a mere bystander seen in profile, but his prestige was incomparable, and the salons fell at his feet.

Socially speaking, the British contingent was not a great success. The commanding gestures of the coachmen who evidently expected all other traffic to melt at their approach, gave offence. The women marched with enormous, hearty strides through the drawing-rooms, and a confidant of Hager's was scandalized by the crude manners of the Englishmen at Court. 'They give no thought to the precedence due to the ladies of Vienna, and proffering their arm to their wives, lead them straight through the Great Hall, carving for themselves a passage through the throng from the entrance door-

---

[1] Wilhelm von Humboldt, 1767–1835, scholar and statesman. Karl August Prince Hardenberg, 1750–1822, Prussian Minister of State.

way up to the Imperial dais.' Both sexes were sometimes heard to complain that few efforts were made by Viennese society to accommodate itself to English ways. There was really nowhere for them to meet. Why could not Prince Liechtenstein, for instance, arrange a few teas *à l'anglais*? It wouldn't cost him much, and one would gladly give his men the money for candles. 'The grandees of Vienna must show us that they are familiar with our customs. And what do they do? Either they try to impress us, or they skulk like beasts in their caves.' Lady Castlereagh is not listed among the beauties of the Congress. 'Colossal and ungainly, her manner uncivilized and unconcerned', as Count Nostitz put it, she achieved immortality of a sort by borrowing her husband's Garter, which in Isabey's painting is so conspicuously in its right place, and binding it round her head. Wearing this odd decoration she went to a ball given by Princess Metternich. People laughed, but no official umbrage seems to have been taken, as it well might have been since only on 21st September the Emperor had been installed as a member of the Order by Garter King-of-Arms Sir Isaac Heard.[1]

If the place of honour given to Castlereagh seems in retrospect overdone, the prancing figure of Metternich in Isabey's painting only suggests his true position in the eyes of his contemporaries if we allow that the artist may have intended irony. This is unlikely. For if Castlereagh was weighed and found wanting, scarcely anyone would have credited Metternich with more substance than the British statesman. There was certainly plenty of mutual disparagement in the air and the delegates and their principals tended also to underestimate each other. One of the most common complaints was of Metternich's idleness. He rose, at the earliest at ten o'clock, 'spends the rest of the morning sighing at the feet of the Duchess of Sagan' and in the short space of time spent at the Chancellery it might be that out of 40 petitioners, heads of departments and so on who had been hanging about for two or three hours, not more than four were admitted before he left to change for the evening's entertainment.

These complaints, and others like them, were exaggerated but were not entirely without substance, particularly when voiced by

---

[1] Franz I bestowed the Order of the Golden Fleece on the Prince Regent.

Gentz. The Czar conceded that Metternich was an excellent master of ceremonies, but he was not prepared to go further than that. The views of La Harpe, the Frenchman who filled Alexander's mind with revolutionary ideas shorn of any method for their practical fulfilment, reflected widely-held opinions of Metternich's professional standing during the first weeks of the Congress. He possessed, La Harpe considered, brilliant qualities. He was superbly handsome, his manners had a particular flavour of perfection even according to the standards of the day, and he had a penchant for pleasantry: these were things which qualified him more for diplomacy than for statecraft. Neither in respect of his intellectual calibre nor in his conduct of affairs could he hold a candle to Talleyrand; equally, La Harpe thought, he was markedly inferior to Hardenberg and Stein.[1] From all accounts he was coming to the end of his ministry and would very likely be sent as ambassador to Paris, while Stadion would take over. The Spanish ambassador, Labrador, was heard to ask: 'Is Stadion to be prevented from taking part in negotiations at the Congress? In my view Austria would be ill advised to remove the only man who, by his frank and loyal manner, has gained the trust of the ministers of the leading powers.'

No one could have called Labrador a perceptive individual, but the fact that Metternich was so generally underestimated, that at that moment no one would have prophesied that he was quietly to take the reins into his hands and was to guide the affairs of Europe for a generation to come, was partly due to misunderstanding over priorities. Metternich's view of how such a concourse of nations ought to be conducted was entirely his own. He was not interested in the concerns of the mediatized states. In the long run, minor issues, Parma for example, would be dealt with in God's good time, but the face of Europe would receive its stamp from the will of the three or four men who held power. And these visitors to Vienna all failed to notice the skill with which Metternich camouflaged the source of his own power, his hold over Franz I.

They were also leaving out of account the significance of a man who was an incomparable source of strength to the Minister:

[1] Karl Baron vom und zum Stein, 1757–1831, German statesman and reformer of the Prussian administration.

Friedrich von Gentz. Gentz was not only his personal assistant but his confidant, alter ego and a constant stimulant and challenge to his intelligence. Gentz was Secretary to the Congress, but he was more. In his biography of Gentz, Professor Golo Mann pointed to the fact that, whether by chance or design, the statesmen who dominated the Congress were all his old friends. Wilhelm von Humboldt was the much-loved comrade of his youth, Count Nesselrode, the Russian foreign minister, had been 'discovered' by him in Berlin and coached in political science. Stein, now an adviser to the Czar, was an old friend and associate dating back to their days in Prague. Among others prominent in the political life of England, Gentz had met Castlereagh in 1802—he had been enjoying a pension of 800 gulden a year, secured for him by Pitt, ever since. Gentz knew everyone in Europe, he was in correspondence with the leading statesmen, thinkers and writers of his time, and each one of them, crowned heads included, enjoyed his company: with one striking exception—the Emperor Franz was irritated, less by his sparkling intelligence than by his alarming eloquence. The Emperor's mother tongue was Italian, it is doubtful whether he was able to speak high German even had he wished to, and his vocabulary and style would not have done particular credit to a regimental sergeant-major. Gentz was an exceptionally articulate man who would make a fortune in the media today, but Franz I found the ebb and flow of his faultlessly constructed sentences with their unheard-of subjunctives unnerving. Because he was not always sure what the fellow was saying, he disliked him.

Gentz could listen as well as talk, otherwise, his notorious indiscretion notwithstanding, he would not have acquired his probably unrivalled knowledge of current affairs. His rooms in the Seilergasse were visited at most hours of the day and night by representatives of the powers and by all those minor figures who were fighting for the existence of their miniature principalities. Many thought that half an hour in the Seilergasse was worth more than several hours spent pacing up and down hoping for a chance to buttonhole Metternich.

The Prince could no longer do without him, and so close was their relationship that it is impossible to say what the effect on Metternich's development would have been if Gentz had died young or had gone to serve another master. Touchy and possessed of an almost unbelievable intellectual vanity as they both were, they were forever quarrelling, and at intervals down the years, like two stags with interlocked antlers and to the accompaniment of much heavy breathing and stamping of hooves, their in-fighting rocked the town. Not that Gentz was trying to bring, as such, a more liberal attitude to bear upon Metternich's policies. 'Why', he once wrote irritably to Adam Smith, 'should the working classes be better off? It would only put ideas into their heads.'

A final glance at Isabey's painting brings to mind the absence, inevitable since the sovereigns have been left standing in the wings, of the man who as a holder of absolute and unchallenged power weighed down on and hampered the work of the Congress, to whose character with its mass of contradictions it is so hard to do justice, whose hatred of Metternich became a political factor of the utmost importance: Czar Alexander I.

If anyone in Vienna in this autumn of 1814 was entitled to call himself the conqueror of Napoleon it was Alexander, now 37 years old and at the zenith of his power. He had ridden as victor into Paris, London had fêted him though without extravagance. There was no one whose arrival was awaited with greater impatience, not only on account of the nimbus surrounding his name and station but because of the conflicting reports about his character which, even leaving aside the matter of his possible complicity in his father's violent death, were the subject of conversation among the leading families. He was a dreamer who had not hesitated to burn Moscow to the ground, a monarch who was prepared to give a constitution to Poland but had done nothing to alleviate the sufferings of the serfs in Russia, a multitude whose number no one could estimate. The philosopher-czar, to some 'un bon fou', was to others a basically noble and good man who longed for a utopia in which the happiness of all men was safeguarded by their own perfection of character as well as by the benevolence of their princes.

On 23rd September, Franz I rode into Vienna with a sovereign's escort of cavalry, all the archdukes and his field-marshals. On his right rode Czar Alexander, on his left the King of Prussia, instantly nicknamed 'the left-hand robber' by the onlookers. That seductive smile for which the Czar was famous turned their heads completely, and they were not to know how heartily sick of him they were to become. The great hostesses of the Congress, beginning with the Empress, may have guessed it in advance. If Prince Maurice Liechtenstein is to be believed, 'everyone' was saying—and they went on saying it throughout the months which followed—that to have invited the foreign monarchs to Vienna at all was an extraordinary error of judgement. 'Truly, Prince Metternich should have known the Russian Emperor, the King of Prussia and Baron von Humboldt better than that . . .' By 'everyone' he meant the anti-Metternich *fronde*, the Fürstenbergs, Choteks, Wallis, Hatzfelds, Stadions, Schönborns, Colloredos, Starhembergs, Hardeggs; the serried ranks of Austrian society.

Over-exposure can wreak havoc, and the Viennese soon began to see too much of the Czar on, as it were, all levels. He could be very rude, he spat on the Persian carpets and polished parquet floors, and the most beautiful women had to bear it with glassy-eyed composure while he stroked their bare backs with his sweaty hand. Altogether, he could be very crude in his amorous approaches. The German diplomats thought him a great big show-off, and that the Viennese were turning his head with overmuch adulation; they should have taken their cue from London society whose leading members stopped well short of undue flattery.

For his part, the Czar must have known that there were plenty of beautiful women in Vienna and that their number would now inevitably increase. Neither the Duchess of Sagan with her Silesian and Russian estates, still less Princess Bagration, could well afford to deny him anything; she, the 'naked angel', was at his disposal. Yet he came to Vienna as one who must provide against a sexual famine. Madame Schwarz was there, an ample and good-natured woman whose husband, in return for her favours to Alexander I, was steadily amassing an enormous fortune through army contracts. They were with Alexander in Paris, and Schwarz was able to build up a network of business contacts on his own account. In Vienna Madame Schwarz moved in banking circles and spent a great deal of money, buying anything she liked the look of. She was the Czar's sexual bread and butter, and he visited her at least two or three times a week. Countess Narishkine was a far more significant figure owing to the part she came to play in the political intrigues of the

Congress. It could be very useful to know Madame Schwarz, but the two women operated on different social levels. Maria-Antonia Narishkine, *née* Czetwertinska, was closely related to one of Poland's most celebrated families, the princes Czartoryski. She was a beauty of a type described as *éclatante*, and she was one of Alexander's favourites over a long period. Her husband, too, the Imperial Master of the Chase, is unlikely to have been the loser in any material sense. The Poles, indefatigable in their search for protectors and clinging always to any ray of hope, now clustered round Countess Narishkine: perhaps she could achieve through Alexander the realization of Poland's aspirations for freedom which Marie Walewska had once dreamed of attaining in the arms of Napoleon? Countess Narishkine took an apartment in the Paniglgasse, near the Karlskirche, and Hager's agents duly took up their posts.

Baron Hager, for his own part sick with unrequited love for his cousin Lulu Thürheim, was soon having to read and pass on to Metternich and Kaiser Franz other reports about the Czar. He and Eugène Beauharnais were becoming inseparable companions: arm-in-arm in the gathering darkness, the Czar and Napoleon's brother-in-law strolled off to the red light and cut-throat districts, becoming for Hager not so much a moral as a security problem of some difficulty. If it was not Beauharnais it was 'that insane hyena',[1] Alexander's brother the Grand Duke Constantine, a man who possessed few redeeming features. He was the perfect picture-book Asiatic tyrant: a completely untrammelled temperament, wild and vicious, making no attempt to adapt himself to western ways, and the announcement of his arrival struck dread into the bosom of every hostess. He had a childish passion for military exercises, and he treated the unfortunate cuirassier regiment stationed in Vienna of which he was Colonel-in-Chief like a collection of toy soldiers. Officers and men and their mounts were called out almost daily for interminable sessions of drill and filing up and down, until at last they could bear it no longer and the commanding officer complained to the General Commandant, Prince Ferdinand of Württemberg, who saw to it that the nonsense was stopped. The Grand Duke's sexual inclinations may also have run on military lines, or vice versa; it is this, probably, which the discreet language of the

[1] Harold Nicolson, *The Congress of Vienna*.

time is trying to convey when talking of batches of unfortunate young soldiers being detailed to go up to the Grand Duke's rooms in the Hofburg.

The more grubby aspects of the Czar's sex life and of his closest associates were very soon the talk of the town, but in themselves they would not have accounted for his unpopularity among the ordinary people. His treatment of the Czarina Elizabeth, formerly Princess Louise, sister of the Grand Duke of Baden, was brutal in private and unbearably humiliating in public, and was widely resented as she was known to be a kind and unassuming woman. Vienna's disappointment in the Czar is visible in innumerable comments in the censorship intercepts. The curly-haired Apollo was better appreciated at a distance. A conquering hero should have better manners: at Countess Sandor's ball he exchanged not one word with his hostess, left after only a few minutes and spent the rest of the night dancing with the daughter of a chemist. Was this the way to behave? He was a barbarian with no interest in the arts. The more perceptive noticed that he was singularly awkward and ill at ease in the sophisticated drawing-rooms of Vienna. Half the time he seemed to be acting a character part, but then he would gradually forget his role and what then emerged was 'le bon fou', a rather mediocre individual lacking in originality, wit or depth.

It was seldom noticed that few men at the Congress worked harder than Alexander I, and Nesselrode's complaint that he was left with almost nothing to do was less amusing to listen to than the opinions of other members of his entourage which reflect the tragedy of his situation. They confided in their eager listeners—the Czar is slightly deranged and will end up like his father; all across Europe, in London, Paris and Vienna, he has accumulated such a reputation for loose living that the news has even penetrated into Russia and discredited his image. Neither his ministers, nor the army, nor the people have any confidence in him. They reproach him for the defeat at Tilsit, for the burning of Moscow, and the events of 1813 and 1814 prove that he is no general, not even a good soldier, but a simpleton and a bungler, a man without character who veers without transition from one extreme to another. Now, they went on, Vienna is littered with caricatures of this *honteux libertin.* Even more damaging, there was the way he went on in Paris about a constitution.

This was the crux of the matter. Alexander came to Vienna to get Poland. When he got it he meant to give it a constitution, a plan with which his own nobility, fearing the intelligence and adaptability of the Poles and consequent disaffection through contact with people in their own domains, were by no means in sympathy. Alexander I was a dreamer, yearning for the love of the masses, floating on a soft cloud of benevolence. Count Capo d'Istria, the future President of Greece, gives this picture of him: he was the personification of those philosophers' dreams of a love which would unite mankind, a utopia of happiness on earth which, however, presupposes the perfectibility both of subjects and of their rulers. The Czar was not unintelligent but he lacked the ability to see things in the round—Capo d'Istria called it the *coup d'œil*—and he lacked confidence in his own convictions, preferring to be led by others.

Alexander the sexual athlete, the poseur, the lover of all humanity who could yet cause the whole population of Moscow to be made homeless in the depth of winter, a man of immense physical and mental energy, an autocrat, but uncertain and hesitant. There was yet another side to this bizarre individual: the religious mystic, childlike and impulsive, who not a year later would be 'kneeling down and opening his heart in a cottage by the Neckar and receiving reproof and instruction with all the contrition and self-abandonment of a Salvation Army convert at the penitent's bench'[1] from that extraordinary prophetess Madame de Krüdener. The Congress was spared her disturbing presence.

A friend wrote to Count Nicolas Esterházy from London that he was scouring the gazettes for news of the goings on in Vienna. 'How all heads are up in the air! How each person listens to the conversation of his neighbour! What plans! What projects! What a focus of affairs it has become, our dear Vienna! The Emperor of Russia has said such and such a thing. The King of Prussia has greeted such and such a person. The King of Bavaria has laughed. The gross King of Württemberg has danced. Mon Dieu! How important this all is. Myself, I tremble in my corner.'

[1] M. Montgomery-Campbell, *Records of Stirring Times, 1726–1822.*

He might well have trembled to learn that it was costing Franz I 15,000 gulden per day to maintain the imperial table. At the end of October Count Stadion, talking of the customary 'fabrication of money' and the absence of any hope that there might be an end to it, said that the Congress was 'nothing but an intermezzo in the great tragedy of the history of the world, an armistice in the *bellum omnium contra omnes*. It permits other countries to study and to watch at close quarters our ministers, our finances and our administration, and it is to this end that we have just released a fresh issue of 500 million gulden in paper money.' This gloomy view was not yet shared by the public: the Viennese were delighted with the magnificent and dignified role played by the Court. No one could remember the like. The équipages—horses, carriages and liveried coachmen —were so elegant, everything was so solid and real, not just for show and in good taste as well—you wouldn't know the place. And it flattered them to see how deferential the visiting sovereigns were towards the Emperor.

In the immediate post-Napoleonic era the Habsburg Court effortlessly outshone all the others: London, Paris, St. Petersburg. It was undoubtedly a fact that among the grandees of the Austrian Empire and their satellites this was on the whole a most impressive generation. There was more beauty about, standards were higher in every way than was the case in other capitals, or in Vienna itself twenty years later when many of the same beauties still reigned and it would be said that hardly one of the younger women possessed anything approaching the looks of her parents. The legendary planets of the Congress possessed not only good looks but something more, their secret lay in their triumphant bearing, their inner fire and individuality. It was not a question of riches. Some of the first families, the Schwarzenbergs, Esterházys and Liechtensteins possessed, as was said earlier, far more ready cash than the Emperor himself. But they had been very rich for a long time and they would remain so for another hundred years and more; not all the most sought-after women were wealthy, while one or two were not even beautiful but possessed magnetism nevertheless. They were aware that they were a good vintage and that even the brilliant court of Charles II of England could not have competed with them. The quantity and quality of their jewellery surprised even the

Grand Duchess Catherine, the Czar's adored but really far from adorable younger sister (generally assumed to be engaged to the Archduke Karl, she had now set her mind on the Crown Prince of Württemberg). At one of the almost nightly balls of that autumn she remarked on the jewellery to an Englishwoman, saying that she had seen nothing like it at any other court, not even in London. 'The reason for that', snapped the good lady, 'is that *our* wealth is displayed in our subsidies.' It was not a bad retort, and one would like to know who made it, if indeed the story was not invented by the Prince de Ligne. But if even the Grand Duchess was impressed, how much more so were the visitors from less flamboyant courts. A startled Prussian was heard to exclaim, 'Good God, you could run three campaigns on this!'

The Empress Maria Ludovica was the mind behind all the entertainments of the Congress. Backed by her lady in waiting Countess 'Pepi' O'Donnell, widow of the former Minister of Finance, she displayed an inventiveness and a pronounced talent for organization, as well as sheer endurance which, in view of her increasing physical weakness, astonished and alarmed those who realized how ill she was. She repeatedly fainted dead away in the middle of her state duties and had to be carried off to her rooms, but in no time she was back again, and this supreme effort she kept up for six months. She had only about another year to live.

Entry to these official balls and *Redouten* was naturally meant to be confined to those whose names were on the Lord Chamberlain's lists, but it will be remembered that many Viennese families could look back on a long experience of the art of gate-crashing. Seeing no reason why the Congress should form an exception, they turned up with wives and marriageable daughters, and as the titled throng moved in, so they moved in on their heels, buying back the already-handed-in tickets from the attendants at high prices. At the first *Redoute*, 8,000 guests were expected, and 12,000 were present. The crush was intense and to dance almost impossible, but the attendants made a nice profit. There was another flourishing trade, in the uneaten food from the tables of all the monarchs and their suites in the Hofburg. Course after obligatory course marched through the dining-rooms and out again where the food at once became the perquisite of one or another Court official. It now left the building by a predetermined route and passed through practised hands, which often conveyed it right out of the walled town, across the Glacis and in at the back door of a restaurant. For the poor, or in fact for anyone who cared to help themselves, there were titbits to be had for nothing. On the evening of a ball at Court, whole tubs of half-squeezed lemons, prepared and uneaten strawberries, oranges and ground almonds were put out in the courtyard. The really needy could in any case always present themselves at the Hofburg kitchens, or, for that matter, at the Hofapotheke, the Court pharmacy. A contemporary remembered a quite well-situated widow who, for years, whenever she walked into town in the morning, called in at the imperial kitchens for a cup of beef tea.

It was during the crisp, dry autumn weather, while the Vienna Woods were a sea of crimson and gold, that the Augarten with its halls for dancing and dining, was brought into play. The party for 400 hundred army veterans held on 6th October with its sack races, climbing the pole and other innocent amusements followed by illuminations and fireworks was not quite the magnificent occasion that the *Wiener Zeitung* made it out to be next day, as a sudden collapse in the weather extinguished the illuminations and turned the ground into a swamp. Altogether, a cloud of ill-fortune seemed to be hanging over the Augarten where Sir Sidney Smith gave a dinner and dance which must have stayed in his memory for a long time. Admiral Sir (William) Sidney Smith was that great English eccentric who, for two months from 19th March to 20th May, 1799, successfully held Acre against Napoleon and could therefore claim, ten years before Aspern, to be Napoleon's first undefeated opponent. Croker[1] called him 'that mere vaporizer', but Napoleon, although he thought him '*mezzo pazzo*', admired him greatly. Smith was very far from being a member of the British delegation. He appeared to be holding a watching brief for the old Swedish royal house of Vasa, but while this was the diplomatic justification for his presence, his declared purpose was to organize concerted measures against those Algerian and Tunisian pirates known as the Barbary corsairs who were raising hell up and down the Mediterranean. The Viennese liked Sir Sidney who, with his wild shock of white hair and Admiral's uniform with cut-throat collar (known in

[1] J. Wilson Croker, M.P.

14. *Congress Beauties*
(a) (opposite) Wilhelmine,
Duchess of Sagan
(b) (below left)
Princess Catherine Bagration
(c) (below right)
Metternich's niece,
Countess Flora Wrbna,
née Kagenegg

15. Czar Alexander I

16. Archduke Joseph,
     Palatine of Hungary

German by the curiously Freudian term *Vatermörder*), was soon a familiar landmark, and his Wednesday after-theatre *soirées* were packed out. A fund-raising dinner for captive Christian slaves was another matter; not until another generation had gone by was this type of charitable activity to be introduced into Vienna by Princess Pauline Metternich and raised to dazzling heights. Smith invited 150 people to his 'picnic' in the Augarten, but—according to Austrian sources—as he belonged to the opposition party in London not one single Englishman turned up. This was unfortunate for his 40 Austrian guests, who, not realizing in the first place that they were to pay for their dinners, and in many cases having little or no money with them, now found themselves having to pay for 110 English Tories and other absentees as well. Altogether the party was not a success, and by 11 o'clock the lights were extinguished and the last guest had gone.

There was perhaps only one really popular entertainment in the true sense, and that was the sit-down dinner in the Prater on 18th October for 20,000 officers and men in commemoration of the Battle of Leipzig. At that time, the Lusthaus was surrounded by water and for the occasion it was joined to the mainland by decorated pontoon bridges. Here the kings and emperors and the chiefs-of-staff dined, and from where they sat they looked out on a series of ever-widening rings of tables at which sat the officers and men who fought Napoleon at Leipzig, their weapons forming an immense pyramid in the centre. The toasts given by the Emperor and his guests in the Lusthaus were brought to the tables by riders at full gallop, and if they looked towards the island as the cannon crashed out a signal in response, the soldiers could just see a tiny, white-uniformed figure in the far distance, holding a glass in his upraised hand. Thousands more soldiers were there who were not included in the feast, and who knows how many Viennese as well, 150,000 at least, perhaps a quarter of a million, who had streamed out to the Prater to watch a spectacle (parades, on the whole, bored them) which they would talk about for many years to come. There was no need for them to go hungry: in the *Wurstelprater* close by 40 inns and five coffee-houses were waiting for them.

A variety of entertainments were laid on. Whether or not constant preoccupation with catering for large numbers, culminating in the mass feeding operation in the Prater, caused the idea to spread that size is in itself a virtue, on the morning of 30th October a concert was given on 20 pianos, two players at each, which adds up to 80 hands or 400 fingers. It was an early precursor of the dreadful Victorian fashion for blown-up music performed by massed bands and vast choirs.

The Habsburgs were always proud of the shooting which they could offer guests at their very doorstep, but it has often happened that in the Court's anxiety to provide visiting royalty who were doubtful shots with the large bags their self-esteem demanded—the hosts, too, have occasionally been notorious butchers—what took place could not accurately be described as sport. The Swiss delegate J. G. Eynard described the shooting of wild boar in the Lainzer Tiergarten, a game reserve in the Vienna Woods. A fortnight beforehand, 600 wild boar were driven into a fenced-in space beside which there was another cage 300 or 400 paces long and 150 wide. 'The monarchs placed themselves a few paces apart along the length of this rectangle. From time to time five or six boar were released which were compelled to pass the guns. The monarchs were placed according to their precedence, so that if the emperors missed these unhappy beasts, the kings enjoyed the honour of aiming at them. Should the kings also miss, it was the turn of the imperial and the royal highnesses, after them the dukes and marshals, and finally their subordinates. This shoot, which is nothing more than a massacre of wild pig, lasted the whole morning, and the monarchs have earned the reputation of having killed five hundred head. The fat King of Württemberg, who himself much resembles a wild boar, accounted for thirty-five of them, the Emperor of Austria for thirty-three.'

It was the presence of all these monarchs which set the Lord Chamberlain's machinery in motion, and once started, it acquired a momentum of its own. But it was Alexander's insatiable love of dancing which gave the Congress its particular image, so that by the end of October, when the work could hardly be said to have begun, the women were already telling their husbands that their allowances were exhausted and they must have more money for ball dresses, while the smaller delegations, although they were doing little or nothing in the way of entertaining, had run out of ready cash and were wondering how to extend their credit. Advent was not far off, many could hardly wait for the enforced end of balls and *Redouten*, and for the return of a comparative calm lasting until after the twelve days of Christmas. One more entertainment lay ahead on 23rd November, at the thought of which the ladies and their husbands too were moaning. There was to be a carousel, and the cheapest sash that a woman could possibly give to her cavalier cost 1,000 gulden: 'Elles ne font que gémir des dépenses enormes . . .'

23rd November: it was just two months since the Czar and King Frederick William had ridden into Vienna, and what had been achieved? Countless notes had gone round in circles, there had been talks, arguments, intrigues, lovemaking. The King of Württemberg, of all people, bellowed that it was a disgrace: it was taking longer to share out the conquered countries than it took to defeat the tyrant. 'What has been done since the Treaty of Paris? Hey? What?' Even Princess Bagration had worked that one out, saying archly to Metternich: 'Confess that it cost you less trouble to defeat Napoleon than it is costing you now to agree over the spoils.'

The Congress had ballooned into something which it was never intended to be. The Swedish Chargé d'Affaires, von Hegardt, summed it up in a letter to Foreign Minister Engeström: 'The princelings and dynasties of Germany, forming coteries by the dozen and by the score, have also sent their plenipotentiaries to the Congress. There are people who have formed a conception of the Congress of Vienna as a court of law before which all kinds of pretensions and claims, however superannuated, may be brought.' All these things wasted time, and meanwhile the two really intractable problems had to be pushed and dragged along, week after week, like laden sledges on wet snow; the Polish question and the determination of Prussia to form an undivided, viable state, at the expense of the King of Saxony. 'It's a shame', pondered Franz I, 'to dethrone a fellow monarch.' And this was another grudge held against Metternich, that he should wish to dethrone a Catholic and incorporate his lands in those of a Protestant sovereign.

By mid-November the tension between Metternich and the Czar was approaching its first climax. In a heated exchange in which Metternich nearly lost his composure—even Napoleon never brought him to this point—the Chancellor told the Czar that Vienna could not see its way to agree to Russia's policy to annex Poland; it was incompatible with peace in Europe, with equilibrium and with the security of Austria. If he, Alexander, wished for good relations with foreign powers, he must abandon this policy. Alexander I was furious. Did Metternich wish to dictate his foreign policy to him, and to defraud him of what he possessed? If the Prince thought that this was what he had come to Vienna for he was much mistaken! Let Metternich send someone to Poland to count the Russian troops there, then he would talk in a different tone of voice altogether! Metternich, said Hegardt, was so disconcerted by this attack that he could hardly find the doorhandle.

Even if the chief delegate of France had been a political nitwit he must have seen that his chance had come. Talleyrand saw the allies at loggerheads over Saxony and Poland, he saw England and Austria faced by the threatening attitudes of Russia and Prussia, and he moved unobtrusively into the front seat and stayed there, oblivious or indifferent to the fact that this unique piece of effrontery on the part of a representative of a defeated nation united all the delegates in Vienna in the one emotion of extreme annoyance. 'Fattish for a Frenchman,' said Croker, 'his ankles weak and his feet deformed', with 'a face not at all expressive except it be of a kind of drunken stupor', he was indeed, 'altogether like an old, fuddled, lame village schoolmaster'. But Alexander listened to him. When the Czar exploded: 'So be it—you shall have war!' he said quietly: 'Sire, you will lose your glory as the peacemaker of the world, the sole glory to which, according to your words in Paris, you aspired.' In addition to nerves like whipcord, Talleyrand had other weapons. He held in his possession a letter from Metternich to Caulaincourt written in March 1814, begging him to do all in his power to keep Napoleon on the throne of France. Metternich knew very well that Talleyrand had the letter and would use it the moment it suited him. This was the kind of thing which aroused such intense dislike in Alexander I, and not in him alone: Metternich's eternal deviousness, the fact that no one ever knew where they were with him, and then his air of amused calm, shaken only on that one occasion. It drove the Czar frantic, Metternich returned the Czar's dislike in full measure, he only concealed it better. He knew very well that in its more acute form Alexander's hostility began in 1813 over the issue of the march through Switzerland,[1] he knew the Czar's violent temperament, and he undoubtedly over-estimated his own ability to deal with him. It was also obvious that sexual jealousy was likely to aggravate the situation in no small degree.

For a start, there was Princess Bagration. On her mother's side, Catherine Bagration *née* Countess Skavronskij, was a niece of Potemkin and on her father's a great-niece of Catherine I (not to be confused with Catherine II, the Great) whose origins are worth recalling. A Latvian peasant, Samuel Skavronskij, had a beautiful daughter who married a Swedish Dragoon in Marienburg. After the capture of this town by the Russians she became the mistress of Prince Menshikov who later relinquished her to Peter the Great. So far, conventional enough, but what follows could only have happened in Russia. Peter the Great married her, and after his death she ruled as Catherine I. She had a much-loved brother, and saw to it that riches flowed into the hands of this direct ancestor (he was her great grandfather) of plump little Catherine Skavronskij. Rich beyond the range of her own comprehension and by no means modest in her demands upon her lovers, by the time she arrived in Vienna at the age of 31 she had nevertheless worked her way through a considerable portion of her fortune. She had presented Metternich with a daughter in 1802, in 1803 she was having an affair with the Duke of Gloucester and in 1805 with Gentz; in 1806, in Dresden, Prince Louis Ferdinand, a nephew of Frederick II (the Great) fell into her arms and immediately afterwards was killed in battle. These names were but the tips of icebergs, as it were her battle honours; her mother saw her disorderly life and would have nothing more to do with her. We are told that her skin was alabaster touched by a rose. Her eyes were large and beseeching, her lips full and sensual, and she fluttered about like a moth uttering political banalities. When the Czar arrived in Vienna he went to her apartment and shut himself up with her for several hours until well into the night—it was thought that what he was doing was instructing her in the art of espionage. Society considered her a tart, all the same it was she and none other who give the first ball of the Congress of Vienna on 1st October, and it must be assumed that Society

[1] The Austrian troops committed a breach of Swiss neutrality in spite of the Czar's undertaking that it be respected.

went to it. But to her unbounded fury she was not on the list of guests invited to the exclusive Court ball on 5th October, and it was only through the direct intervention of the Czar that Franz I was forced to relent. She now began to draw all the Russian and Prussian contingent into her net, and her drawing-rooms became something resembling a headquarters of the pro-Alexander faction—an odd situation in view of the undoubted virtue of many of these diplomats and that one or two of the inner rooms were set aside for sex. The house in which she lived was the palais Palm which stood conveniently close to the Ballhausplatz on the present site of the Burgtheater. In the very same house, on the very same floor, front doors face to face, lived Wilhelmine, Duchess of Sagan.

Wilhelmine and Catherine possessed nothing in common which they would have cared to discuss. The origins of the Duchess's principal source of income were however not dissimilar. Whether the ancestor who made good was a forester or a student, whether his name was Bühren or Bieren is immaterial: Anna, widow of the Duke of Courland (or Kurland) fancied him, and when she came to the throne of Russia in 1730 as Anna I she took her secretary-chamberlain-lover with her. Biron, as he now called himself, was left to run the affairs of the Empire much as he pleased and to accumulate riches as he did so. The son whom the Czarina is believed to have borne him she created Duke of Courland, and in 1795 his descendant Peter Duke of Courland allowed himself to be bought out of this duchy by the Czar and in its place bought the Duchy of Sagan in Silesia. The Duke died in 1800 leaving a widow and four redoubtable daughters, the 'Courland whores'; the term was understood to include the widow.

In a way both Wilhelmine and Catherine got off to a bad start: Catherine Skavronskij because on the orders of Czar Paul I she was married off at seventeen to a middle-aged man whom, as he was almost continually on active service, she rarely saw; Wilhelmine because she was unable to marry the man she loved. She had known Prince Louis Ferdinand of Prussia (later to be consoled by Catherine) since they were both children, and the fact that for reasons of state he was forbidden to marry her hurt more than Wilhelmine's *amour propre*; she was deeply upset. At once, she accepted Prince Julius Rohan. It was a great name, but one of her sisters, by now Duchess of

Dino, thought nothing of him: he 'lacked spirit and nobility of character'. In 1805 she divorced him and tried marriage to Prince Vassilji Troubetzkoj, but within a year she was rid of him as well. Her sisters were also divorcing their husbands, Pauline a Prince Hohenzollern-Hechingen and Jeanne the Duke of Acerenza. All this activity was possible because the Courlands were Protestants, but since both Rohan and Troubetskoj had to be bought off in hard cash it was expensive. 'Je me ruine en maris,' sighed Wilhelmine. As in the meantime she had inherited the Duchy of Sagan from now on it became the custom to call her by that name.

Princess Bagration was small, fair and fluffy, and her *décolletés* were a miracle of brinkmanship. The Duchess of Sagan could hardly have presented a greater contrast. She was of medium height, her hair was plentiful, dark and wavy, her skin flawless. The stillness of her sometimes almost mask-like face contrasted with her large and expressive eyes. Even as a girl an indefinable aura surrounded her: a youthful *grande dame*, she never was touched by the fatal cheapness of her rival.

The complaint that Metternich spent his mornings during the first weeks of the Congress sighing at her feet was not literally true, but it had this foundation in fact, that they were locked in a battle of wills of a kind which Metternich had never experienced before. For some time the Duchess had been feeling dissatisfied with her role as Metternich's mistress, she had dropped hints in plenty but the lack of response failed to put her off. On the contrary. Whether it was the irksome presence of the Prince's earlier love across the landing with whom he and Gentz had the effrontery to spend a whole evening alone, or whether the whole erotic circus offended her sense of dignity, she now decided that it was all or nothing. Clemens Metternich must divorce his wife and marry Wilhelmine Sagan. To go along with her point of view for a moment: it is true that with her intelligence and political insight the two of them would have made a formidable combination, and in retrospect it may be thought that if she could have brought that element of self-criticism into play which was so entirely lacking in Metternich's intellectual make-up, she might have preserved him from some of the follies of his later career. But it is surprising that she could have been so naïve. At 41, Metternich was now approaching, had in fact reached though not all could see it, the summit of his career, yet he was surrounded by enemies. His one sheet-anchor was the Emperor. His wife was beyond reproach and it was a Catholic marriage. Did Wilhelmine really believe that Clemens Metternich could divorce Lorel and marry her without sacrificing his ambitions? Clearly, she did. There was one single meeting between them when she brought the matter to a head, and after that her manner towards him, which latterly had been cool and distant, became just one degree less than icy; it was not prudent to make an enemy of the Emperor's first minister.

Metternich's anguish may well have been largely compounded of injured pride, as never before had it been the woman who set the pace, and to a man of his staggering conceit that a woman should withdraw from his embraces was an unthinkable occurrence. All the same, suddenly to lose an intoxicating woman of her calibre was hard indeed. Gentz, bored beyond endurance, had to listen to his moans for hours at a time, and he also had to put up with being told by the Duchess, in reply to a letter in which he remonstrated with her, to mind his own business. After this Gentz could never say anything bad enough about her, not so much from personal conviction as because he was an expert at relieving his master's feelings by putting them into words which Metternich himself would have been too fastidious to use. The Czar, however, told Princess Bagration: 'Metternich never loved either you or Sagan, that's an ice-cold fellow, believe me—he loves no one!'

Though it may well be suspected that the Duchess of Sagan loved Metternich more genuinely than he loved her, both suffered excruciating pangs yet both made a complete and even fairly rapid recovery. Her position was now considerably eased, as the Czar's almost frantic hostility towards Metternich was now coming to a head, culminating in a determined attempt to unseat him from office. It is usually said, Gentz being quoted as the authority, that the Czar put pressure upon Sagan to drop Metternich, but this seems unlikely because it would have been unnecessary. To begin with, Alexander largely ignored her, while arousing her jealousy with his long visits to Catherine Bagration, and it was she who restored herself to favour by asking him for an audience, whereupon he gallantly came to breakfast. From now on the two female rivals struggled to outbid one another in the service of Alexander I who, for his part, severed all social relations with Metternich. He went out of his way to be polite to the Princess and her eldest daughter, but he never attended another ball at their palais on the Rennweg, of which there were to be no less than 19. The Duchess, who could well claim to have placed a drag brake under the wheels of the Congress all through the autumn, now threw herself into an affair with the British Ambassador, Lord Charles Stewart, while Metternich switched his charm on to the virtuous *beauté céleste*, Countess Julie Zichy, to the mortal distress of King Frederick William of Prussia who was so much in love with her that he sat, evening after evening, gazing at her in helpless adoration.

Apart from the official entertaining by the Court, the Metternichs were almost the only members of Viennese society to entertain consistently and on a comprehensive scale. As a result, running parallel with the ever-growing criticism of non-stop frivolity there was a constant undercurrent of complaint to be heard among the minor delegations that not enough notice was being taken of them. They were not, they felt, being entertained by the leading hostesses, or when they were, a lurking suspicion remained that they were left to stand around in listless groups while the real fun was going on in another room. They were not altogether mistaken. The 'first society' hostesses were as a rule remarkably generous towards foreigners with a personal introduction, and usually admitted them at once to their circle. But now they felt swamped. They continued with their *jours*, increasing as well the number and scope of other forms of entertaining, but there were limits to what they could do, and most salons cut even kings from their list if they were unendurable: the King of Denmark, for instance, was so hideous that he had to buy female company on the open market. The King of Württemberg, owing to his seniority (an extremely sensible rule settled precedence by age) became a monotonously regular burden for the Empress.

Congress was now overtaken by Christmas, a reminder to all the delegates that they were still far from hearth and home with nothing settled. It brought the first Christmas tree to a Viennese home: not, as is usually said, to that of Archduke Karl who was then still a bachelor, nor to that of the banker Geymüller. The record is held[1] by

[1] Hilde Spiel, *Fanny von Arnstein.*

Fanny Arnstein. This striking figure of the age of Jewish emancipation, born an Itzig of Berlin, was a Napoleon-hater no less impassioned than Germaine de Staël, or Maria Ludovica. She married the merchant Nathan Adam Arnsteiner, who as Baron Arnstein was the first Jew to be raised to that rank of the Austrian peerage. Throughout most of the reign of Franz I her houses on the Hohe Markt and on the road to Schönbrunn were a focus of the intellectual life of the capital. Almost every day of the week her drawing-room was the place where anyone who had something of interest to say—on politics, poetry, philosophy or whatever it might be—was made welcome. As though all this were not enough to cause the authorities to keep an eye on her, Fanny's glowing Prussian patriotism was apt to create dissension even within her own circle. During the Congress the Prussians and their allies were naturally to be found at the Arnsteins, and that Christmas, in addition to 'all the circumcised and baptized relatives of the house', Prince Hardenberg and Prince Radziwill were there to join in the Berlin custom of singing comic songs and carrying their presents in procession through all the adjoining rooms. 'Prince Hardenberg was infinitely diverted.'

Entirely owing to her personality, the Arnsteins' situation was exceptional, but it had this in common with other families of the 'second society' and the bourgeoisie: there was no social mingling with the top nobility as a whole, and yet the rigidly separated groups interacted like communicating vessels in some laboratory experiment. A great deal of private entertaining, of stag dinners and quiet discussion went on in the houses of bankers and merchants, both Jewish and Christian. Aristocrats never took their wives with them, but (not only during the Congress) these contacts were essential to them for the invaluable opportunity they gave of hearing news of the outside world. The host, meanwhile, was placing his powerful guests in his debt; satisfaction was mutual. Vienna's intellectuals, however, its world-famous scientists and scholars such as the Jacquins and Hammer-Purgstall, were not in evidence at the Congress. Not that they would have had much to contribute to an exercise in power politics, but some discerning foreigners who sought them out noticed their apparent social irrelevance and wondered at it.

The work of the Congress was going on in scores of rooms in

hotels and lodgings, in the guest apartments of the Hofburg, in the drawing-rooms of the Duchess of Sagan and Princess Bagration, of Countess Fuchs and Countess Molly Zichy-Ferraris, and Baroness von Arnstein, in Gentz's study and in Metternich's. There was also that attic bedroom referred to earlier as a refuge from Baron Hager's espionage system. Its occupant was the Countess Aurore de Marassé.

Aurore was the daughter of a French general who at the time of Dumouriez's defection left his troops standing and fled. He settled in Temesvár on a small pension from Franz I and died in 1805. A penniless refugee and alone, Aurore was evidently unable to find settled employment as a companion or governess, and it is clear why. She was too outspoken, too witty, too good-looking, too vague and erratic to hold down such a job for more than a week. The Congress found her acting as lady companion to Princess Bagration, but although that apartment was looked on by many as little better than a brothel her reputation suffered not at all. 'For some women,' they said, 'it is as difficult to lose their reputation as for others to keep theirs.' Too thin, elongated, beautiful, in a tattered balldress and a borrowed tiara, she drifted from one palais to another, exchanging repartee with kings and princes, dignified and undoubtedly virtuous. The Congress offers no more unconventional scene than that shabby attic room with its row of ambassadors perched on Aurore's bed.

Before the Viennese saw the old year out a major sensation lay in store for them.

Count Andreas Razumovsky, now mainly remembered as a patron of Beethoven, was the Czar's Ambassador to the Habsburg Court between 1792 and 1807 when he was dismissed for his unconcealed dislike of the Franco-Russian alliance. At that time an immeasurably wealthy man and related by marriage to the Austrian aristocracy,[1] he stayed on in Vienna where his house became a rallying point of the anti-Bonapartist war party. Disagreements notwithstanding, he was too good a man to be overlooked and he became Russian plenipotentiary to the Congress in company with Count Stackelberg and the Foreign Minister Nesselrode.

---

[1] He married first Elisabeth Thun-Hohenstein-Klösterle, secondly in 1816 Constantine Thürheim, elder sister of Lulu.

On an area of waste land outside the town walls, between the road to Hungary and the Danube canal and only a stone's throw from the spot where Richard Cœur de Lion was arrested, Razumovsky was building a palace. Already he had laid it at the feet of the Czar as a residence for future ambassadors, and the Czar had raised him to the rank of prince. He could hardly do less. Now that the great project was completed the Viennese were stunned by the splendour of the palace and its grounds, a new-style Winter Palace in which, said the popular press, it was inconceivable that ordinary mortals could live. The approach was through an arch and along an avenue, and there was not one mansion but three main blocks with extensive buildings for domestic servants, a riding school, chapel, stables and glass houses, all set in a landscaped park from which a bridge led across the Danube canal into the Prater. Unlimited wealth and the work of superb craftsmen—plasterers, gilders, cabinet-makers, upholsterers and the rest—had made of the palace a dwelling place of infinite luxury, beauty and comfort. There were priceless oriental carpets, tapestries, old masters and valuable sculptures, a comprehensive library and many musical instruments including a small organ. Cool air could be pumped with bellows into the rooms in summer, scented air in winter; pipes laid inside the walls brought warmth to all the rooms.

On 30th December the workmen had nearly all gone, only a few upholsterers were still sewing, nailing and glueing in upper rooms. The principal scene of activity was the kitchens, more particularly that section of the bakery in which pastrycooks and confectioners were preparing for the great house-warming party on New Year's Eve. They had been working round the clock for days, not knowing that they had overheated a baking oven, which being badly insulated had caused a beam to start smouldering. All unsuspected, the fire ate its way along the walls until a sudden draught made it burst into flames. It was now the central heating system which sealed the fate of the great house as currents of air swept through the walls carrying the fire from one end of the building to the other.

The flames were seen from the watch-towers of the city and soon all the fire engines in Vienna were being drawn at a gallop or manhandled towards the palace on the Landstrasse, while sappers were brought along to hack a way for the fire engines through the exotic shrubs on the park side. Prinze Razumovsky, exhausted and ill from the double strain of work and festivity on top of the anxieties of house building, was in bed and had to be hastily dressed and helped downstairs by his valets. His domestic staff appear to have lost their heads completely, as no organized efforts to save some of the invaluable contents of the buildings were made. No one seems to have carried pictures, tapestries or gold and silver ware to a safe place. Instead, the Prince's underwear was hurled out of one upper window, followed by alabaster lamps, silk, velvet and brocade soft furnishings out of another, where they were either trampled underfoot in the morass which quickly formed near the walls or were swiftly removed to some other place of permanent safety in the house of a Viennese citizen. For the townspeople were there in their thousands, and although it is perhaps hard to blame them, they did get hopelessly in the way of the fire engines, as crowds always have and always will. The mounted police had a practised technique for dispersing crowds whereby they cut off small sections at a time and drove the people away, but this was of little use as more crowds, more fire engines and more soldiers were coming up behind, as well as important personages on horseback, then the archdukes, and finally the Emperor with Alexander I. They found Prince Razumovsky sitting on a bench far out in the park under a plane tree on a patch of raised ground, huddled in sables and with a velvet cap on his head, a figure paralysed with misery watching his dream go up in flames. Everywhere the ground was soaking wet and planks were laid down for the Emperor to walk on after he dismounted. Now even the immense copper roof was glowing as though in the light of the midday sun. There was really nothing that anyone could have said at this moment, but Franz I did his best and said what came into his mind. Touched, Razumovsky made to kiss his hand, but the Emperor nervously snatched it back. It is a characteristic little gesture.

By eight o'clock in the morning the whole palace was destroyed with all its contents. The sole consolation was that it had at least given employment to a large number of people from labourers to skilled craftsmen. So far, the Congress was bringing prosperity only to those trades which were directly involved, leaving the rest of the population relatively unaffected. The bankers—Arnstein,

Elkan and Geymüller—could assess the amount of money actually brought into the town as opposed to the debased paper money with which the government was paying for the Congress: all the delegations had deposited letters of credit with one or other of them, and their withdrawals were of course known. Compared with the brief séjour of the allied sovereigns in Paris which brought 20 million gulden into the town, the visitors to Vienna were keeping their pockets fairly tightly buttoned up, understandably, since the plenipotentiaries—Talleyrand, Hardenberg, Labrador, Castlereagh, Loewenhielm—had no real domestic staff and did no large-scale formal entertaining. The King of Württemberg, Elkan thought, was simply speculating on the exchange. The Congress, however, still had some way to go, and Prince Hardenberg thought it worth while sending to Paris for his mistress the actress Jubille. She arrived at the end of December.

By the New Year there was no concealing the fact that, in the eyes of nearly all concerned, and of the public, the monarchs had outstayed their welcome, and the imposition of a 50 per cent tax on trading profits only confirmed the view that it was high time they went home, leaving the field to those who were doing the work. On 22nd January, the day after Talleyrand's own bizarre theatrical performance, a full-scale memorial service for Louis XVI which cost him the equivalent of 40,000 francs, the Court held a sledging party. The celebrated *Schlittage* consisted of a trip to Schönbrunn for the royalties and the reigning beauties in the ornate imperial sledges. Etiquette notwithstanding, the King of Prussia was able to sit with his adored Julie Zichy, and Alexander I with Princess Gabriele Auersperg. She was a 20-year-old widow who is believed to have withstood his onslaughts on her virtue to the very end—'not much of an achievement', it was said, as 'she is cold and lacks passion'. The bystanders watched as the coachmen whipped up their horses and the 34 sledges, scraping and grinding on the packing stones as the one essential prop, snow, had failed to materialize, and one embittered citizen spoke for all the rest: 'There they go with our 50 per cent!'

The monarchs and other royal personages had, in any case, no intention of leaving Vienna. The carnival season was in full swing, and how pleasant it was to exchange banter with those famed society beauties: there was Thèrese Esterházy *née* Thurn und Taxis, Caroline Szechenyi *née* Lady Caroline Meade, Gabriele Saurau *née* Hunyady de Kethely and so on, and at the back of one's mind there was the knowledge that the little woman was waiting patiently in those cosy rooms which her patron had booked for her in a quiet street. Rosalie Morel fell into the little woman category. She was the daughter of an officer in a Hungarian regiment of Hussars, but was brought up in France, and she possessed not only beauty but distinction and reserve; she was generally considered to put all the other courtesans of the Congress into the shade. Rosalie sounds a little too good for the Grand Duke Charles of Baden, and perhaps she felt this herself, because having deposited her husband and children at Baden near Vienna she also had an affair with an unnamed count, a fact which the Grand Duke discovered. He forgave her, as well he might, as in December we find him 'favouring' a maid[1] in the service of Baron Gärtner 'who appears to be equally to the taste of the hereditary Prince of Hesse-Darmstadt'; already Charles of Baden had debts all over Vienna. Throughout the winter his chief equerry Baron Geusau would arrange intimate little dinner parties for him, and on the night of 12th–13th February the party (said the secret police agent) was so exhausting that the Grand Duke was unable to get up until four o'clock in the afternoon. He was spending at the rate of 1,000 to 1,200 ducats per week for his private entertainment alone.

Prince Ludwig of Hesse-Darmstadt was not necessarily reduced to sharing Baron Gärtner's maid with the Grand Duke as he had his own Mlle Toussaint, now passing herself off as Countess von Waffenberg, whom he had taken over from Prince Starhemberg. This was the moment when Friedrich von Gentz took up with that exceptionally gifted courtesan Johanna Desfours-Walderode who had been playing Tom Tiddler's Ground with the police for years, a contest which she invariably won. Gentz's relationship with her lasted until 1823. A glimpse is caught of Prince Wolkonsky's mistress Josephine Wolters as she slips into the Hofburg in men's

---

[1] The Viennese *Stubenmädchen* were a celebrated institution. Chosen for their looks and agreeable temperament, impeccably dressed in the local style, their duty was to initiate the young men of the family. One legendary figure, 'Nanderl', was immortalized on Augarten china.

clothing. King Frederick of Denmark found himself a truly magnificent creature on the streets, and throughout the Congress he spent the better part of his time with her, becoming thinner, more haggard and ashen as time went on. The King's enthusiasm for his splendid Viennese beauty was such that he rented a luxuriously furnished apartment for her in the town house of Princess Paar. The girl, by now a celebrity who was followed by an admiring throng whenever she took the air on the bastions and was known to every urchin in town as the 'Queen of Denmark', entered into the spirit of it all and gave this as her name on taking up residence, to the fury of Princess Paar who forbade her to enter the house. King Frederick was by far the most popular among the prominent visitors in the eyes of the general public, although he was not welcome in the best salons, particularly in that of Molly Zichy-Ferraris where the younger princes and the statesmen and diplomats regularly forgathered. Lulu Thürheim is much more generous in her comments: 'He is a disgusting person, and yet the best king in the world, noble, bountiful, charitable, intelligent and continually concerned for the well-being of his people.'

Eugène Beauharnais exercised his sexual athleticism over so wide a field that the agents hardly bothered to identify the woman whom, as the contemporary euphemism had it, he was pleased to distinguish. The careful researcher is thus left wondering whether the Madame Suzanne in the Färbergasse whose daughter was Beauharnais's mistress is identical with Suzanne Lamberg, and what Madame Lambert has to do with a Séraphine (?) Lambert living in the 'Römischer Kaiser'. One is on safe ground in saying that it was Madame Orondi, wife of a Karlsruhe merchant, who followed Beauharnais's call to Vienna and promptly sent him to Herr Neuling to buy jewels worth 32,000 ducats. These were paid for partly in cash, partly with a sword set in precious stones given to him by Napoleon, together with three tiaras and assorted diamond buttons. While this gives some idea of the scale on which the brother of the Empress Josephine and son-in-law of the King of Bavaria was expected to reward his favourites, it may be hoped that he was not shopping solely for Mme Orondi but was keeping something for his other regulars—even for Suzanne Lambert although two days running, 'la place étant déjà occupée,' she was unable to receive him.

17. Villa Metternich on the Rennweg. Behind: Salesianerkirche

18. Karlskirche

19. Archduke Karl, his wife
Henriette and their children at
Weilburg Castle, 1830

She may have been genuinely sorry to have to put him off. For depraved he might be, the Nuncio might call him 'ce coquin de batârd, ce friseur parisien',[1] his voice was disagreeable and some laughed at him behind his back. But Eugène de Beauharnais was a spellbinder all the same: it was his quick wit, his well-stocked mind, his looks and elegance and that quality, 'le grand air', which disarmed men as well as women and gave him, if they were not constantly on their guard, a hold over them all. That he should entirely win over Alexander I was understandable, but to have cast his spell over Lady Castlereagh was an achievement of a different order.

Debts were piling up in the palais Palm where Princess Bagration threw one party after another and danced wild Cossack dances with Count Potocki. Whose mistress she was now, during the first months of 1815, who knows? Those young Counts Schönfeld and Schulenburg, *faiblesses passagères*, were long since forgotten, and she was having an affair with the Crown Prince of Württemberg even when he was engaged to the Grand Duchess Catherine. Alexander I was not always her lover—perhaps he never was with any consistency—many of those withdrawals to her bedroom at odd times of the day and night had the different purpose of political rendezvous as the Czar's increasing deafness made it necessary to shout at him. By the spring her great love was Charles of Bavaria, second son of King Maximilian, but the end of the Congress found her in the arms of the Crown Prince of Denmark. Nothing and no one stayed in her mind for long unless it was her hatred of Wilhelmine Sagan. Her moods and her hypochondria fluctuated with almost manic rapidity: 'One moment she's at death's door, the next she's dancing like a wild woman'; Lorel Metternich thought her a bit mad.

Madame Grassini must not be forgotten, sweeping into Vienna on 3rd February at the side of the Duke of Wellington as though she were the Duchess herself. Grassini was a celebrity in her own right. She had been, for a time, Napoleon's mistress, but he is unlikely to have spoken to her as peremptorily as he did to the Parisian actress Mlle Mézeray: 'Sit down, undress, lie down.' She was a prima

---

[1] This harsh view was not shared by the public. During the march on Vienna in 1809 and throughout the six months of occupation, Beauharnais, in striking contrast to, for instance, Marshal Davout, behaved towards the local inhabitants with kindness and chivalry, paying in cash for his lodging and provisions.

donna, a member of the Scala of Milan, of whom Auguste Fournier wrote 'Grassini had been the belle of the universe from the bumbailiffs of Salò to the English princes of the blood royal and to the emperors and kings of the new creation. An entertaining woman, agreeable, gay, an excellent actress, the possessor of a unique physical constitution, generous rather than mean and at bottom a decent woman, she was never considered *intrigante*.'

The Duke of Wellington's arrival and the departure of the Castlereaghs had been the talk of Vienna for the past fortnight. There was a general feeling of expectancy, but as usual, hardly had he embarked on his round of visits before the chatter began again about the total disregard of the British for international etiquette. Calls were paid on kings and sovereign princes without a previous appointment, as if he were their social equal; it was thought that here the usually tight, 'half crazy' Sir Charles Stewart was really to blame. Metternich, however, annoyed these royalties in just the same way: overfamiliarity and a tendency to sit down before he was invited to do so. Absurd though these sensibilities may seem they do bring to mind two points about the Congress. To begin with, converse between nations in the modern world is often more bound by etiquette than ever it was. The faintest appearance of a slight towards a statesman or towards a public hero in the realm of sport is liable to be seen as an insult to the whole nation which he represents. In the early nineteenth century this was by no means the case. The Congress of Vienna was different from anything which the twentieth century could mount, being of its essence aristocratic, which is a different thing from saying that most of the men and women involved were aristocrats, often intricately related (Franz I with Alexander I, the Duchess of Sagan with Talleyrand and so on ad lib) and that these relationships intercrossed with no regard for political convenience. Few of those present, that is to say, would have to justify their actions before an elected legislature. It follows therefore that although the Duke of Wellington and Castlereagh were both aristocrats, to most people in Vienna at that time the autocratic Duke was a more comprehensible figure than the Leader of the House of Commons, Viscount Castlereagh.

Secondly, among all those who came together in Vienna in 1815 there were few to whom it occurred that what was happening in

North America had any particular relevance to the manner in which Europe was ordering its affairs. But one evening Gentz gave one of his exclusive dinners to which he invited Prince Reuss, Humboldt, the Danish ambassador Count Bernstorff, Prince Ferdinand of Coburg-Gotha, Count and Countess Fuchs and Karl Varnhagen von Ense with his wife Rahel Levin to meet an American doctor by the name of Bollmann. When the last dishes had been cleared away the company fell silent while Bollmann began to tell of the wonders of the new society in the United States of America. 'The whole country', wrote Varnhagen, 'had become strange to us on account of the long sea war, stranger still was the conception of a free state whose development presented a fabulous, indeed a terrifying model of the manner in which common citizens may bring about an accumulation of power which we in Europe are accustomed to associate solely with nobility and kings. The naiveté of one of the diplomats present whose untiring lust for knowledge could with difficulty be satiated, caused the discourse to expand more and more until at last, furnished as it was with striking examples, it became a course in the theory and practice of republicanism such as one would least have expected to find at this Congress of monarchs. Gentz was like one shattered by the weight of these matters and was as ill at ease as though an assassination had been attempted in his presence. The good Bollmann had no malicious intent . . .'

Wilhelm von Humboldt's brother Alexander was a close friend of President Jefferson, Countess Fuchs was a woman as intelligent as she was beloved, while Rahel Levin was one of the leading personalities of her time. They, and Varnhagen, could hardly have been as upset as their host who, for his part, must have congratulated himself on not having invited Metternich.

But why was Castlereagh now recalled to London? According to Harold Nicolson, in his in many ways still unexcelled account of the Congress, it was the clamour in the Cabinet for Castlereagh to come back and take his part in defending the Government against the increasingly vehement attacks of the Opposition—not that Castlereagh, by temperament or inclination, was a gifted speaker able to sway opinion in Parliament. For some reason Harold Nicolson says nothing about the other aspect, referred to earlier: that Castlereagh carried insufficient weight. Benzel the society spy jotted down the consensus of opinion as it came to his ears, and there is confirmation for this view. 'Lord Castlereagh is no negotiator, he is too light-weight for Humboldt and company, he has felt it himself, Talleyrand has made the point in London; France, England, Austria cannot allow themselves to be dominated and insulted by the combined Russians and Prussians. Humboldt has presumed too far; C. makes little impression, he swallows everything; Lord Wellington will swallow nothing, will impress people.'[1]

This hurried note, probably written late at night just before Benzel blew out the candle, points to the great crisis which had come over the Congress: the growing hostility between the former allies and the emergence of a new grouping, England, Austria and France against Prussia and Russia. The Duke of Wellington, coming fresh to the scene, his enormous prestige untarnished by overmuch ex-posure, swallowed nothing; he impressed people. For a day or two the Congress was very near to war, but a compromise was found. Had it not been, an express despatch from the Austrian Consulate-General at Genoa would have effected it.

Metternich's account of what happened in the early hours of 7th March is well known. There had been a meeting of the Five Power plenipotentiaries in his room which only broke up at 3 o'clock in the morning, and he told his valet not to wake him if a courier arrived in the early hours. Disregarding this order, the valet brought in an express despatch marked 'Urgent' from the 'Imperial and Royal Consulate-General at Genoa'. It was only 6 a.m. and Metternich tossed the letter unopened on the bedside table and tried to go back to sleep, but in vain. 'At about 7.30 I decided to open the envelope. It contained only the following six lines: "The English commissioner Campbell has just entered the harbour enquiring whether anyone had seen Napoleon at Genoa, in view of the fact that he had disappeared from the island of Elba. The answer being in the nega-tive, the English frigate put to sea without further delay."' Metter-nich leaped out of bed. By 8 o'clock he was reporting to the Em-peror Franz, fifteen minutes later he was with the Czar, at 8.30 with

[1] These derogatory views of Castlereagh are not presented as historical fact but for their interest as the opinion of men who were there. Plenty of accounts of the Congress give a very different assessment of Castlereagh's stature and achievements, notably Henry Kissinger in his *A World Restored*.

the King of Prussia. At 10 a.m. Talleyrand, Hardenberg, Nesselrode and the Duke of Wellington assembled in his room, but the fundamental decision had been reached during the Chancellor's early morning dash and almost within half an hour. Metternich could be a fast mover if he had to be.

All that day the news was kept quiet; not even Marie Louise was told. For that evening at Court, a ballet-cum-pantomime was arranged called 'Les Noces de Psyché', and the whole of Olympus was represented in it. Jupiter was played by Prince Leopold of Saxe-Coburg, later to become King of the Belgians, Juno was Thérèse Kinsky, Amor, Count Tolstoy. Neither the monarchs nor their plenipotentiaries can have had their minds on it, but they played their part. Lulu Thürheim was watching them: 'These lords of creation gave nothing away. With light-hearted mien, lorgnon in hand, they gave the appearance of paying attention solely to the performance.'

Napoleon's consort heard the news 24 hours after the arrival of the official despatch, but from an entirely unofficial source. Anatole de Montesquiou, the son of her lady-in-waiting, may have been informed by Napoleon's agent Charles Schulmeister who, according to his own statement made later, was in Vienna at the time. Hager's agent reported: 'Madame de Montesquiou went . . . straight to H.M. the Empress to convey the news from her son. H.M. listened to her without speaking one word in reply, retired to her room and wept for some time so loudly that it could be heard in the anteroom. H.M. then came out of her room and gave the order that all the servants, the coachman also who customarily drives Count Neipperg into the town, be strictly forbidden to speak a word of the matter.'

As soon as the news got round a hubbub broke out. Everyone blamed the British. It was unpardonable to be so negligent. Normally moderate, reasonable people were even saying that Bonaparte could never have done it without the connivance of the English: this was no secret flight, but a departure with three frigates and a whole cortège. The anti-British reaction only lasted for a short time, however, and was silenced by the realization that England was making active preparation for war. Comte Alexis de Noailles, on the other hand, said 'This is the best thing that could have happened. Bonaparte has placed himself outside the law.' The King of

Prussia: 'We should have treated him more severely.' And Talleyrand: 'He has pronounced sentence upon himself.' Alexander said nothing for the record. The most practical reaction was the Emperor Franz's comment: 'How lucky that it has happened while we are all assembled here!' All were in fact profoundly shaken, but the hesitation and confusion which would inevitably have resulted if the Congress had already dispersed were avoided.

In this connection, the idiocy and worse of the whole system of espionage in Vienna seems to be thrown into relief by a report dated 18th December, 1814. It records that a certain Marquise Maria (Mme de Brignole) has said: 'I often have news from Elba. Napoleon has completely stopped the building and furnishing of his castle and the work of laying out his large garden.' The hint was repeated in mid-February when in the entourage of the ex-Empress at Schönbrunn it was being said, meaningly, 'The bird will take flight in good time.' To the Austrian authorities this possibly vital piece of intelligence need not have been seen as more than a straw in the wind. It allowed of more than one interpretation: Napoleon, for example, was short of money. But there is nothing to show that it was given any particular treatment to raise it above the puerile level of this kind of imperial *Morgenplaisir*: 'King Frederick William went out in the evening with Prince Wittgenstein[1] in civilian clothes, a round hat pressed down upon his eyes. He was still not back at 10 o'clock.' If the Congress was imperfectly informed concerning Napoleon's intentions, and if important hints were neglected, he himself was amply furnished with first-class intelligence on the Congress.

On 13th March the proclamation was signed which declared Napoleon to be an outlaw. On the following day an anachronism was rectified. By imperial command the Duchess of Parma's suite exchanged Napoleonic for Habsburg livery, and the Napoleonic coat of arms was removed from her carriages. A few days later the Wellington household was beginning to pack, and on the 29th at 4 a.m. the Duke left Vienna to take command in the Low Countries.

The work of drafting, now the main concern of the professionals at the Congress, was time-consuming and monotonous. In May,

[1] Prince Sayn-Wittgenstein, Prussian Grand Chamberlain, Minister of State and Police.

the society hostesses began their annual move out of Vienna, the Liechtensteins and Batthyanys to Hinterbrühl, the Esterházys to Meidling, the Zichys to Baden. There were plenty of country house parties. Countess Flora Wrbna-Kageneck gave a dinner for Alexander I at Greifenstein Castle which caused great excitement in the surrounding villages. At last, with the coming of June, bags were being packed, farewells were said and suitable largesse handed out for services rendered. These varied greatly in kind and in degree.

What did Metternich get out of the Congress?

To the question whether, by the standards of the time, Metternich was venial there is no plain answer, but if the generally prevailing usage is taken as a guiding line for the men at the top, the picture emerges: a modest salary, reimbursement of expenses on demand, bonus according to results—paid by the interested party. The principle governing this last item was: it is usual for a statesman to accept money for doing something which he considers it is his duty to do, but less so for not doing what he thinks he ought to do. Alexander I certainly thought, not necessarily correctly, that Metternich would accept a bribe. On 20th July 1813, during the negotiations in Prague, he wrote to his sister the Grand Duchess Catherine who was there at the time: 'I regret that you have still told me nothing regarding Metternich. I have the necessary funds, you are empowered to proceed with these tactics which are always the best when required . . .' But this was a mere assumption on the Czar's part, it is not evidence. Even by his most bitter detractors it is considered that Metternich was not, in the sense described, corrupt.

Perhaps he had no need to be. Franz I reimbursed 56,000 gulden for expenses which probably came nowhere near covering them. The City of Frankfurt gave him 10,000 ducats. But the big money lay in the restoration of the Bourbons. From King Ferdinand of Naples, preferred at last over the Murats though with restricted authority, came the offers of a pension of 60,000 francs per annum and the title of Duke of Macaroni. The first suggestion was acceptable, the second, even assuming a perfectly straight face on the donor's part, was not, and in 1818 the more euphonious title of Duke of Portella was agreed upon. It has been said with some justice that never has a man received title and hard cash so undeservedly as did Clemens Metternich in this case: ever since he came to power and until January 1815 when he, Louis XVIII and Castlereagh secretly agreed to depose Joachim Murat, he had left nothing undone which ran counter to the interests of the old Bourbon royal couple and hindered their reinstatement on the throne of Naples. True, he had a motive over and above that loyalty to Caroline Murat which so scandalized his contemporaries who saw in it a shameless intrusion of the bedroom into European politics: he hoped that the Murats' small army would always be available to Austria and unavailable to the French. King Ferdinand certainly displayed unusual generosity and possibly a shrewd assessment of the odds in the international stakes.

Both Nesselrode and Metternich are believed to have received a million gulden each from King Louis XVIII. According to the Austrian historian Viktor Bibl, this has never been proved, but the source is Vaulabelle, a distinguished historian and politician who later became Minister of Education. Bibl added that Gentz undoubtedly received 24,000 gulden from Louis XVIII. Metternich must inevitably have been given substantial gratuities by a variety of European sovereigns. And one may be sure that plenty of those nice little jewelled boxes filled with golden ducats, a favourite royal gift, were also changing hands while packing proceeded.

Alexander I gave Prince Razumovsky an interest-free loan variously estimated at 120,000 or 150,000 ducats, plus 15,000 ducats as payment for his services in 1812–1813; all this probably under pressure from his sister the Grand Duchess Catherine, as in spite of Razumovsky's loyalty and great generosity towards the throne, the Czar never cared for him. The great fire nevertheless marked the beginning of a gradual decline in Razumovsky's fortunes. He continued to live not only as though no searing rent had been made in his enormous resources but also as though no term had been placed on the loan. Yet it had, and when soon after he succeeded to the throne in 1825 Czar Nicholas demanded repayment and threatened to foreclose on his estates, his consternation was entirely genuine. Razumovsky was 62 at the time of the fire. If it had not occurred to him before to pay regular and prolonged visits to his estates, he was not likely to start now, nor could he do anything other than try to fight off foreclosure when he was an old man, by then in his seventies. He could hardly indulge in the splendid effrontery of Molly

Zichy-Ferraris who, well on her way to financial ruin during the Congress and having borrowed a million rubles from Alexander I, sent the reply back to Czar Nicholas when he demanded repayment: 'If Your Majesty wants the million back you only need to declare war on me.'

Princess Bagration was now completely broke. Her debts came to 21,811 ducats, 18,121 gulden in paper money and 7,860 gulden in goods. Her credit was exhausted, her creditors were foreclosing and her only hope was that her stepfather, the Russian Vice-Admiral Count Jules Litta Visconti Arese would come, as so often before, to her rescue. Aurore de Marassé was pouring all this out to a friend. She was afraid that the stepfather, 'a mean and selfish man', might refuse to help, and would repudiate the bill of exchange which the Princess had drawn on his account in St. Petersburg. If he did—all her jewellery, furniture, china and so on had already been impounded—they would put her in jail. These were the straits to which *cette malheureuse folle* had reduced herself. Consider, Aurore went on, how the *beau monde* used to run after her, and how they leave her in the lurch now that she is in distress! On the other hand: 'now she is dissolved in tears, but if you help her out of this predicament she'll be off again. . . . She should be sent home to her mother.'

The banker Elkan advanced 7,000 ducats, but it is thought that in the end the Czar paid her debts. It was only right that he should; in her own way the 'naked angel' had worked hard for her country.

Meanwhile Aurore herself was selling off the last of her presents from those who had sat, though never lain, on her bed. Catherine Bagration's bankruptcy and her departure from Vienna were a disaster to her too; worse still the disappearance from the scene of the Courland sisters who had always helped her. The Baronne de Montet wrote in her memoirs: '. . . One morning she came to me, pale, distraught, prostrated, begging me to give her, quickly, a dish of beef tea as she had eaten nothing since Princess Sagan left the day before. I hastened to comply. She wept, spoke with despair of her deplorable situation. That evening I saw her, as sprightly as could be, at a soirée at the Razumovskys.' Miraculously, the story of this delightful eccentric ends happily. After a time, friends managed to place her as *grande maitresse* with the sovereign Prince of Coburg when he married Princess Saxe-Coburg-Gotha; the Prince had jokingly promised her the job when he was courting Princess Bagration. Although the Prince kept his word, the young bride was jealous and Aurore was soon on the road once more. A whim decided her to take the waters at Aix-les-Bains, and here Providence came up with the Comte de Venanson, a Sardinian and an excellent man who married her and with whom she lived happily ever after.

Princess Bagration went to live in Paris, where in 1830 at the age of 47 she tried to settle down in holy matrimony with Colonel, later General, Sir John Hobart Caradoc, afterwards Lord Howden. She visited Vienna once or twice in middle age, still swathed in revealing materials, an overblown rose at her throat. In 1852 we catch a last glimpse of this Congress beauty as she was seen by a Frenchman in Berlin. '. . . Princess Bagration is staying at the Hotel Meinhardt. We found her reclining on a couch . . . this would be a woman worth studying. She is near to 82,[1] has all her teeth, and fair hair; these things are left of a beauty once so celebrated . . . her gleaming, yellow brow is excessively high. Her fingers are like a game of knuckle-bones. She has retained for her feet an adoration which they justify by their whiteness and their small size. She only walks supported by two servants.' A suspicion cannot be wholly dismissed that this was one of Catherine Bagration's 'at death's door' acts, and that she was still perfectly capable, if not of a Cossack dance, of waltzing all through the night.

The fact is undeniable that among the Viennese public Princess Bagration was extremely unpopular and that they delighted in her humiliation when the bailiffs moved in. They thought little better of the Duchess of Sagan: both, in their eyes, were no better than Russian spies, working against the Emperor Franz. Wilhelmine Sagan had now wholly taken up with the British Ambassador. Sir Charles Stewart, subsequently Lord Stewart and finally 3rd Marquis of Londonderry, was Lord Castlereagh's half-brother. Described by British sources as a vain, quarrelsome and ostentatious man, opinion in Vienna went so far as to say that he was unworthy of his post and that his presence amounted to a slight against the Austrian Court and the Congress of Vienna. He had a few mildly endearing traits: one day in May he rode along the Kohlmarkt and Graben, his horse's head covered in lilies of the valley while he carried an enor-

[1] A very wide miss, she was 69 or 70.

mous bunch in one hand, laughing his head off the while and clearly a little drunk. He had 20 couples of foxhounds sent out from England, and explained that Austrian *Jagdhunde* were hopeless and the English hounds would teach them what to do. The project was a disaster. In the end Sir Charles tried to sell them, but hardly a purchaser came forward. Few diplomats ever made more ample use of their diplomatic privileges, and some years later when he was again Ambassador in Vienna and his wife was earning the heartfelt loathing of the British colony, he imported no less than 504 gallons of Austrian wine into England without paying duty. His appreciation of these excellent wines is praiseworthy, also his determination never to be without them, but the indignation of the Chancellor of the Exchequer and his protest in the House led to a limitation of such privileges. Congress Vienna called him 'Lord Pumpernickel' or, on account of his yellow boots, 'Goldfasan' (golden pheasant) and much else of a less attractive order. The stories about his undiplomatic behaviour are endless and he even got into a brawl with a cab driver and threw him into the Danube. And yet the Duke of Wellington considered that he 'procured more information and obtained more insight into the affairs of a foreign court than anybody, and that he was the best relater of what passed at a conference, and wrote the best account of a conversation of any man I knew.'

During May and June he and Sagan were inseparable. They found an inn close to Laxenburg which, said unfriendly tongues, they turned into a gambling den and a brothel. The Duchess had survived the Congress with at any rate her finances in fair order. On 22nd July, that faintly whore-like aura which some older men had always detected in her in no way diminished, she left Vienna for Switzerland and Paris in the wake of Sir Charles Stewart.

King Frederick VI of Denmark gave to Baron Arnstein a snuffbox worth 6,000 florins and to the 'Queen of Denmark' a pension for life of 2,000 gulden. The 'insane hyena' left an accumulation of debts behind him and his servants in the Hofburg received not a single kreuzer. King Frederick William of Prussia gave generous presents to all his attendants and left in floods of tears at being torn from the side of Julie Zichy. Alexander I, too, distributed superb presents among all who had worked for him. It was widely believed that only the prostitutes of Vienna would regret his departure, but

3. Europe after the Congress of Vienna, 1815

on the day that he left, a friend found Princess Gabriele Auersperg weeping in her boudoir. Had there been something between them after all? Countess Fifi Palffy-de Ligne thought that there could often be two possible reasons for crying one's eyes out: 'Hélas, ce ne sont pas toujours les remords, mais les regrets.'

The Master of Ceremonies Count Wurmbrand was totting up the cost of the whole Congress, including the expenses for the foreign

KINGDOM
OF POLAND
(To Russia)

RUSSIA

...STRIAN

...EMPIRE

Danube

Black Sea

MONTENEGRO

...DOM

...HE

...WO

...ILIES

O T T O M A N   E M P I R E

Ionian Is. (Br.)

sovereigns, all the festivities, new liveries, food, rent of houses and
other accommodation, and stabling. He had not got the final figures,
but up to the end of May it came to 8½ million gulden,[1] or approximately £850,000, and the Court seemed to be surprised that it was
not more. The Congress of Vienna was one of the most successful
and enduring pieces of publicity ever undertaken, but at the time

[1] 15 million, an unofficial total figure, is probably an over-estimate.

this aspect occurred to no one, alive though they were to everything which concerned prestige, and even at the farewell dinner at the Razumovskys on 8th June the assembled diplomats were still talking of Metternich's blindness, superficiality and inconsequence in staging the Congress in Vienna. In retrospect, what did the Congress achieve?[1]

The order laid down by the Congress of Vienna endured for a lifetime, many frontiers remained where they were for a century. The wisdom of the final Act of Congress lay in its moderation towards the defeated aggressor: apart from the loss of Savoy and one or two minor frontier adjustments France retained her pre-revolutionary figure. Even after the Hundred Days, after Waterloo, the British government insisted that France be allowed to keep Alsace-Lorraine against the wishes of Prussia. But three fundamental problems were only half solved, therefore not really solved at all: Poland, Germany and Italy. Poland was divided between Russia and Prussia, but it was very largely Metternich's achievement to have prevented Prussia from swallowing up the ancient kingdom of Saxony. He was able to mobilize Bavaria and Hanover to resist the territorial ambitions of the Hohenzollerns, yet the problem of the German nation as a whole remained. Should it unite, and under whom? The German peoples had been spurred on to fight the Wars of Liberation by the promise of constitutional liberties, which, it now appeared, their rulers had already forgotten. At best they might be palmed off with essentially medieval Estates of the Realm. A deputation of princes besought Franz I to accept the crown of the Holy Roman Empire of the German Nation, that is, sovereignty over the Congress's creation, the Germanic Confederation. Whatever his true motives, Franz declined the honour; Metternich's reasoning was that Prussia would never again accept Austrian supremacy in Germany. It seemed that for the moment the history of Germany was able to move neither backwards nor forwards. It was Metternich's belief, and the army high command agreed with him, that Austria should consolidate its possessions, turning its back on areas which, however long they might have belonged to the Habsburgs, were too exposed and therefore difficult to defend. This applied to the Netherlands, but also to the so-called Habs-

[1] See map of post-Congress Europe.

burg Forelands, the (Swiss) Aargau, and Breisgau which was in one-time Swabia, the original home of the Habsburgs. In Italy on the other hand, the whole of Lombardy-Venetia became a kingdom directly under the crown of Austria, Tuscany was ruled by Emperor Franz's brother, Archduke Ferdinand III, Modena by Franz IV of Habsburg-Este, Parma and Piacenza by the Archduchess Marie Louise. This was not quite what Metternich had intended. More far-seeing than the Emperor, he had visualized a *Lega Italica* on the lines of the Germanic Confederation, closely linked to the Austrian Empire but in most respects autonomous. Unfortunately, the Emperor and the archdukes most concerned were adamant. At the risk of over-simplification: if the Austrians ruled without consultation with the people, so did the Bourbons in the Kingdom of the Two Sicilies. So did the Pope. The Habsburgs ruled for the most part with benevolence and tact, but their position was undermined by the lower ranks of the Austrian civil service whose members, throughout Lombardy and Venetia, came to personify alien rule. How much wiser was the Empress Maria Theresa (founder of la Scala in Milan) whose firm policy, in Italy as in the Netherlands, had been the greatest possible degree of political and cultural autonomy, inconspicuous government from Vienna and sensitivity towards the feelings of all classes of the people.

No one can have been more thankful to see the visitors to the Congress go than the Empress Maria Ludovica, but it had taken all too great a toll of her strength. One more supreme effort lay ahead of her: a state tour of northern Italy. Modena, Venice—here she was able to rest, but her weakness was such that it was obvious to all her family and household that her life would be in immediate danger if she went on with her official programme. Archduke Franz d'Este protested to Franz I, emphasizing her medical adviser's opinion, but it was no use, and undoubtedly nothing except the Emperor's insistence would have deflected Maria Ludovica from doing what she saw as her duty. On New Year's Eve the tour began with the formal entry into Milan, and now there were receptions, state banquets, speeches, audiences, a solemn Te Deum in the Cathedral, and on rolled the machinery of protocol to Bergamo, Brescia, Verona, with long drives to smaller towns on the way. At an earlier state of the tour she wrote to the Emperor during a brief separation, thanking him for a kind word or two that he had managed to say to her: 'You have given me great joy by your assurance that I have brought much happiness into your life. . . . Had I but better health, or were the evil but confined to such complaints as I could have suffered without becoming useless to you, how gladly would I have borne with my fate and had then been of good cheer.' Soon her weakness was such that she could hardly stand up, and one of her women said that she was falling out of the carriage and into bed, then out of bed and into the carriage. Did the doctors, the Empress asked them again and again, think that they could save her? And at last: 'Then I must really die?' Even now all her letters were being intercepted and copies laid before the Emperor, including two from the Czarina.

Maria Ludovica died in Verona on Palm Sunday, 7th April. She was 29. Virulently attacked by Bonapartists even down to the present day, among all the kings, statesmen and field-marshals she was, rightly or wrongly, almost alone in her unfaltering opposition to Napoleon. When she died, Goethe felt that one of the most shining stars in the firmament was suddenly missing from its place, but on the whole this was not the feeling in Vienna where she was not greatly missed except by her friends. One of them said of her: 'She had not only an unlimited need to love but also the unlimited strength to do so.'

Had she lived, she might have played a vital role in the life of a boy who, like herself, chafed and wilted at a Court where mediocrity reigned and where there was too little love: the Duke of Reichstadt.

20. The Duke of Reichstadt (L'Aiglon)

21. Archduchess Sophie (wife of Archduke Franz Karl) with her son, the future Franz Joseph I

22. Count Franz Anton Kolowrat, Metternich's rival in home affairs

23. Empress Caroline Augusta fourth wife of Franz I, leader of the Catholic party

7
L'Aiglon

As the sound of guns reverberated round Paris, the newborn child whose advent they saluted had already survived an experience which would come to symbolize his whole relatively short and tragic life. It had been a prolonged and exceptionally difficult birth, accomplished with the help of instruments, and for several minutes while the doctors bent over the Empress, her son was left for dead.

Napoleon was adamant that his son must never fall into the hands of the Austrians. Twice, in the secret instructions to his brother Joseph on 8th February, 1813, and again in his message from Rheims on 16th March to King Louis XVIII and to the Lieutenant-General who was guarding Marie Louise and the child in Paris, he used almost identical words: 'As far as I am concerned I would rather my son were strangled than see him brought up as an Austrian Prince in Vienna. . . . I could never watch a performance of Andromache without lamenting the fate of Astyanax who survived the downfall of his house without considering him fortunate not to have outlived his father.'

It was certainly a worthy descendant of Hector and Andromache who fought with such desperation and fury before the party left Paris, a tiny figure yelling and stamping, refusing to budge, flinging himself on the ground, shouting 'I won't leave my house, I won't go away! As Papa is not here it is I who give the orders!' At that moment he was indeed in the right mood to cast himself, with assistance from no one, from the walls of Troy.

This scene tells one more about the inner life of this child in the years to come, about his character and development and the frustrations which were to beset him than any other evidence that we have. It shows that in his mind there was no dawning realization of his identity as the son of Napoleon, on the contrary he knew perfectly well who he was, he could not remember a time when he had not known it, but for his understanding of the political situation and of himself as a factor in it he was now to be dependent on his Austrian advisers, and they might deceive him, just as the French were intentionally deceived as to his attitude towards them.

The child whom the Viennese always called 'der kleine Napoleon', christened Franz after his grandfather, now settled into the routine laid down for a Habsburg Archduke. Or was he, on the contrary, a prisoner of state?

Metternich's 'system', the policy of Talleyrand and the principle underlying the Congress of Vienna can be summed up in the one word 'legitimacy'. It was a concept which could be bent at will—Metternich's efforts to keep the Murats on the throne of Naples at the expense of the deposed sovereign, who was moreover a daughter of the Empress Maria Theresa and one of the successive mothers-in-law of Franz I, are an example—but the principle remained. There were many people who saw no advantage whatever, least of all to France itself, in a return of the hopelessly inadequate Bourbons. Gentz, and whatever his faults may have been no man in his time possessed sharper faculties of political analysis, considered the restoration of the Bourbons to be an unmitigated disaster. He favoured a regency in the person of Marie Louise. It was no solution, he believed, and many agreed, merely to put the ship of state into reverse. The events of a lifetime were not to be obliterated in such a way that they might never have happened, and in any case, it was entirely in Austria's interest to put Napoleon II on the throne of France, as the two countries together would have ruled Europe. Needless to say this was not a prospect likely to appeal to other European nations, in particular to Prussia. Archduke Johann agreed with Gentz. He was delighted with the lively, gifted child and thought it would have been very much better to put him on the throne of France under a regency instead of 'that weak Bourbon'. To the Emperor he pointed out the effect that this would have in power-political terms, but he only received the oracular reply: 'I have nothing against Franz being chosen to mount the throne of France—but I wish to know nothing about it.'

Spoken by a monarch without whose *placet* nothing of any consequence was allowed to happen, this was an extraordinary statement. Metternich was against a regency for another reason which was just as weighty as the principle of legitimacy and of greater practical importance. More than anything else, Europe needed peace, and Napoleon had proved that he would never keep quiet so long as he could make his presence felt. Franz I was, in fact, against it, and the British would never have given their consent. As for Marie Louise herself, at no time would she have willingly returned to Paris to bear, even assisted by the wisest of statesmen, the onus of responsibility for the government of France; she was appalled at the very idea.

It is another question altogether to ask—as people were doing everywhere—whether Napoleon should have been robbed of his wife and child. Should they not have been sent to join him on Elba? Was it humane to separate them? And was it wise? Those who, after the Hundred Days, questioned the wisdom of this action were thinking that if Napoleon had had his family with him he might never have broken out into his final frenzy of activity. The theory seems hardly to have logic on its side, but it also leaves Marie Louise's feelings, which had undergone a rapid change, out of account. When Napoleon wrote to her from the Tuileries and asked her to join him, she wept. Her acquiescence in the allied proscription of Napoleon is considered to have been given of her own free will. Her declarations of submission to the will of her father were probably no less voluntary for having been dictated, as she repeated them on a number of occasions. 'I place our destiny in Your hands and under Your fatherly protection,' she wrote, and to Metternich, that Napoleon's intentions were wholly alien to her and she put herself under the protection of the allies. And when the news reached her at Schönbrunn that on 22nd June, 1815, four days after the Battle of Waterloo, Bonaparte had abdicated and had proclaimed his son Emperor of the French, she was frozen with horror. When the next courier brought news of the sequel, that the provisional government had declared the proclamation to be a farce, and she was told that the allied monarchs intended to bring back Louis XVIII, no one was more profoundly relieved than Marie Louise. She was forgetting the husband who had given her such complete sexual satisfaction, she also forgot the letters in which she had told the world of her happiness.

Marie Louise did not fall into bed with Count Albert Adam Neipperg quite as soon as this celebrated breaker of hearts expected, nor of course anything like as fast as the gossips believed. But she was falling in love with him, at any rate as far as her nature permitted, he represented a safe haven and quiet domesticity after the terrifying uncertainties of public life. It is possible that they became lovers on 27th September, 1814, during an excursion from Aix while they were marooned in a storm,[1] but Austrian biographers maintain that she 'gave herself' to her dashing cavalry officer only in February 1815. The French historian Frédéric Masson believed that Napoleon never knew about this liaison, and attributed her switch in loyalty entirely to the influence of her advisers in Vienna. At all events, Metternich's plan to detach her emotionally from Napoleon was completely successful. All she now wanted was to settle down in her Duchy—away from her father's capital in which she had so strangely, so totally failed to re-acclimatize herself. There is a secret agent's report to Hager on 14th April, 1815, which describes her as depressed and preoccupied. To a Councillor of the Teutonic Knights, Sommer, she said that she was upset over the severity and the injustice towards her of the public. What had she done, she asked, to cause this animosity? If only her true sentiments could get through to them—if only they could understand that in no circumstances would she return to France; sooner would she enter a convent than return to live with Napoleon! Her son was her only consolation, and for her nothing could be more cruel than to have to be separated from him.

Here the Duchess was being a little less than candid. Or to come rather closer to the truth: she almost certainly meant what she said at the moment that she said it. A biographer tried to define the essence of her character: 'It is in the nature of some individuals that, seized by a momentary emotion, they appear to be totally dissolved in joy

[1] André Castelot, *l'Aiglon*.

or sorrow, but after perhaps half an hour the feeling has almost departed—it was simply all on the surface.'[1]

The Duchess was soon to settle down with Count Neipperg as snug as could be in her own little sovereign state. Metternich and Franz I never allowed her son to visit her—Hager was always warning them of the danger of abduction by Bonapartists—and from then on she would find that unsurmountable difficulties stood in the way of her making frequent visits to the son who, in all truth, could have said that she was all he had. One of her undisclosed reasons, in fact three of them, were to be the births of her children by Neipperg.

Franz Karl Joseph: no longer King of Rome, no longer allowed to be called Napoleon, among his other baptismal names 'Franz' found most favour. What was to be the future identity, the title, the property of the child whom Gentz described as being in the eyes of allied statesmen 'un object d'alarme et de terreur'? The fact that Talleyrand was a signatory to the Treaty of Fontainebleau, Article V of which guaranteed Parma, Guastalla and Piacenza to Marie Louise and her son, disturbed that statesman not at all once he had decided at the Congress of Vienna to support the cause of the Spanish Bourbons. Marie Louise could have Lucca, and he suggested that she be given fiefs in Bohemia which would bring her in 400,000 gulden a year. This scheme, he wrote to Louis XVIII on 15th February, 1815, would reduce the number of petty sovereign states in Italy and would have an even greater advantage in 'keeping the Archduchess's son out of the way and depriving him of all expectation of ever reigning'. Talleyrand had the entire support of Metternich, of Castlereagh and of King Frederick William of Prussia. It was on Neipperg's suggestion that Marie Louise implored Alexander I to champion her cause, and it was on the Czar's insistence that, after endless wrangling, the ex-Empress of the French and ex-Queen of Italy was granted the Duchy of Parma. On 31st May, 1815, Alexander, Metternich and the King of Prussia signed a secret treaty securing the hereditary and sovereign rights of the Duke of Parma, but the Acts of Congress signed on 9th June omit any reference to the treaty. On 10th June, 1817, the allies signed a contract which disinherited him altogether: after the death

[1] Viktor Bibl, *Marie Louise.*

of Marie Louise, Parma was to revert to the Spanish Bourbons. This piece of statecraft left the Emperor and Metternich with a royal personage on their hands who, since he was not Napoleon II, had no identity, no function and no inheritance. Who and what was he?

Whether or not Marie Louise really believed that by accepting the Duchy she was saving something from the wreckage for her son, it is impossible to say with any complete certainty. Like her contemporaries, posterity, too, has been hard on Marie Louise, and one must try to understand her. Her protestations of gratitude towards her father, her apparent blind trust that everything would turn out for the best, are open to charitable interpretation, particularly when we remember that she was not a very intelligent young woman. But she positively yearned to live in Parma, and her instinct guided her rightly because she lived there in complete happiness with Neipperg for 12 years until his death. She knew perfectly well, however, that this meant parting from her small son—the signatories were unanimous on this point—and she shed tears at the thought. What she was doing to him she seemed in her egotism not to have realized at all.

On Franz's fourth birthday, 20th March, 1815, two days after he was removed for safety from Schönbrunn to the Hofburg, Madame de Montesquiou, 'Maman Quiou', was given her *congé* by the Emperor; although Marie Louise disliked her child's governess intensely she could not have denied that this passionate Bonapartist loved him devotedly and that he loved her in return. He had lost his father, he was now to lose his mother. He would see her again in the late summer of 1818, in the summer of 1820, then not at all until 1828; all were happy occasions and the latter visit extended through most of the summer, but to a child such intervals are an eternity. He lost his governess and, though not all at once, his French attendants who, at least, were familiar faces. All reminders of his past including toys bearing Napoleonic emblems were removed, his principal language was switched from French to German. All this Marie Louise knew before she left Vienna. Allowing for the emotions of a man such as Napoleon's former private secretary, Baron de Méneval, who accompanied Marie Louise to Vienna, and therefore for the possibility that he might have invented this little scene, it is still not only moving but convincing. De Méneval went to say goodbye to l'Aiglon. 'When I entered, he gave no sign of welcome. I went up to him, took him by the hand and asked if he had a message for his father who I would soon be seeing. He withdrew his hand, looking at me sadly, and walked over to a window. After a few words with his entourage, I followed him to where he was apart, all by himself, staring at us. As I stooped towards him to say farewell, he drew me to the window and whispered with the most touching expression: "Monsieur Méva, tell him that I still love him very much." '[1]

Within the limits of his personality the Emperor Franz I was a kind grandfather. The child was admitted to his presence, they went for walks hand-in-hand in the grounds of Schönbrunn, and that direct and simple way of speaking which Franz used to everyone since it was the only one he knew gained the child's affection. Franz I meant him to be treated with all the honour due to a member of the imperial family. He ranked for precedence immediately after the archdukes and was entitled to a coach and six. But as soon as the tenuous claim to Parma was finally abandoned, the title had to be dropped as well and another found. Was there no territory in the furthest corner of the monarchy over which he might acquire sovereign rights? Understandably perhaps, Metternich would have none of this. Should he be destined for the priesthood? This was the suggestion of Joseph von Hudelist, a most able diplomat who acted as notary to the imperial family at the time of the marriage of Franz I to Maria Ludovica and again when Marie Louise married Napoleon, and who acted as Metternich's right hand in the Chancellery throughout the Congress. Fortunately this problem could be shelved, but a title must be found without delay. Many were proposed and rejected, but one found favour with Metternich: let him be created Duke of Buschtiehrad. The suggestion was laid in all seriousness before Marie Louise, who rejected it on the grounds that no one in the world outside Bohemia would know how to pronounce it. One is bound to agree with her—the name would have made him all but invisible; was this not what Metternich meant to happen? At last a title was found: Reichstadt, a duchy to be found on no map. When the contents of the Imperial Letters Patent became known there was a stir of interest abroad. This seven-year-old

[1] Patrick Turnbull, *Napoleon's Second Empress.*

boy, born in wedlock to the Emperor and Empress of the French, suddenly appeared to have no father, as though he were the unsought-for consequence of a fleeting liaison. He was 'the Son of Our most Beloved Daughter Marie Louise, Archduchess of Austria, Duchess of Parma, Piacenza and Guastalla.' Napoleon was not mentioned.

The child who had been called King of Rome, briefly Duke of Parma, who to all loyal Bonapartists would always be Napoleon II and whom romantics would call l'Aiglon, was now the Duke of Reichstadt. The name was more euphonious than Buschtiehrad but the one cast no more light on the bearer's putative future than did the other. He was not quite an archduke, but for all essential purposes this made little difference. He would be put through the customary routine which made up the education and general upbringing of a royal prince, a routine which in the past had deformed the character and weighed upon the spirit of many an archduke, but which was planned and carried out with the best of intentions. It had been the custom at all the courts of Europe, to look no further than that, to remove the male children at an early age, usually at six, from the care of women, and to hand them over to whiskered warriors, to courtiers and clerks, who usually had one thing in common, that they were old. No one would have thought of questioning the practice, not, at any rate, in England where the upper classes have always thought it vital to eject their male children from the nest at the age of eight and a half. The young Duke of Reichstadt was never brutally treated. His childhood cannot for one moment be compared with the harshness suffered by Frederick II of Prussia in an earlier generation or with the lot of thousands of other boys, of royal or noble birth, who were subjected to the full rigour of nineteenth-century ideas on education. But inevitably he was lonely, much more lonely than he need have been. As time went on it was not so much that l'Aiglon occasionally needed a shoulder to howl on: he needed, and knew that he lacked, someone who would tell him the truth.

Truth was not a commodity which was easy to come by. If Franz Duke of Reichstadt still had a dim recollection of his own tempestuous protest as he was dragged from the place where, some flash of insight must have told him, he had a right to be and which he left at his peril, the events of the Hundred Days had largely passed over his head. The acute tension in his mother's household, her tears, the forced appearance of calm, the pursed lips, broken off conversations: he had been too young at the time to make much of all this and no one attempted to explain. One thing an intelligent four-year-old in his situation would be sure to notice: the sudden metamorphosis of the menservants' livery and the corresponding disappearance of his father's crest from the carriages.

The boy's education was placed in the hands of tutors, chief among whom was Count Maurice Dietrichstein. There is a description of Dietrichstein which takes one back to the childhood of the boy's grandfather; for a moment we seem to see Colloredo and the future Emperor wrestling with the classics in the schoolroom in the Palazzo Pitti. He was an over-anxious, fussy man, pedantic and excessively strict. But Dietrichstein had a far better mind than Colloredo and he was a lover of the arts. And the Duke of Reichstadt was a better scholar than his grandfather was, with a marked sense of the ridiculous, a quality which among royalty and courtiers he would find difficulty in matching; Dietrichstein had no sense of humour whatsoever. Inevitably, what Reichstadt suffered from most in his early years was the lack of candour on the part of his tutors, their evasiveness in the face of his incessant questions about his father: where is he? What is he doing? Does he know where I am? Does he want to see me? And questions about the past which were very difficult to answer, even given the will and the authority to do so. As children habitually insist on a clear distinction between friends and foes, the world of their imagination being peopled by good men and bad men and woe betide any adult who brings in an element of doubt, it would be insensitive to deny that to have to explain the phenomenon Napoleon to his own son was a peculiarly unenviable task. It is not surprising that his tutors, fending off these sharp enquiries, deflecting as they must every whiff of criticism of the allied cause in general and the House of Austria in particular, did little to help the questioner.

In time, Count Dietrichstein did come round to discussing the Napoleonic era with his pupil, and he was willing to talk over the campaigns and re-fight the battles, a subject which, all too much so, fascinated Reichstadt. By the time he reached his teens he knew every detail of his father's campaigns off by heart. But by that time the damage was done. He led a very solitary existence and had no one to play with. The Archduke Franz Karl, one day to be the father of the Emperor Franz Joseph, was nine years older than he, and Ferdinand, the heir to the throne, was a simpleton; neither was of much use to the son of Napoleon. Thrown back on his own company, he responded to the lies, half-truths and stone-walling to which he had been subjected all his life, in the obvious way: the truth should be *his* servant. In short, he lied, usually in all those ways which serve to prop up a child's self-esteem. The onset of puberty brought a change for the better. By the age of 14 he had stopped telling lies, although, sighed Dietrichstein, 'he has a spiteful way of discovering the weaknesses or the ingenuousness of others, to profit by them in order to place himself at an advantage'. He had also stopped bed-wetting, an affliction which his tutor Baron Obenaus cured by getting him out of bed twice in the night, at 2 and 5 a.m.

The disappearance of these two so obvious distress signals by no means meant that the fundamental conflict no longer existed. The belief that he might yet be wafted by some miraculous agency on to the throne of France was one that the boy had not ceased to cherish in spite of all Dietrichstein's arguments to the contrary. The Count followed political trends in France very closely, he was able to assess his pupil's chances with some accuracy, and believing as he did that these chances were almost non-existent he thought it would be cruel to allow the boy to spend all his nervous energy in chasing a rainbow. The difficulty was: what positive alternative had he, in however relatively humble a capacity, in the service of the House of Habsburg? The boy's undoubted intelligence and his inherited military talent would ultimately, Dietrichstein thought, be sure to lead to a brilliant career: he might become, and this was Reichstadt's own dream, a new Prince Eugen of Savoy, a one-time foreigner leading the imperial troops to resounding victories. But against whom? This, as is the way with dreams, was not clearly spelled out, and of course the monarchy no longer needed a Prince Eugen. The threat of Islam had sunk back into history, the time of that other power whose menace Metternich foresaw, Prussia, had not yet come. Count Dietrichstein's greatest mistake was to feel perfectly confident that the Chancellor had some kind of master-plan in mind for the boy's future. He could not have been more wrong: Metternich had no plans whatever.

One or two people were coming into the Duke's life who were to make him feel less isolated. He was 13 when, in November 1824, the rather dreary Franz Karl married Princess Sophie of Bavaria. It was to be a momentous union as it was she who, as the Empress Elisabeth's mother-in-law, was to exert such a baneful influence at the outset of the girl's marriage to Franz Joseph, causing never-ending trouble. As a young girl Sophie was a totally different person from the dragon of a mother-in-law that she became in later years: a friendly, lively young bride who at last brought warmth and laughter into the rather arid group around Reichstadt. Habsburg dynastic marriages were often so closely interlocked that the underlying policy seemed to be to keep the whole thing within the family, and in this case the new Archduchess was the youngest half-sister of the over-pious Empress Caroline-Augusta, fourth wife of Franz I. For much of the year she and her husband lived at Persenbeug Castle on the Danube, and here Reichstadt often stayed with them, loving the complete informality of life. There was no 'court' and no formality whatever: the boy must have felt that he had escaped from prison. How far this informality went, whether it brought the Archduchess Sophie and the adolescent Duke into bed together, will never be known. Some people, however, appear to have believed that he may well have been the father, not, mercifully, of the future Emperor Franz Joseph, but of Sophie's second son Maximilian, the ill-fated Emperor of Mexico. It will be best to examine this possible liaison later on in the light of what has been said about Reichstadt's sex life in general.

The only member of the imperial family to take a real interest in Reichstadt from the beginning was Archduke Johann, who, with his intelligence and common sense, understood the boy's predicament and was touched by it. His affection was felt and returned, and he could have done much to make the boy's life more tolerable because more purposeful. But living as he was under a cloud, considered by the Emperor, by Metternich and by many others to be politically unreliable, eccentric and immoral to boot, he was hardly likely to be allowed to take a hand in the upbringing of such a tricky public figure. Since the Alpenbund affair he had spent his whole time and energy on developing the industrial areas of Styria which had lain in the grip of a depression ever since the seams of precious metals petered out 300 years before. The Erzberg, a mountain of iron ore which has been worked since Celtic times, was inexhaustible, but the methods used were primitive and unco-ordinated. In 1815 the Archduke accepted an invitation by the Prince Regent to have a look at the revolution in technology in England. Few royal personages of the day can have been as capable as Johann was of absorbing what he saw in the factories and mines of England, fewer still would have thrown themselves personally into industrial production. Later, the Archduke was able to buy a house and a disused foundry at Vordernberg, the predecessor of today's iron and steel town of Donawitz, and persuaded the other small owners to join him in forming a co-operative society. There was hardly a craft in the land to which he did not, at some time, set his mind to see in what way it could be made more efficient. A very high proportion of the people of Styria must at least have known him by sight if they had not actually spoken to him: he lived among the people and he chose his friends mainly though not solely from among them. His monuments are the University of Graz, the Joanneum, the College of Technology and the College of Mines at Leoben, all of which owed their existence, directly or indirectly, to his initiative and untiring work for education.

To Archduke Johann, hanging around at Court was a sheer waste of time. He was distinctly persona non grata, but in any case he shared Count Dietrichstein's view that the intellectual level at Court was low, the conversation alarmingly trivial, and both felt that for Franz von Reichstadt this was a great pity. Dietrichstein, also, could escape. In 1819 the Count became Intendant of Music to the Court, and two years later the appointment of Director of the Court Theatres was added to the first. Later he would administer all the vast art collections of the crown and he was in frequent contact with Beethoven who often played in his house, and with Schubert who dedicated to him one of his most famous lieder, the 'Erlkönig'. He lived a full life independently of the benumbingly constricting circle of the imperial family.

Archduke Johann had yet another reason for avoiding Vienna.

His romance with the postmaster's daughter from Bad Aussee, Anna Plochl, is, with the exception of Crown Prince Rudolf's affair with Marie Vetsera, the most famous in the history of the Habsburg dynasty. The stories could hardly be more different: the Mayerling tragedy was a turgid event in which nearly everyone concerned appears in a bad light. By comparison, the Johann-Anna romance was a picture-book story for Victorian misses. But it is not a senti-mental tale. The depth of character of both parties, her courage and the religious faith which sustained them during their long wait while Franz I procrastinated—he gave his written consent and then withdrew it verbally—the deep depressions, the accidie into which, like his brother Karl, the Archduke was prone to fall, all these things dispel the roseate hues. During Reichstadt's adolescent years, at the time when, in theory, Archduke Johann could have been doing so much, walking and climbing with him in the Alps, taking his mind off history and politics and giving him something solid to bite on, more than likely in fact saving his life, 'Nani' Plochl had taken over the reins of her future husband's households in Vordernberg and at the Brandhof. This was a step which was taken, not as a gesture to flaunt public opinion but, on the contrary, with great care to safe-guard her reputation, since the time had come when she could no longer be left to live at home among her companions, gossiped about, followed by police agents, in the eyes of the Styrian people a constant reproach. The Archduke's memoirs make it clear (he would hardly lie to his own diary) that they were not living 'in sin'. The future Countess Meran was not just his paramour, she had to gain the respect of those circles in the aristocracy whose opinion in the eyes of Archduke Johann mattered, and to this there was no short cut. She succeeded, Franz I (gloomily remarking to his brother 'I can see you're pretty well at the end of your tether') at last gave way so that they were able to marry in 1829.

Martha Bradford, wife of the Chaplain to the British Embassy in Vienna, was staying in Ischl in the summer of 1827 when two men came to the door of her house. They spoke to the maid, asking the whereabouts of a man they were seeking. Mrs. Bradford went to see what was going on. 'It was the Archduke . . . whose passion for a mountain life is such that he lives constantly in the Tyrol [*sic*], adored by the peasantry among whom he lived familiarly, they calling him "Herr Johann" and addressing him as thee and thou. This mountain life is not relished at Court, and as far as I have learnt, such familiarity is not without its demoralizing consequences.' Styrian folklore puts it like this: it was not so much Anna Plochl whom the nobility had in mind when they talked of over-familiarity with the peasantry, but fleeting relationships, and the consequences of this 'demoralization' are said to have been fairly numerous. Be all that as it may, it is the last on the list of reasons why this man, who might have been the saving of Reichstadt, was given no chance to help him.

Yet Franz did at last find a real friend. He was a member of the minor aristocracy, Anton Prokesch von Osten, who was beginning to make a name for himself in the diplomatic service. He was a most attractive personality, this comes through in his diaries and gives one confidence in his judgement. The difference in ages hardly mattered to Franz who spent so much of his time with middle-aged men (in 1825 Dietrichstein was 50), and to a young man of Reichstadt's intelligence and intense preoccupation with the affairs of the day this wideawake, liberal-minded and generally sympathetic young diplomat was a life-line. Soon Prokesch-Osten became a close confidant and Franz told him everything which came into his head; if not face to face, because Prokesch-Osten was liable to be away from Vienna for months at a time, then by letter. As a result, he became far and away the most convincing source of information on Reichstadt's brief adult life and the responsibility of his mentors for the brevity of it.

On 31st December, 1828, a Frenchman saw the New Year in in Vienna: Auguste Barthélémy, the poet and Bonapartist who had made the long journey from Paris to learn what people could tell him about young Napoleon. Was he a Frenchman, eating his heart out in captivity? Or had he become an Austrian, a *German* prince, knowing nothing of his origins, caring nothing for them, for his father, for France? Barthélémy failed to see Reichstadt, had an unsatisfactory interview with Count Dietrichstein, and for the rest relied on gossip and oversimplified what he had heard. The result was the lengthy poem, 'Le fils de l'homme', a piece of damaging political propaganda. 'Barthélémy's tale deprived many who were faithful to the great Emperor of their last hope of seeing Napoleon II mount his father's throne.'[1] In France even historical scholarship adopted the extreme view of Reichstadt's position. The 1854 edition of the *Biographie Universelle Ancienne et Moderne* gives the impression that Reichstadt was a complete prisoner, brought up in a state of docility, 'vivant dans l'ignorance et l'abnegation la plus complète de tout interest politique . . . colonel d'un régiment qu'il n'avais jamais vu . . .'

Within four days of each other two events took place of which the Court took no official cognizance. On 18th February, at 11 p.m., in the chapel of the Brandhof in the Styrian Alps, with only two witnesses, Archduke Johann and Anna married. On 22nd February, far away in Parma, Field-Marshal Count Neipperg died. He was one of the most skilful, tactful and just administrators that Parma ever had, and under his hand the province flourished. But Parma was not so far from Vienna that the Duchess could not receive immediate instructions forbidding her to wear mourning. It was a piece of characteristic hypocrisy which wounded her deeply.

A month later, a third non-event took place: the eighteenth birthday of the Duke of Reichstadt. At 18, l'Aiglon was an unusually mature youth. That he was lonely and frustrated is undeniable: it was not so much that he sat about indulging in dreams of glory, his frustration was physical as well as mental and he longed for activity of any sort, while Dietrichstein's panacea for restlessness, unremitting study, only made matters worse. He was not discontented, however, and touchingly grateful to his well-meaning 'preceptors', though his gratitude may not have extended to Baron Obenaus who is reliably reported as having whipped his 18-year-old charge. Dietrichstein certainly beat him soundly when he was a small boy. One of the Duke's most marked characteristics was kindness, sometimes of that impulsive royal nature which likes to scatter money at the feet of the poor. The Emperor gave him some newly-minted gold ducats which were not yet legal tender, and Reichstadt immediately gave them away; it was left to the police to trace them. His tutors fussed over him unendingly, and their reports are full of complaints, for the most part of the pettiest description, such as that he had been caught reading a history book during a long religious ceremony.

[1] Jean de Bourgoing, *Le Fils de Napoléon*.

His popularity among the public was enormous, and his every public appearance was greeted with far more enthusiasm, and inevitably, curiosity, than the younger Archdukes drew upon themselves. Martha Bradford saw him on 22nd September, 1828, when army manœuvres were held on the plain south of Vienna between Neudorf and Mödling. The weather, as it usually is at this time of the year, was brilliant, and so was the occasion as the Emperor, his consort and all the Court were present. Mrs. Bradford was close enough to the imperial party to pick out 'young Napoleon in his Captain's uniform, and the Duke of Wellington's sons, Lord Douro and Lord Charles Wellesley.' Other, unofficial, appearances, were noted with disapproval in some circles at Court and in society. It was not thought *comme if faut* that the Emperor's grandson should be seen about the place at all hours without an official escort in the company of a young man like the Prince of Salerno '*tres peu considéré*' or Maurice Esterházy. He was evidently not a prisoner in the sense that many people in France imagined.

In the following year the destiny of Franz von Reichstadt was bound up in one brief moment of suspense with that of his father's great adversary, Archduke Karl.

24. The Stephansplatz with market stalls

25. Entrance to the Hofburg (Michaelertor), and the old Burgtheater

26. Emperor Ferdinand with Empress Maria Anna, at the theatre

27. Metternich in old age

8

'Vienna heals all wounds'

Although his adoptive mother Archduchess Marie-Christine had tried often enough to marry him off, women had played all too small a part in the life of Archduke Karl. Throughout the Napoleonic wars, if he was not campaigning himself, his mind was filled with his army reforms, with study and with writing. His three-volume *Principles of Strategy*, published in 1813, was a contribution to the science of warfare which for the quality of its thought is widely considered to be equal if not superior to the great Prussian classic of the later nineteenth century, von Clausewitz. In their edited and condensed form his war memoirs run to six volumes. All this material was originally published anonymously, and a censor was sufficiently worried by the stern criticism of Archduke Karl which a particular volume contained to recommend its suppression. Perhaps the Archduke was a man *moyen sensuel*; he was neither a womanizer nor was he indifferent to women. How far his friendship with Baroness Clémence Vay went there is no way of knowing. They met at a ball at Pressburg and they wrote many letters to each other, one of his was written while leaning on a gun carriage during the Battle of Aspern. None of these letters have survived, but Clémence Vay never married, and to the end of her life she talked of Karl as '*mon héros*'. For him to have married a Baroness would not, of course, have been so very much easier than it was to be for his brother Johann to marry the postmaster's daughter from Aussee. It was only a matter of degree.

With Napoleon apparently safely established on Elba, Karl decided to look around for a wife, and methodical as he was, he set

o

about the business in the way used before and since by innumerable aristocratic marriage makers in Central Europe. He enlisted the help of Archduke Johann, and together with his friend Baron von Gagern they sat down with their Almanachs de Gotha and pencil and paper. It must have been tiring, thirsty work and one wonders whether either of the royal brothers knew the European marriage market intimately enough, even though they were naturally confining their search to the princely houses. Finally it was Gagern, who, persisting, discovered an 18-year-old girl among the family of Duke Frederick William of Nassau-Weilburg. Archduke Karl—he was at his army headquarters at Mainz—got into his coach and made for Weilburg, a small town about 30 miles north of Frankfurt, near Wetzlar. He had never cared for pomp, and now he walked into something which he found utterly delightful: a completely informal, easy-going way of life, 'the pattern of homely happiness'. Karl fell into it as into a hot bath after a day's shooting. Princess Henriette smiled upon him, the whole family of Nassau-Weilburg beamed and it was all fixed up without delay. Karl wrote to Johann: 'I should wish to see you in similar case, it would not, believe me, be at all injurious to your hypochondria, more particularly if you were to find a woman such as I have found. Even were she a termagant, she would set your gallbladder in motion, to great curative effect. Mind: never take a woman who is neither fish nor fowl.'

Henriette, while certainly not a termagant, was a Protestant, a fact guaranteed to set quite a number of Viennese gallbladders in motion and keep them going all the years of her life, as ensuing events proved. Meanwhile, Archduke Karl acted quickly. He went home, drafted a marriage contract and laid it before the Emperor Franz without waiting to consult Metternich who at the time was in Paris. When the Chancellor returned he found himself faced with a *fait accompli* in that Franz (he did the same for his brother the Palatine Joseph) had granted permission to Karl to negotiate his own contract. In this way Metternich was robbed of the pleasure of drawing the whole thing out like a sheet of strudel pastry, making the most of it, acquiring kudos, receiving presents from the grateful Duke of Nassau-Weilburg, and so on. But this was the kind of situation which Franz I understood and with which he sympathized:

his brother was coming to him as head of the family and there was nothing in it all to arouse the old suspicion and jealousy.

Archduke Karl now entered on the happiest, probably the only really happy period of his life. In 1822 the man died to whom he had opened his heart ever since he was 17, who had encouraged him and built up his confidence in all those intermittent emotional and nervous crises when he was at cross purposes with the war party at Court, alternately wooed and cold-shouldered by the Emperor, when he was attempting to carry out his army reforms with hardly any money and surrounded by intrigues: Duke Albert of Sachsen-Teschen. He left his entire estate to Karl. The landed property consisted of the Duchy of Teschen, the manors of Ungarisch-Altenburg, Bellye, Seelowitz, Saybusch and Friedeck, and his palace on the Augustiner Bastion in Vienna. The great art collection, one of the most important of its kind in the world for which Karl was now responsible and which he made accessible to the public, consisted of 160,000 etchings and prints and about 15,000 drawings of all schools and epochs.

It was a characteristic of the Archduke, one not shared by very many men in his position, that he liked the company of writers and scholars, intellectuals whom Franz I disliked so much, calling them 'bookmakers' and 'scribblers'. At bottom Archduke Karl had a great deal in common with them, and Franz Grillparzer was often at his table until the playwright sank into depression and neurasthenia and shunned all his friends, even his fellow playwright, the prolific Bauernfeld; and the poet, Nikolaus Lenau, until his mind went. These writers and several others were gathered up by Karl into a prominent literary society, the 'Shakespeare Club', and this inevitably meant that now he too was giving sympathy and support to men who, while certainly not enemies of the state, must be considered in varying degrees as in opposition to Metternich's system. Karl spent much of his time in Baden near Vienna where he had built a miniature version of the Archduchess's home, the Weilburg, for her pleasure. But in his absence a square meal was still to be had in the Annagasse where his principal secretary and land agent Councillor Kleyle carried on the good work of entertaining men of the arts and sciences to the tune of 16,000 gulden per annum.

In 1829 Karl and Henriette, their two children Albrecht and

Karl Ferdinand and their household celebrated Christmas round their Christmas tree. Henriette was not feeling well. By night-time she had a high temperature and on 30th December she died, of scarlet fever.

There could hardly be a more inconvenient corpse than that of a Protestant Archduchess. Her poor widower would have been better advised to arrange a quiet funeral in Baden or at one of their other country seats, anywhere rather than among the tombs of the Habsburgs in the vaults of the Kapuzinerkirche, but he wished to lie one day among his ancestors, his wife at his side. The Capuchin friars at first violently resisted the suggestion that they should accept a Protestant into their care, but they were overruled by the Emperor himself and gave way ungracefully. It was always supposed that Baron Hormayr, sitting in Munich with poised pen, was behind a report on the obsequies which appeared in the newspaper *Der Bazar* on 3rd January, 1830. It said that there had been insulting incidents during the service, and the whole report was slanted in such a way as to cause grave ill-feeling in the Protestant areas of Germany. The only man in the Austrian Empire whose pen was mightier than Hormayr's was of course Friedrich von Gentz, and Metternich at once set him to work to counter all these 'wicked lies'. Neither the Nuncio, the public now read in the *Wiener Zeitung*, nor the Archbishop of Vienna, nor yet the Capuchins had raised one finger in protest against the committal of the mortal remains of Henriette, consort of Archduke Karl, in the Kapuzinerkirche, nor had any 'incidents' taken place during the obsequies. Unfortunately the only effect of these denials was that informed opinion, not only at home but throughout Germany, was more convinced than ever before that all these things had indeed happened.

Summer came. The first families, the second families and the also-rans moved out to Baden, to Hinterbrühl, the nearer to the Court the better. Vienna lay under a hundred thousand dust sheets, the blinds on all the *bel-étages* were down. In the storm which on 27th July swept Charles X of France from his throne and set the shutters banging throughout Europe, wiser men than the Duke of Reichstadt shielded their eyes and waited. For him, the *fils de l'homme*, it was destiny's last mocking gesture, misunderstood at first: might he not yet be called upon? But if the Bonapartist poet had been in

the pay of Metternich he could not have written to better effect—
history swept past Napoleon II and chose Louis Philippe of Orleans.
Franz von Reichstadt turned his attention to humble regimental
duties. For him it was the end, a closed chapter. When the news was
brought to Metternich he collapsed, half unconscious, at his desk,
muttering, 'My life's work is destroyed!' But for him the chapter
was far from closed; a bare 15 years after the Congress of Vienna
there were faults in the structure, and the intensity of his emotion
was due to his clear realization that this was no crackle effect, no
series of shallow fissures such as might appear on mud banks at low
tide and would disappear when the waters returned. In the old conservative Europe, restored as best might be in 1815, this was the
first rift, and Metternich had no need of the news that the Poles were
rising against Russia and the Belgians against the Dutch to know
that the rift was deep. Once the first shock had passed off, the 'coachman of Europe's' impulse was to repair the storm damage by putting
everything back where it was before, if necessary by force of arms.
There are perhaps few moments in his career when Metternich's
life-long policy is so clearly displayed as in 1830. The years of
finassieren, of tacking against the wind, lie far behind him, and now
it is a matter of imposing his will by force. But not for sheer love of
it, not from megalomania. Here too the profound difference between
his mentality and that of Franz I is shown up with considerable
clarity.

To the Emperor liberalism was a threat to the throne and to the
state, therefore to himself personally since the state and his person
were one. Liberal ideas frightened him, and in any case he was not,
by the standards of those days which were extremely high, an educated man. Metternich on the other hand was familiar with the
thought and writings of the leading writers of the day and he could
recite Byron's poetry by the page. It was his conviction, however,
that between conservatism and anarchy there was no middle way;
liberalism was a soft option, a feeble compromise which, having no
practical substance, led only to disaster. He saw the English experience as conditioned by a different set of historical circumstances and
as having no relevance for continental Europe.

No prizes were offered to those who could see what was coming
for Archduke Karl. The Poles, tragically fighting for their lives and

the liberty of their country, called him to come and be their king.
Metternich had another plan. It was—war on France, with the ever-
popular Archduke at the head of the Austrian armies. He should
march on Paris, push Louis Philippe off the throne, and put back
the 'legitimate' Bourbons. While he was at it he could intimidate
and suppress those constitutional governments which were beginning to pop up like mushrooms in southern Germany. A proposal
was placed before Karl and his reply, addressed to the Emperor,
shows how fundamental was his disagreement with Prince Metternich. He saw that what was involved was a war of principles, a new
crusade against the Revolution, and to oppose opinions in this way
was, he said, a highly dubious and perilous undertaking. He asked
the Emperor to consider for himself 'whether after the melancholy
experiences of the past 40 years one would be in a position, mili-
tarily and financially, to plunge into an enterprise for which there
would be very little enthusiasm.' This apart, a war of this kind
would drag even the victor into the depths; one should therefore
beware of entering lightly, without exigency or forethought, upon
an adventure the consequences of which were quite unforeseeable.
War, he argued, is not the way to crush revolution, you only cause
it to spread and it unites the people against you. Meanwhile, in the
well-ordered states opposing it, the war effort reduces all the means
towards betterment of the condition of the people, and demoralizes
them while estranging them from their government.

This reaction can hardly have come as a surprise to the Emperor.
He knew his brother well enough: when had the country ever embarked upon a campaign with, at any rate in the opinion of the
Commander-in-Chief, sufficient resources? When had he not
placed the economy of the country before military intervention
abroad? And as for his liberal views, these were notorious. The
Emperor Franz however took Karl's refusal with equanimity. Not
so Metternich, who saw the Archduke's memorandum as a total
rejection of his own foreign policy. 'It is a fight', he declared, 'between anarchy and the existing order, a battle to the death on the
part of all the states of Europe for their existence, which we have to
pursue . . .' Yet again, he told the Emperor, the Archduke was trying to usurp the office of Minister of Foreign Affairs. The two men
were totally at cross purposes, the statesman seeing, as in an apoca-

lyptic vision, the downfall of the old order in Europe, profoundly convinced that once the principle, not so much of legitimacy as of absolute authority, was tampered with, the dams would burst. And the Habsburg prince, brought up on the divine right of kings, what was his comment while the normally impassive Metternich whom neither a lost battle nor the whole force of Napoleon's personality could shatter, gave way to despair?

His reaction to the deposition of Charles X is contained in a letter to his brother Joseph. 'This is what happens when the men in power and their associates are unfamiliar with the people and their circumstances and at the same time overestimate their own strength!' He did not believe that, whether they were right or wrong, ideas could be suppressed by armies; he knew the 'common' people as Metternich did not, and he knew them at first hand and not from censorship intercepts. In any case he had not been willing to lend his good name to a turncoat escapade, unavoidable and brilliantly managed though it may have been, in 1812, and he was not willing to emerge from retirement now to fight an aggressive war. Metternich's feelings contained an element of personal vindictiveness, for there was no justification for his wish to press the issue to its furthest extent. To brand Archduke Karl publicly as a man who refused to respond to the Emperor's call to arms, a man little better than a traitor: this would show once and for all that it was not the Emperor who ever failed his brother, but the Archduke who failed the *Casa d'Austria*. It was Metternich's military adviser Count Clam-Martinitz who pointed out what would happen if Metternich did this; he saw that the damage caused by creating a public scandal would not be confined to the target, and he was certain that owing to Karl's popularity great offence would be caused in army circles. Finally the idea was dropped and Metternich confined himself to overthrowing risings in the Papal States, in Modena, and also in Parma where from now on the governors would lack Neipperg's flair.

Even this was not to be the last time that Karl would be asked to lead the Austrian armies into the field.

Metternich's attitude towards the Duke of Reichstadt, too, contained an element of malevolence. Now nearly 20, Reichstadt was far from being the same person in the Chancellor's eyes that he was in his grandfather's. Franz I undoubtedly loved Marie Louise and he was fond of her son. The ex-Empress of the French had placed her life and that of her infant son in her father's hands, and this trust he would and did betray where Reichstadt's destiny entered the sphere of foreign affairs, for here Metternich (though speaking always of 'my Lord') was master; all the same, the boy was his grandson. Inconvenient he might be, but the Habsburg dynasty had infinite experience in dealing with its more decadent or tiresome members, be they mentally retarded, halt or maim, epileptic, homosexual or indeed illegitimate. A niche was found, their *faiblesses* were disregarded. To Metternich on the other hand, the young man was a constant reminder of unpleasant matters and doubtfully successful enterprises, an unperson who must not be allowed to acquire a personality of his own; a discarded pawn, a political nuisance.

In Vienna all this was no secret. Anton Prokesch-Osten says that to the Chancellor even to be reminded of Reichstadt's existence was disagreeable, and 'his flatterers took good care not to mention his name.' During the events of 1830 'because of France and the selection of officers he was several times forced to think of him, and he did so with the expression of a man who is swallowing bitter medicine.' Prokesch-Osten is commenting on Count Dietrichstein's complaint that Metternich did nothing for Reichstadt's political education when he says flatly: 'Between 1815 and 1830 the Prince did not occupy himself with the Duke in the slightest degree . . . . So as to pass the lie round Vienna that he himself initiated the Duke into a superior conception of the history of the epoch he countered Count Maurice's reproaches [with]: "The Count is a fool; it is not a question of hours of study", for during his meetings with the Duke, the latter "learnt more in a few words than with his professor of history." In reality, during the course of 17 years the Prince has spoken to the Duke but five times, and has placed not one document before him.' Prokesch-Osten may well be considered biased, but in March 1831 Gentz said to him: 'If such a thing were possible, the Prince's antipathy towards Reichstadt has increased. The young man is a *plaie grave* in the system of Metternich . . . The Prince detests in him all that he has committed against the son of Napoleon. The very fact that he has to pay attention to him renders him disagreeable.' And Reichstadt saw in Metternich 'the irreconcilable enemy of his father and of himself, the man to whom he owed his sad lot.'[1]

Reichstadt's attendance at a ball at the British Embassy on 25th January, 1831, was the sensation of the season. The aura, the glamour surrounding his name and person were unique, all the more so for the rarity of his appearance at important social functions. He was the golden boy of his epoch, curly-haired, slender, ethereally handsome—qualities common enough if it had not been for his alert manner and that sudden piercing glance which was so characteristic of Napoleon. Lulu Thürheim was there; needless to say they exchanged a little drawing-room banter. It ended with this exchange:

'Your Highness appears to be intending to become serious as from tonight?'

'You will think perhaps that I am lying, but I swear to you that I am accustomed to solitude, in such a way that I do not fear it. I am always alone, my situation is as singular as—er——'

'As that of an eagle on a fowl-house perch?'

'Let us rather say like a chicken shut up in a back yard . . .'

The evening brought a far more interesting encounter. Marshal Marmont, one of Napoleon's oldest companions in arms and a political surf-rider of distinction, was now Ambassador in Vienna. The number of masters whom he had survived to serve was of no concern to Reichstadt. Here was a man who had stood beside his father in battle, who could quote his words, explain his every action. Reichstadt grabbed him. For an hour, the two men stood engrossed in each other's company, talking in lowered tones so that, stretch their ears as they might, neither tutors nor adjutants, neither diplomats nor police agents could pick up a word. But this was nothing like enough. Reichstadt asked the Comte de Marmont to come and see him two or three times a week and go over it all with him, blow by blow, from the earliest beginnings up to Waterloo. This he did, visiting Reichstadt for long sessions in the Hofburg where the two bent over maps at long tables, working out logistics. Marmont had no less than 17 meetings with the young prince; this was not complete freedom, but it was something.[2]

[1] Jean de Bourgoing, *Le Fils de Napoléon.*
[2] André Castelot, *l'Aiglon.*

'Vienna heals all wounds'

Reichstadt's health was beginning to give cause for anxiety. During 1830 the Emperor's medical adviser Malfatti was already warning that he must on no account be subjected to physical over-exertion, nor be allowed to get over-heated and catch chills, and he pointed out that all the more care must be taken in view of the Duke's fiery temperament and strong desire to do all these things. Particular attention, he said on another occasion must be paid to his chest and vocal chords. Franz's evident delicacy caused a frustrating hiatus during the winter of 1830–1831 when he was not allowed to begin his army duties. Meanwhile three officers had been appointed to his household. General Hartmann was a stereotype regimental officer, worthy but boneheaded, Captain Standeiski too was totally out of his depth, but Captain Charles von Moll was better company for the Duke and he kept a diary which is the principal historical record of the end of Reichstadt's life.

The summer of 1831 came and he was posted to his regiment. He was looking ill and he often lost his voice while giving commands, but he shared in all the fatigues normally carried out by other young officers but to which it was not the usual practice to subject arch-dukes. A great deal has been made of this point, too much perhaps. Far more care should have been taken of him, and the warnings of the Court's medical advisers were disregarded or forgotten. But remembering his longing for action of any kind, his loathing of being 'mollycoddled', the fact that he wanted above all to learn his trade and rise by means of the great talent which he hoped and believed that he had inherited, was it not right (and with hindsight, infinitely more merciful) to let him have his head? It is difficult wholly to accept the reproach that Reichstadt, *le fils de l'homme*, should have been treated in the manner customary with royalty: given the honorary rank of General with no closer peacetime ex-perience of soldiering than an occasional inspection of troops or an afternoon watching manœuvres from a convenient hillock. He was of course under orders, and those who were responsible for him carried their burden lightly. It has been said that if a hundredth part of the passionate concern expended on shielding him from contact with Bonapartist plotters had been devoted to intelligent care for his health, his life might have been considerably lengthened. But this argument is of doubtful value: tuberculosis was a scourge the nature of which was not fully understood, and Metternich himself lost most of his family from the same cause. Certain it is that after a six-month postponement insisted upon by Dr. Malfatti no precautions whatever were taken. On 6th November, 1831, Reichstadt was given command of a battalion of the 60th regiment of foot, 'Graf Gyulayi', with the rank of Lieutenant-Colonel.[1] The battalion was located in the Alserkaserne barracks. The Duke was now fighting illness day by day, forcing his body, trying by every means to toughen it and overcome weakness. Something of this, and the seriousness with which he took his regimental duties, clearly got through to his men; there would otherwise be no explanation for what happened one day on the barrack square. The battalion was drawn up for inspection, every man standing rigidly to attention, eyes front. 'He was proceeding on horseback along the ranks when the expression of deep seriousness on his young face, his martial bearing, made such a powerful impression on the troops, accustomed though they were to complete silence and absolute immobility, that they burst out into loud and prolonged cheering.'[2]

In the depth of winter, 16th January, 1832, Reichstadt was detailed to carry out a military conduct at the head of his battalion. He had a heavy cold and his voice failed him as he gave the commands. By April Dr. Malfatti had to admit that his charge was seriously ill. But it was his 'liver'; tuberculosis was never officially diagnosed. He was not allowed to travel to a drier climate, he was not even given permission to go to Bad Ischl, or not until he was too ill to travel.

He died on 22nd July at Schönbrunn, in the same room that his father had slept in 22 years before, in the presence of his mother. It was hardly thanks to Marie Louise that she got there at all. Since the death of Neipperg she had been engulfed in a cloud of misery and hypochondria, but she was not unaware of the situation because for a long time Malfatti's mendaciously reassuring letters were alternating with anxious, entirely realistic assessments from Dietrichstein. She may have thought that he was merely an old fuss-pot, which indeed he was. Never brisk and decisive when decisions

[1] Archduke Albrecht, Karl's son, who was some years younger than Reichstadt, was at this time already a Colonel Commandant.
[2] Jean de Bourgoing, *Le Fils de Napoléon.*

involving action had to be taken, if it had not been for Metternich's insistent warnings that he was desperately ill and she must not delay her journey (he knew that if she failed to arrive in time the public would never forget it and would never forgive him either) she might never have left Parma. Even then, if Baron Marschall, the Administrator in Parma, is to be believed, the Duchess accompanied by her lover of the moment—her views on sex were eminently practical—could only with difficulty be persuaded to proceed beyond Trieste. Marschall was a hard man and he hated Marie Louise; a percentage of his report may be put down to prejudice.

There was not much that she could do when she did arrive, and her presence was not comforting to the dying Duke.

Should Marie Louise have sacrificed her happiness to stay with her son? If so, then at least the extent of the sacrifice must be admitted: on the one hand, long years spent moping around at Schönbrunn, on the other, a life with the man she loved in her own small but sovereign state. Later on, there was her responsibility towards her children by Neipperg to be considered. Until Napoleon died and their position could be legalized their situation was pathetic: a fiction had to be maintained and they called her La Signora, but she was devoted to them and her affection was returned in full; she launched the princely family Montenuovo (the Italian translation of Neipperg) and they never had cause to reproach her. But embarrassment over these children when the facts about their ages came out certainly increased her awkwardness in her relations with Reichstadt and this in turn contributed to her reluctance to travel to Vienna during the time between Neipperg's death in 1829 and the onset of her son's last illness. Their last and happiest meeting before these events was in 1828. What did he think of her? In spite of his frequent letters in which through the conventionally florid style a note of genuine affection and even of kindness seems to be detectable, his comment on her was damning. 'If Josephine had been my mother,' he told Prokesch-Osten, 'I should not be in the sorry plight in which I find myself at the present time.'

The Viennese had known for some time that *der kleine Napoleon* was dying. And as the news of his death spread, so did the rumours, casting as they went an odd light on Metternich's supposed attitude towards Reichstadt: the public had little or no hesitation in crediting him with murder, the preferred version being that Reichstadt had died of arsenic poisoning. The ripples expanded, by no means only on the housemaid circuit, and it was not long before King Ludwig of Bavaria was asking the Austrian chargé d'affaires quite openly: 'Tell me, did the Duke of Reichstadt die a natural death?'

The rather better informed believed that over-indulgence in sex had undermined his health (this was in any case always a prevalent superstition) and that this round of dissipation was encouraged by Metternich with the intention of shortening his life. The more recent biographies dismiss this theory, in one case with evident reluctance because although if Metternich had been an African witch-doctor Reichstadt would surely have wasted away long ago, no evidence of the kind has ever been produced.

When Reichstadt grew up, the long reign of the waltz had begun, the reign of Lanner, Ziehrer and the Strauss family. More than a fashion, more than a new craze, it was almost a social revolution and it seized hold of all classes of the population. Before it began, dancing had seemed almost to be on the way out, so boring and pointless were the old formal, stately dances which had come down from a time when a woman's *grande toilette* gave her little freedom of movement. Now at last a man could take a girl in his arms, lightly corsetted as she now was and wearing some soft, flowing material allowing unlimited freedom of movement, and rotate like a top all the night long. More often than not Reichstadt was clasping Countess Nandine Károlyi. Prokesch-Osten never much cared for her, she was 'frivolous, light-headed' and had been more or less 'brought up in the salons' of Vienna; far from giving stability to his character she would simply cast over it a veil of banality. To begin with Reichstadt took no notice of anyone's opinion and he met her at the masked ball in the Redoutensaal; there were one or two evenings, too, at Sperl's famous establishment beyond the Ferdinand Bridge. How far did the friendship go? Dietrichstein's warnings that he was damaging her reputation brought an end to it, and he switched his attention to less conspicuous circles. A dancer, Thérèse Peche, caught his attention at the ballet, a meeting was arranged at her home and he went along taking a friend, probably the ubiquitous Maurice Esterházy. He had no intention of treating the girl as though she were a prostitute, but wanted to see what she was like at closer range. Unfortunately, Thérèse, or more likely her mother, mistook the situation altogether and, anticipating not tea and talk but instant coitus, dressed in a manner appropriate to the second contingency, and Reichstadt, thoroughly put off, left after a polite interval without making a further date.

Legend has always linked the Duke of Reichstadt's name with the great dancer Fanny Elssler, but the difficulty about involving her in the frantic excesses is that if anyone's life was shortened by love for Fanny Elssler it was that of Friedrich von Gentz. When Gentz fell in love with Fanny he was an elderly man of 66; she was the love of his life and there can have been no one in Vienna who was not aware of it. In it all there is a slight element of burlesque, not because of his age but his vanity. So besotted was he that he could announce 'I have won her solely and alone by the magic power of my love'—this when he was casting money, pearls and precious stones at her feet with gay abandon. Metternich was as irritated by the emotions of his assistant as Gentz had once been by those of the Chancellor; not even the approach of cholera could disturb his euphoria. On 16th August, 1830, Metternich wrote to Mélanie Zichy, 'Revolutions are attacking my front and the cholera amoebus my back . . . This sickness is spreading across one Russian province after another [it was to reach Vienna in September 1831]. I have just imparted this news to Gentz, but he laughed in my face. "What are revolutions, what is the cholera!" he cried. "Long live Fanny!"' (There was something rather attractive about Gentz after all.) Fanny always denied that she had an affair with Reichstadt, but it is in any case hardly conceivable that such a wildly emotional man, deeply in love and mortally jealous, would have allowed himself to be deceived, or that knowing about it, he would not in his misery have lifted up his voice and howled so that all Europe heard him.

The opinion of the one man who was wholly in Reichstadt's confidence must carry great weight, and he talked to Prokesch-Osten about his sexual desires and what he should do about them, always with such frankness that his inexperience was obvious: Prokesch was perfectly convinced that Reichstadt—and this would of course dispose of the story about the Archduchess Sophie—never had any sexual intercourse with a woman in his life. In his opinion, the causes which brought about his physical decline and death were these, and this view is echoed in several contemporary memoirs: 'The Prince died consumed by mental distress over his situation and over the disuse of his most noble talents. I cannot but believe that a happy and active youth would have favourably affected his physique and that the defects in his development were the results of a sickness of the spirit. I knew his disposition well enough to understand how his body should have succumbed to it.'[1]

Friedrich von Gentz, Golo Mann calls him '*der freche Wunderknabe*', died on 9th June, 1832, within six weeks of Reichstadt. The politically turbulent thirties and forties would have to do without his voice. One could do without him, but one would miss him; this applied in particular to the Rothschilds.

Gentz could never hold on to money, and he was a generous man, kind to his employees. Apart from his salary and emoluments from his own employer Franz I, however, he was never averse to selling information for cash and for many years he drew (see p. 152) a regular salary from the British Government. Concurrently, but increasingly during the 1820s, Gentz was working for the Rothschilds. After the Napoleonic era the Austro-Hungarian Empire was put back on its feet by the genius of the Rothschild brothers, and Count Stadion said that the finances of the state could not have been run without them. In his history of the Rothschild family Egon Caesar, Conte Corti, describes the mutual dependence of Metternich and the bankers: upon his tacit or active support their existence depended once the death of the Elector of Hesse had deprived them of their original patron. But for their financial operations the Rothschilds' imperative need was for reliable inside information, and this Gentz gave them. In return, they at first merely arranged for him to win on the stock exchange, later he was nothing less than their official agent with a fixed salary of 10,000 gulden a year; a strange position indeed for a man through whose hands every single day any amount of state secrets passed, although Metternich was certainly not only aware of the fact but sometimes used the situation for his own purposes. 'During his last years', says Corti, 'Gentz divided up his services between the State Chancellery, the Rothschilds and the

[1] For the autopsy report, see *Franzisceische Curiosa* by F. Gräffer, Vienna, 1849.

charming artiste. Now no sum of money . . . was large enough, for he carried everything to his beloved Fanny.'

Gentz had hardly ceased to breathe before Metternich ordered a search to be made through all his private papers for anything of a displeasing nature concerning himself. Gentz was known to have written an account of the Congress of Vienna, and it was on this in particular that Metternich wanted to lay his hands. But Gentz had burned the manuscript, apparently not long before he died. What a loss this was to posterity Metternich's junior colleague Baron Wessenberg appreciated at once. He said that it was a loss similar to that of the annals of Titus Livius.

9

Biedermeier Man:
an Introspective Society

During the years which lay between 1815 and 1848, between the Congress of Vienna and the year of revolutions, profound changes came over the prevailing way of life and the intellectual climate in Vienna, but with marginal exceptions these changes were scarcely influenced by those highly-placed persons whom we have been discussing, nor were they themselves much affected. That Clemens Metternich influenced the course of events, that he was responsible for much that happened and for yet more that did not, goes without saying. Yet it will emerge that there were limits even to his power; and no one could possibly see in him a representative of the Biedermeier era.

Biedermeier: the term is not Austrian, but derives from a fictitious character, a small-town Swabian schoolmaster, the alleged author of a series of poems published in 1850 in the satirical journal *Fliegende Blätter*. Correspondingly, the term is used throughout the German-speaking countries of Europe, but owing to the pressures which were peculiar to the Habsburg Empire, here the period acquired characteristics of its own. Those characteristics were certainly not confined to the capital and they may even be seen as a pan-Austrian phenomenon. There are few Biedermeier houses in the central districts of modern Vienna (though in innumerable drawing-rooms, if the owners' great-grandparents were to walk into them today, they would find little to startle them), but there are many in prosperous suburbs such as Hietzing. Baden bei Wien was, and partly still is, Biedermeier, and that quiet, reserved style can be

P   *225*

seen anywhere between Ljubljana and Czernowitz. At the time, the
same plays with similar dress and settings were being put on in
Graz and in Lemberg. Was it all a little too smug? Many a family
portrait of a simpering welterweight Hausfrau holding a rose between the tips of her podgy fingers would lead one to suppose so,
but this is a highly complex as well as an unusually self-conscious
epoch. Chronologically it falls into two halves; from the dispersal of
the guests after the Congress, to Metternich's cry of despair in 1830,
and then the all-important period when, with the coming of the
railway age, and—from 1835—with a simpleton on the throne,
Metternich's 'system' became ever more of an anachronism. The
period contains strands of liberalism, which in Austria always im-
plies more than a touch of anti-clericalism and even a turning away
from religion, but strands too of a religious revival. It was above all
a seminal era within which the great explosion of genius originated
that, as the century advanced, was to cast its glow over the dying
Empire.

In retrospect, it can be seen that as the shutters closed on the
Congress the Biedermeier age began, but elderly inhabitants of
Vienna today are adamant that their grandparents never used the
term and that it only came into general currency after the turn of
this century. Until then, *Vormärz*, pre-March, which today still
stands for the times and events leading up to the revolution of which
the first outbreak was in March 1848, was the only expression in
general currency. The attribute *bieder*, hence *Biedermann*, were
approving or mildly pejorative terms according to taste, and the
image has many of the qualities of John Bull: solid, respectable,
reliable. Just off the Graben in Vienna there was a Gasthaus *Zum
Biedermann*, and Archduke Johann in a letter of condolence to the
family of one of his former tutors said of him, 'The deceased was a
Biedermann.' In this period there are many traps for the unwary:
the tendentious travel-writers of those times seeing on the one hand
the horrors, mitigated by unbridled sensual uproar, of Metternich's
'China in Europe', or, alternatively, seeing a dignified, benevolent
paternalism ruling over a horde of merry, apple-cheeked, touchingly devoted subjects from whose minds, assuming that they had
any, nothing could be further than politics; all this, moreover, on
the eve of revolution. Charles Sealsfield's *Austria As It Is*—occa-

226

sionally wildly funny though in its cumulative effect deeply depressing—and the writings of Josef Hormayr, seem to be talking of a different Vienna to that of young Henrich Laube, in later life Director of the Burgtheater, and of Adolf Glassbrenner, who—neither the first nor the last journalist to whom this has happened—was sent to Vienna by his employers in Berlin to write a series of articles of a more or less polemical nature, and fell in love with the place.

In her invaluable work *Vienna, Legend and Reality* Ilse Barea made the point that 'it was impossible for travellers coming to Vienna in the late twenties and thirties to be unbiased, to have the innocent eye, even if they came on a purely musical pilgrimage. They had heard too much'—of Metternich's support of every reactionary régime in Europe and from reports of the Emperor's rigid administration at home. They came agog to see what it was all about, and as writers with pronounced liberal views would not have been given an entry visa, their testimony is not to be trusted. All the same, among the cloud of witnesses, not all are disingenuous. While the exasperating Mrs. Frances Trollope, mother of the novelist, was clearly given the *entrée* to high society and allowed to go over a prison because her Tory views were known and she was sure to believe anything she was told by a count or even by a baron provided that the title were of feudal, not stock exchange origin, even her sententiousness was sometimes shaken by a whiff of common sense. Her *Vienna and the Austrians* gives a description of what it was like to travel on the Danube in an *ordinari*, and tells of the all-pervading *odeur continentale* in general, and the stench rising from the River Wien on its course between Schönbrunn and Vienna in particular. There exist many descriptions of the catacombs under St. Stephen's Cathedral before the piles of semi-preserved corpses were tidied away, but none is more hair-raising than hers, and if she had never heard of Grillparzer we have her account of a performance by the great tragedienne Madame Rettich. We have much to thank her for. In 1836, Mrs. Trollope gave it as her considered opinion that the Viennese were the happiest people she had ever known. Within less than a decade of the social explosion, Peter Turnbull, F.R.S., also found them 'a most happy and enjoyable people . . . Frugal, cheerful and contented, they (the working classes) seek no alteration in their conditions . . . they dread change of any kind as fraught with evil.'

The explanation of this apparent blindness, at least in part, is that those people, however numerous, who in the eyes of both authors made up the Viennese 'working classes' had little in common with either layer of the population which, actively or latently, carried in its heart the seeds of revolution. More difficult to assess at their true value are the writings of the Viennese themselves, not only because of the 'good old days' syndrome by which all writers of memoirs are threatened, but by a feed-back mechanism to which the Viennese have been particularly prone. They were always theatre mad, a fact which it is not too far-fetched to relate to their passion for watching the world go by. It was a peculiar 'pleasure in everything which shimmers in colour, which unfolds before him in pictures, and precisely because he lacks passion he seeks to intensify his inner life through the passions on the stage.'[1] Their native dramatists showed them to themselves in a mirror which, slanted now this way, now that, so caught their fancy that soon every tinker or tailor was a 'character'. The playwright Johannes Nestroy confronted the Viennese with the demonic undertones in their psychology, a phenomenon with which Grillparzer was all too familiar; later, the great student of the Austrian character on all social levels was to be Arthur Schnitzler. But this is to run on too fast. *Were* the Viennese a happy people, or was it all a propaganda gimmick thought up by Metternich and Franz I?

Writing in the forties about the aristocracy in the post-Congress period, Lulu Thürheim wrote: 'During that winter of 1816–1817 Vienna was brilliant. Generally speaking it was quite unlike the Vienna of today. If a few joyless balls, a few gatherings without interest beyond a contest over jewellery among the women and over luxury on the part of the hosts, if several [*sic*] doyens of the diplomatic corps, one or two coteries, a mediocre theatre, many *têtes-à-têtes* and numerous scandals provided the programme for society in the year 1847 and lent it a European reputation for tastelessness, at the time of which I was speaking foreigners thronged to take part in all the entertainments which social life and the prominent houses offered. Apart from the palaces of the ambassadors and ministers

---

[1] Claudio Magris, *Der Habsburgische Mythos in der österreichischen Literatur.*

who gave *soirées* several times a week for all who had made themselves known to them, apart from the many dinners in the town and uncounted balls and festivities in private houses, there was many a small supper party for exclusive, elegant circles. It was mainly there that gaiety, piquant, instructive talk, charming coquetry and the delicately veiled intrigues of love propagated a feeling . . . of *"gai-vivre"*, combined with a sense of affinity, of *"rapport"* such as could not have been found in any other great capital but Vienna. I remember that the week was too short for all these delightful suppers. The Tuesday suppers at the Razumovsky's were among the most pleasant of all, especially in Spring, when the music in the gardens, the illuminated terraces with many small laid and decorated tables, the quantities of flowers standing all about and often the light of the moon invited dalliance in the shrubbery [with, for example, the Prince's secretary Charles Thirion whom she married secretly] gave the Palais Razumovsky quite an oriental appearance.'[1]

During this same winter the owners of textile mills where calico, all kinds of cloth and silk materials were woven, were faced with such a slump in demand that by December 1816, of 10,000 looms, two-thirds were standing idle and soon nearly the entire labour force was on the streets. This frightful alternation of boom and slump which was such a familiar element of post-Napoleonic Europe, fell, in Vienna, principally on the rootless industrial proletariat on the outskirts of the town, for the most part unwelcome immigrants from Bohemia and Moravia who had succumbed to the draw of the capital. But in the years after the Congress, with the return to a peace economy, small tradesmen were in trouble as well, and master craftsmen were going begging or working in the moat and on the roads as unskilled labourers. To make matters worse,

---

[1] Outlandish, if not oriental, in blue silk pantaloons and a little short skirt, with flaming red face and bristly hair, Queen Caroline, spurned wife of George IV, turned up in one of the Court theatres on 8th April. Members of the audience were aware that she had been living in the house of a General in Austrian service, Domenico Pino, in Milan, where she had taken a fancy to a fine upstanding lackey called Bergami. In 1816 as a reward for personal services she organized for him the title of Baron della Froncini and the Cross of the Knights of Malta, and they were living together on a property which she bought at Pesaro in the Vatican States. Her request for an audience with the Emperor was refused, and at the news of her arrival the British Ambassador fled from Vienna with his whole entourage.

there had been a bad harvest. Beggars were always a feature of Viennese street life and travellers who failed to see them should be viewed with suspicion. Now, women and children among them, they filled the courtyards and lay about on the stairways, they pushed their way into the churches during the services and importuned the members of the congregation to such an extent that since church premises were sacrosanct the Archbishop demanded that a special *Religionspolizei* be appointed to deal with them. But the police were helpless in the face of distress on such a scale, and though they herded the beggars to and fro and arrested them by the thousand, they were not without sympathy for the plight of these people, and were well aware that all this was no solution to the problem.

In the spring of 1817 Emperor Franz visited the poorhouses and issued an order that all beggars were to be admitted—but there was to be no overcrowding. At this time the government's charity fund had a deficit of 614,000 florins and the Minister of Finance hardly knew how to cover the daily overheads. At this very same time reports from Lombardy and censorship of the soldiers' mails showed that the army was in little better heart than it had been in 1812. The President of the War Council had tried to make his voice heard in March 1815: officers and men must be put on a reasonable subsistence level if sickness and lack of discipline are not to go beyond all bounds and lead to chaos, and he called attention to the far better conditions prevailing in the armies of other nations. In 1817 there was again talk of the 'boundless misery' of the junior officers, who, messing together with the non-commissioned officers, seldom saw much meat. They were living mainly on potatoes, sharing their bread with their soldier servants, and could accept no invitations because in their ragged uniforms they were not presentable. How dreadful is the Emperor's reaction, reminiscent of his injunctions years before to his underpaid civil servants. He was greatly put out by the sample intercepts put before him: the soldiers' letters home should be 'cleansed of all forward and insolent remarks' such as were liable to cause 'untimely anxiety' and to give an 'untoward impression of the circumstances'. Did he sometimes think that his great forbear the Empress Maria Theresa was imprudent in introducing compulsory primary education throughout her dominions, thereby all but abolishing illiteracy?

Biedermeier Man: an Introspective Society

The morale of the students of Vienna University, too, was indifferent. On 8th June, 1815, as it chanced the day before the signing of the Final Act of Congress, an agent of the secret police was talking to a librarian in the University Library, who told him: 'There is no courage, neither among the students nor the teachers. It is because of the rise in prices, and the rates of exchange; the subsidy [an extra allowance for civil servants and teachers granted in the autumn of 1814] does not help, the professors are turning of necessity to other activities in order just to keep themselves and their families afloat; the young people are studying badly and less; they can see that no one can live on his earnings. All those large-scale publications and the periodicals which must be paid for in cash and kept up, are not being continued, the rate of exchange will not allow of it.'

Family papers published in Austria a few years ago[1] begin with a vivid picture of student life in Vienna in the mid-eighteenth century and show precisely what it meant to be a 'beggar student'; perhaps it is a pardonable digression to mention these papers here as they describe aspects of life in Vienna which were still unaltered in the early nineteenth century. By no means simply a sad predicament, the social status of a *Bettelstudent* was one which conferred certain privileges. Johann Georg Obermayer ran away from the monastery school at Passau to avoid entry into the priesthood and travelled down the Danube with the help of a sympathetic ship's captain. He walked into the city through the Rotenturm Gate, and after attending High Mass in St. Stephen's, went straight on to the University and reported his wish to register as a *Bettelstudent*. The beadle told him that he was almost too late, but two other students were also asking for admission and they would all three be accepted. The free places—provided by wealthy burghers and some of the monasteries, and offering meals and sometimes free lodging—were, however, all taken: they would have to chance their luck when soup was dished out to the poor. Each was issued with a long cloth coat, a tricorn hat, a pair of grey woollen stockings and sturdy shoes (swords were forbidden). The duty of feeding the poor was carried out in turn by the Dominicans, Jesuits, Capuchins and the Friars Minor on the Minoritenplatz, and the students' distinctive clothing and identification cards gave them precedence over others. The

[1] Wilhelm Weckbecker, *Die Weckbeckers, Karriere einer Familie.*

Biedermeier Man: an Introspective Society

Pauline Fathers in the district of Wieden had no kitchen of their own, it being their custom to ring the church bell for half an hour, after which, at 10 a.m., they sat down at their table and waited to see what their charitable neighbours would place before them. Whatever was brought in excess of their needs was given to the people who, in bad times, thronged the gateway. The *Bettelstudenten* were also allowed to go about as 'gospellers', reading the Gospel in public places on Saturdays, Sundays and holy days, and they might, without damage to their honour, pick up the coins thrown to them by their listeners.

The three young men swore eternal friendship, pooled their tiny resources and set forth. Obermayer and Bernhard Jenisch rose to the top of the civil service; the last of the trio was Franz Thugut who became Minister of Foreign Affairs in 1793, remaining in office until his dismissal at the end of the Second Coalition War in 1803. Their careers show that in the apparently so rigid social structure of those times, in some ways hardly altered since the Middle Ages, it was nevertheless possible, Dick Whittington-like, to walk into the capital of the Holy Roman Empire with a spare shirt and pair of socks rolled up in a bundle and to end up at the top. A hand-to-mouth existence was taken as a matter of course, and until the industrial proletariat came upon the scene, poverty was not always oppressive, particularly as accepted attitudes towards life, death and the hereafter were not those of a later age. The Viennese were a volatile people with a capacity for instant enjoyment which ran side by side with one of the highest suicide rates in Europe, a distinction which Vienna has retained to this day though the *joie de vivre* has gone. A member of the aristocracy visited Prague and found it deadly. The people were quiet and industrious, nothing ever seemed to be going on in the street outside her window, there was no music, no song. 'How I long to be back in dear Vienna', she wrote, 'where hardly have two men sat down at a table in the open air but a third arrives with his fiddle . . .'

In the air of Vienna there was a touch of the South. The long hours of work were softened by the slow pace of life and by passive resistance. The surprise of visitors at the number of people who had all the time in the world to stand around staring has been mentioned earlier; it is not to be assumed that they were all unemployed. An

English traveller asked his Viennese companion what holiday it was, 'since everywhere people are lounging idly on the windowsills; in England or in Holland I should not have seen this.' Until the number of 'holy days' was curtailed by Joseph II the feasts of the Church and an occasional pilgrimage brought relief and colour into the lives of the poor. But there was no interference with the major feast days, and in the private sphere the pagan element flourished as it always had: Hugo von Schönholz describes how on All Hallows Eve the maids in his grandmother's house, not daring to go to bed, spent the night on their knees in the kitchen, wailing and praying for deliverance from evil spirits.

Adalbert Stifter the novelist noticed the truly baroque sense of theatre which in his time still accompanied the ceremonies of Holy Week. On Good Friday immense catafalques were built up in the Cathedral, in St. Maria am Gestade, the Peterskirche and other large churches. '. . . on Good Friday and Saturday towards sundown it is the custom to go walking in one's Sunday best along the Kohlmarkt, Graben and the Stephansplatz. It is a custom of which such ample use is made that people literally walk shoulder to shoulder, and those who would normally always use a carriage, now appear on foot and a broad, brilliant stream of people is poured out upon the whole street, which is seldom disturbed by any vehicle . . .' And with a touch of sententiousness: 'In spite of the striking tendency to display clothing of the richer sort, even an eye accustomed to harmony and beauty remarks no discordance . . . for in our capital the female sex possesses the remarkable tact to select at this time garments which, while being the most beautiful that she has, are yet such as are not only without detriment to the solemnity, the calm and the festive character of the occasion but even exalt it.'

On Easter Saturday all these crowds in their Easter bonnets were on their way to the Resurrection services, and Stifter saw it as the most animated day in the whole year, with every church a sea of candles and a mass of flowers. 'The Resurrection is celebrated in more than a hundred churches, in each with the greatest possible magnificence, and as this does not occur at the same hour in all places, the crowds on the streets are forming at two or three in the afternoon; it is a crush through which it is sometimes hard to force a passage; mounted police and the military must be on duty . . . in particular when towards 4 o'clock the pushing, scintillating throng moves down the Kohlmarkt towards the Hofburg, where the Resurrection will be celebrated with a solemn procession in the Burghof in the presence of the All-Highest Family, the dignitaries and the military in their most brilliant uniforms: of all the sights to be seen today this is the most beautiful and festive.' Church bells, says the novelist, are ringing all over the town, dominated by the bass roar of the Pummerin, the great bell of St. Stephen's, outside which thousands are standing for whom there is no room inside. As the services end a run begins on the shops which will stay open until late. Every shopping street is filled with scurrying figures, housewives and cooks with large baskets on their arms are off to buy the roast, and the Naschmarkt, the fruit and vegetable market, is bathed in the light of a thousand lamps.

The Prater Corso was a tradition which only died with the monarchy. There was one on Easter Sunday, another on 1st May, and others when a special occasion and fine weather coincided with the presence of the Court and society in the capital. Everyone in Vienna joined in the Corso if they could call a carriage their own or anything else on wheels with a nag to pull it. If not, they walked. Vienna had no more glamorous sight to offer, nor any which united all classes in this way. By 3 and 4 o'clock in the afternoon the broad, handsome thoroughfare called the Jägerstrasse, now the Praterstrasse, was crammed from end to end with carriages, carried along by the drift of the crowd like ships among pack-ice on the Danube. Every window was filled with watchers calling out the names of the famous as they passed in their splendid *équipages*: the Emperor himself in a carriage drawn by six greys, princesses and countesses by the hundred in the latest fashion but with no extravagant display and discreetly bejewelled. A little more ostentatious were the *toilettes* of the prosperous ladies of the town, the actresses, singers and courtesans. Alongside the carriages rode cavalry officers in parade uniforms and splendidly mounted on the finest horses that the Empire could muster. Every scrap of harness had been tended, rubbed and breathed on for months in anticipation of this day. By the time that the outriders were approaching the main avenue of the Prater, the cortège was half a mile long. Moving down the Hauptallee, the nodding, smiling beauties were carried along on carriages so perfectly built that they seemed to float on air; the shimmering stream turned at the Lusthaus and drifted back the way it had come, causing, as the carriages, pony traps and more humble vehicles passed and re-passed during the course of the afternoon, who knows what problems of recognition and non-recognition with endless nuances in between. The riders overflowed into one of the side avenues, the pedestrians into the other, but the desire to see and to be seen was so strong, the only purpose in fact of the whole undertaking, that very few felt inclined to wander off into the cool depths of the forest. Stifter saw a stag standing back in the shadows. It paused for some time, watching the colour and movement of a monarchy on parade before it turned and trotted back to its water meadows.

The Easter Corso was a set piece, but the Prater was always the principal recreation ground of the Viennese, particularly that part known as the Wurstelprater, where an almost non-stop amusement fair has been carried on for centuries. Martha Bradford drove out to the Prater. 'We have hired a carriage by the month which we found indispensable . . . I take the children with Mademoiselle and Nurse alternately to the Prater of a morning. There we get out and walk about the *lovely* grounds which belong to that singular place, which is at once an exquisite retirement and the resort of all that is smart and fashionable in Vienna . . . the deer run wild in one part and there are walks without end in different directions under the shade of trees, and in another part hundreds or I believe thousands of carriages assemble as they do in Hyde Park, fill'd with beauty and rank, smart equipages and the most elegant style of dress. The evening, that is, from five to seven o'c, when all good Germans [*sic*] have eaten and drunk to their heart's content, and their stomach's surprise, is the fashionable time for repairing to this strife of vanity and display; from the Emperor down to the jew pedlar and the bearded Turk everybody assembles there and 'tis the most amusing sight that a stranger can possibly witness.'

Mrs. Bradford, owing no doubt to her connections with the Court of St. Petersburg, was presented to the Empress and consequently was accepted into Austrian society. She is a most valuable foreign source of information on Vienna in the twenties of the nineteenth century, when the grand traditions of the Congress still lingered and Vienna remained the political and social centre of

Europe. She went to a ball at the Spanish Embassy where she saw dresses 'glittering all over with gold or silver, wrought in the most exquisite and *rich* manner. Then the diamonds—I can give you no conception of it, for combs, earrings and necklaces were *nothing*.'[1] Lady Stewart was keeping up British prestige with 'a diamond necklace, under it a necklace of turquoises set in diamonds, a diamond tiara and earrings to match'. She was a byword for hauteur, and the frigid, regal manner in which she liked to receive the British colony, seated on a 'throne' and fawned on by her husband, the Ambassador (the Duchess of Sagan's former lover, who perhaps had much ground to make up in the eyes of Lady Stewart), annoyed Mrs. Bradford exceedingly. It is evidence of the movement of money and goods generated by Court and society in the centre of Vienna that in the early twenties she could already write: 'To be sure it is the best dressed Public I ever beheld. The holydays are endless and then the turn out of finery is past all describing', and one blesses her for this attention to detail: 'My kitchen maid sports eleven flownces of worked muslin at the bottom of her petticoat, and a gold cap on her head which was taken out of pawn on Whit Sunday.'

The feeling akin to claustrophobia which overcame many a visitor inside the walled city assailed Martha also. 'The Town of Vienna is remarkably small, so that when you feel yourself bewildered by the crowds of well-dressed people in Carriages, and the swarms who press forward to all places of amusement, on foot, you are astonished where they come from and how they can find room to exist, till you recollect that Vienna is like a Rabbit Warren above ground, and that from the cellar to the garret, which includes 7 or 8 stories, it is inhabited till every hole and corner is full . . .' Beyond the Glacis she was entranced by the number of gardens, 'and that, none yr pockethandkerchief sized flower gardens, but lovely acres of ground laid out exquisitely in the style of Kingston House gardens and some in the style of Hampton Court grounds.' Moreover, she said, these gardens, belonging to the 'great Princes of the Land' were open to the public every day.

[1] The men were often carrying around as many carats as the women. At his wedding to his first wife Princess Elizabeth of Württemberg, the then Archduke Franz wore diamond buttons worth 1,305,000 florins. Including the sash of the Order of Theresa with its 920 diamonds in four rows, a total of about 4,580,000 gulden.

Biedermeier Man: an Introspective Society

When the Court moved out of Vienna one could only marvel at 'the tastes of the Austrians who have no conception of the country, otherwise than removing them from the town of Vienna to the smaller town of Baden, and from exhibiting their very fine dresses in the Prater to exhibiting them with equally solemn anxiety to the same people in the little Park of Baden, or in the beautiful valley of St. Helena close by the town where they appear to be perfectly insensible of the exquisite scenery, and assemble in gaudily attired multitudes in a particular spot of the Vale, where a sort of Parade is formed every evening regularly, and beyond the limits of which parade, if any creature is seen to wander, you may be quite certain that the courageous being is a stranger! This sameness of amusement is so characteristic of the people of all ranks here, that I do not know any exception to it . . . everybody assembles every evening to *stew* in a small playhouse, looking at very poor acting, and inhaling a pleasing mingle of perfumed gales, where smoke of tobacco, sulphur of the baths and the well known odeur Teutonic struggle for superiority in poisoning the atmosphere.' Martha revised a few of her snap judgments as time went on, such as the idea that Austrians (she meant members of the aristocracy) had no conception of the country. She was to meet, near Bad Aussee, acquaintances whom she might well have last seen, dripping with diamonds, at a ball during *Fasching*, but who were now going for extremely taxing whole-day rambles in the mountains of the Salzkammergut.

The untidy, even neglected approaches to the big country houses in comparison with the neatly-kept drives and lawns in England are mentioned, an exception being the estate of Count Maurice Dietrichstein near Baden: 'the grounds are so beautiful by nature, so finely diversified by hill, dale, rock, wood and water, that art could hardly spoil it.' This reference to the chief tutor of the Duke of Reichstadt is taken up by Lady Londonderry in her introduction to *The Letters of Martha Wilmot* (Martha's maiden name; the letters were published in 1935) who says that the Bradfords' son Wilmot had riding lessons at the royal riding academy in company with the Duke and that he was one of the few playmates whom the Duke was allowed by his Austrian 'captors'.[1]

---

[1] Wilmot inherited his remarkable longevity from his mother who lived to the age of 99. Born in the year of the Congress, 1815, he only failed by a few

Biedermeier Man: an Introspective Society

Martha considered the Viennese shiftless and improvident, present enjoyment being the main object of life 'so that the head of a family seldom dies, without leaving so many debts that the widow and younger children sink at once into distress for which they are ill-prepared by education and habits. This self-indulgence pervades all ranks, and 'tis a fact that there are more suicides in Vienna than in London . . . But they are good-natured people, and their first impulse is always friendly.' Lulled by these fairly conventional views, it comes as quite a shock when in another letter she suddenly refers to cosy, fun-loving Vienna as 'This most vicious place . . . I forget whether I have ever yet expatiated on the demoralized state of this town, on the system of espionage, the bribery, corruption and gallantry[1] from high to low, the churlish inhospitality of the great nobles, and the jealousy or dislike of the English . . .' She had not, and unfortunately she never did.

Her account of the rigid caste system and the way of life of the upper classes is not inaccurate but it is lent a note of desperation by the fact that her nephew Edward had announced his wish to come and stay with the chaplain and his wife for some months. Martha thought him spoilt and a bore, and was determined to put him off. He would not be asked to the best parties, and even if he were, he would feel thoroughly out of it. 'The pride of the aristocracy is by no means greater, but it is more defined, than that of England, and therefore talents, tastes and every natural endowment of a superior caste . . . can *never* break down the barrier of rank or be admitted into its circles.' (In 1836 Mrs. Trollope, too, exclaimed over the contrast with London where men of high achievement in almost every sphere might be seen in the leading houses, but in Vienna practically never.) '. . . A young Englishman arriving in Vienna, if quite unknown, is driven to theatres etc. in very despair; if known and introduced into different houses, he has the honour to sit in

---

months to see the outbreak of the First World War. Lady Londonderry said that he was fond of recalling his association with Reichstadt, and he also remembered the Emperor Franz I. His obituary notice in *The Times* said that he must have been for many years past the only living person who could claim a first-hand knowledge of both l'Aiglon and Metternich. When approaching his century he could still sing Viennese folk songs and he kept up with old friends in Austria, among them a Count Clary.

[1] The contemporary euphemism for extramarital sex.

their drawing-rooms during a quarter of an hour where *nothing* but French or German is spoken [how many languages did she ever hear spoken in a London drawingroom?] and where the young ladies seldom appear . . . all to be over by 8 o'clock when it is supposed each has his private engagement, and this sort of thing lasts till near the Carnival, when gaiety begins. Then come on balls thick and threefold, and woe be to him who does not *Waltz*, for tho' there is a blaze of beauty and the balls are quite lovely to look at once or twice, yet no girl will speak to a man who does not dance, and (the men say) very little to those who do. They dance uninterruptedly . . . The young men of our Embassy give the *ton* to the English, and *they* are notorious for making no acquaintance with any young man who is not a Peer's son. . . . Why not descend a little into more rational, sociable society? I have tried and seen both tried, and I do assure you 'tis the same thing on a more disagreeable scale. . . . Without speaking French', she concluded hopefully, 'he could have no success.' Edward came all the same.

Woe to him who does not waltz!

For many, better times had come. Now, if ever, the Viennese were moving into an epoch when in place of the double eagle we may seem to see a fried chicken rampant: they have always believed in a *Backhendlzeit* while never quite knowing when it was. Martha was seeing the waltz era in its early stages when, a sophisticated refinement on the country dance, the *Ländler*, the waltz was sweeping the tedious old gavottes out of the ballrooms before the disapproving eyes of the dowagers. Now the Strauss dynasty was to hold sway over the hearts and minds of the young in a way for which there is no parallel even in our times. Vienna went mad.

In 1833 Heinrich Laube followed the crowd across the Ferdinand Bridge to Sperl's gardens which he called 'the key to the sensual life of Vienna'. He leant against a tree and watched the throng, seated at what seemed like hundreds of tables, and in spite of the talk and the laughter, the movement and the clink of glasses, there was an underlying tension as they waited with one eye on the central pavilion where their hero was to appear. Even among such an amalgam of nations as the population of Vienna, 'the Austrian Napoleon' seemed alien. Laube's journalese ran away with him as he described the father of the waltz dynasty in action, but it is vivid.

Biedermeier Man: an Introspective Society

'Appearance? African-hot-blooded, crazy with life and the heat of the sun, fidgeting restlessly, bold in his modernity, unattractively passionate. Strauss looks swarthy, his hair is kinky, his mouth melodious and enterprising, he has a snub nose. He conducts his dances with ecstasy. When the storm erupts his limbs are no longer his own. Bow and arm dance in unison, his feet mark the leaping rhythm. Now he is playing a potpourri and the audience greets every brief quotation with thunderous applause . . . this man holds a dangerous power in his hands.' Couples are streaming towards the dancing floor, each young man puts his arm round his girl and they wait, swaying gently while Strauss and his orchestra begin, very softly, one of those tremulous preludes, a long drawn-out sobbing of violins speaking of pain, of sensuality and nostalgia with all the lagoon-like shallowness of the Viennese character. Strauss knew to the very second how long he could keep his dancers in suspense—there comes a triumphant trill and they are off, swept away by that rhythm which no twentieth-century dance has yet driven from the ballrooms of Vienna.

'Vienna heals all wounds': Was this true, or was Laube just seeing Vienna through the usual sentimental haze?

He saw around him, or so he said, no excesses, no drunkenness; Austrian sensuality was not vulgar. Entertainment was business, but the all-pervading impression was of a sense of well-being which he found irresistible. 'Take a deep breath, open your heart, fling wide your arms, you will not do so in vain!' Laube's intoxication is endearing even when it fails to convince, his descriptions of the women, their clothing as fresh and crisp as their manner was free and unaffected, are a social document. He refused to believe that Vienna was a damped-down revolutionary volcano—'the people are as unvolcanic as they could possibly be . . .'—or if a volcano did exist, it was a stove for roasting, boiling and baking. He has quite fallen for the Metternich system of bread and circuses when he exclaims: 'How strange, how foolish did my past life seem to me, with all its learning and science, its theories and ceaseless thinking, and strivings after freedom. . . . Here is Greece, here is the classical world, the moment counts! Things are as they seem . . . and are there to be enjoyed. Here is the true joy on earth. Don your velvet jacket and white trews, go out on to the streets, kiss the girls and eat fried chicken—what concern of yours is the course of the world? Books ruin the belly, thoughts disturb one's sleep and one's career.'

Following on Laube's heels, Adolf Glassbrenner was less ecstatic but he confirmed Laube's view of Viennese women: plump, natural, warm-hearted, with a tremendous vitality, 'they leap rapturously into life as though they can hardly wait for death.' He was not greatly interested either in the lowest class nor the highest which he dismisses with a few generalizations: 'The Viennese aristocracy is utterly innocuous, it enjoys the advantages which the throne bestows, sits at home counting its ancestors, drives through life in its *équipage*, pays for its box at the court theatres and bothers its mind very little with politics, art or science.' Glassbrenner too watches the 'sea' of people in the Prater on Sundays, sitting about, smoking, drinking and flirting, but he is more interested in the coffee houses which the years of peace have evidently improved. They are now clean, elegant, comfortable, and quick and efficient waiters lay the tables with gleaming china and cutlery, although the thousands of inns in the inner and outer suburbs tend to be sleazy, the food offered usually goes little beyond *gulasch* or sausages. The best restaurants in Vienna are 'Der Wilde Mann', 'Erzherzog Karl' and 'Der Schwan', all in the Kärntnerstrasse and very expensive, but the food is superb. The standard of cooking in the private houses is highly professional, which he thinks may help to account for the blandness of the intellectual climate: 'All men become uninteresting as soon as their stomachs have no further wishes.'

Varnhagen von Ense is a more reliable witness than either Laube or Glassbrenner. Ever since he fought in the Austrian army at Aspern he had known Austrians of all classes, and he said himself that he knew Vienna too well to be deceived by superficialities. He noticed the change of mood among the intellectuals after 1830. He himself in 1834 was deeply depressed by the death of his wife Rahel, and yet Vienna cheered him. Seeing his old friends helped: the country house of Fanny Arnstein's sister, Baroness Eskeles, at Hietzing—the whole family and their circle cast a spell which came of a peculiarly fortunate marriage of Berlin with Vienna; and he called on several hostesses of the Congress. It is impossible not to believe him when he says that the whole look of the town and its surroundings possessed a richness, a pleasurable quality both sensual and gay. 'Somewhat like the old French courtesy and good style of living, the Austrian atmosphere of well-being at least has the merit that it points to that which people ought to offer and to bestow upon one another. The life of Vienna has the power to rejoice the heart.'

It also had the power to break it, as Franz Schubert knew, and his close friends the painter Moritz Schwind and the dramatist Eduard von Bauernfeld also. During the post-Congress years until the late twenties the three met almost daily, sometimes wandering about the streets at night, talking endlessly. Their headquarters was Neuner's coffee-house in the Plankengasse, and if one of them had any money in his pocket they might eat at an inn on the Brandstätte, a stone's throw from the cathedral. It would seldom be Schubert; no composer has been more disgracefully treated by his publishers than he, and as time went on the chief earner was Bauernfeld, whose plays, now quite forgotten, covered a span of half a century at the Burgtheater. The poet Nikolaus Lenau who was to end his life insane, Count Anton Alexander Auersperg, writing under the pseudonym Anastasius Grün, whose poems with the harmless-sounding title *Rambles of a Viennese Poet* were a cry for freedom of expression, the physician and poet Ernst von Feuchtersleben, and above all Franz Grillparzer: these men were a group of friends, trying out their work on each other. They were young, they were the Biedermeier era. On 29th March, 1827, Beethoven, of whom when he was 16 Mozart had said, 'Watch him, one day the world will be talking of him', was buried in Währing churchyard. This was no hole-and-corner funeral, as Mozart's was; Vienna came to do him honour. Schubert and Bauernfeld followed the coffin, the actor Heinrich Anschütz read the valediction (as he was a Protestant, outside the gates) written by Grillparzer who in latter years had been one of the few people whom Beethoven was glad to see. Afterwards Schubert drank 'to the one whom we have buried. And to the one who will follow him.' It was not until a year had passed almost to the day, that at Bauernfeld's insistence Schubert put on his first concert. There was a full house, each item brought tremendous applause and the composer was called for a number of times. The box office—800 gulden—was not to be despised. Nine months later Schubert was dead, the first of the species Biedermeier man to go.

What were the characteristics of this species?

Biedermeier Man: an Introspective Society

Seen as a middle-class culture, represented by a wide spectrum of the educated population, the usual image of impeccably-run households, of unruffled calm and serene self-righteousness is acceptable just as the image of a mindless, roistering, beer-swilling public is true also: both up to a point but, even taken together, only partially so.

It was suggested earlier that the complexities of the Biedermeier era begin to fall into a rough semblance of a recognizable pattern when it is realized that while the outward forms remain fairly constant throughout, intellectually and psychologically there is not one Biedermeier era, but two: the periods up to and after 1830, the apolitical era between the Congress and the French July Revolution; and a time of growing political awareness from 1830 to 1848. This second period, though of course fed from abroad, was only in part a change of direction; it was much more a logical development of the *status quo ante*, but it also contained elements which had survived with remarkable tenacity from the last period, in the time of the Josephine reforms, when creative thought was not only permitted but expected. In the history of the West, populations have been politically indoctrinated, they have been forced or urged to voice opinions which they did not hold, but it has been rare indeed for rulers to discourage—to use no stronger term—interest in politics in any form. The rules of a literary group, the *Ludlamshöhle*, expressly forbade political discussion, and Grillparzer's *Bildungsgesellschaft*, a society for the advancement of learning founded in 1808, banned religion as well, in both cases not so as to avoid friction between members, but because otherwise they would not have been allowed to meet. Yet Grillparzer has been called one of the most mature political minds of his time.

It was Metternich's most basic misconception that a population can be educated and raised to a higher level of culture and civilization, while politics are excluded from the curriculum; here he differed from Franz I whose understanding even of the benefits of learning was minimal. Metternich believed in this tenet all his life, not solely in the sense of the dreaded sequence whereby all preoccupation with politics led to revolution—he was convinced that *Ruhe*, repose, is not merely essential for the security of the crown and the whole body politic and therefore the first duty of every citizen, but is synonymous with contentment and even with happiness in the individual. This conviction was fundamental to his own character: he needed smooth-running domesticity, while the effect on his working capacity if his current emotional relationship was disturbed became all too evident during the autumn of 1814. This longing for peace of mind, the belief that inward serenity is an essential point of departure and, for the majority of mankind, sufficient in itself, formed a large part of the philosophical basis of the 'System'. And the mood of the times came half-way to meet it. For many people now approaching middle age, to crawl thankfully back into the womb from whence they came was their most powerful if unconscious desire, so severe was the buffeting to which they had been subjected. To live from day to day, postponing all momentous decisions, in fact abjuring 'greatness' in all things; a profound dislike of *action* was inherent in Franz I, in the whole of the public administration, it was an aspect of Metternich's own character and now it spread through society. It took a variety of forms.

Lack of interest in public affairs, the lack of any sense of personal involvement (Grillparzer once said he believed that Bauernfeld never read a political newspaper until he was 30) was accompanied by a flight from reality, by quietism and by religious revivalism. In the plays of Raimund, the Viennese found themselves in an ideal world: not until the reign of Nestroy in the thirties were they confronted by a realism in which they were forced, though without bitterness, to face the worst sides of their character. There was a craze for trashy novels about the days of chivalry, robber barons and maidens in distress, often with a touch of the supernatural thrown in, and for the more educated public there were novels of a similar type but of higher quality. In the middle-class Biedermeier household the child came into his own, but it is sometimes not so much the individual that we see, as an idealized vision of childhood: Biedermeier man's nostalgia for his lost innocence. Very slowly, nature was being discovered, but generally speaking it was still a domesticated nature. It is not until 1831 that, as the climax of a walking tour through Heiligenkreuz, Lilienfeld, up through the mountains of Lower Austria to Mariazell and on to Aussee and Bad Ischl, Schubert's old friends were to be found in fog and rain struggling up the slopes of the Hochschwab, where Grillparzer, convinced of the imminence of death, was frequently heard to moan 'Mercy on us! Jesus! My end is nigh!' and other pious ejaculations. Caroline Pichler was convinced that, as this scene symbolizes, mankind needed a shield to protect it from raw reality, and she saw religion as this shield. This is not as natural as it may seem. Frau Pichler, the best-selling novelist whose collected works Heinrich Laube found selling like fresh rolls at Herr Gerold's bookshop on the Stephansplatz in competition with Bonaparte's newly-arrived *Letters to Joséphine*, a Burgtheater playwright through whose unassuming salon beyond the Glacis blew every intellectual breeze from northern Europe, need not necessarily have turned to religion seen not as revelation but as a breast-plate.

It is one of the curiosities of that epoch that the Redemptorist father Clemens Maria Hofbauer, who initiated a strong and enduring current of religious renewal in Austria and was canonized by the Catholic Church, was regarded with distaste and mistrust by the Emperor whose interests (law and order, distraction from social evils) religion might be supposed to serve. This was not his view of the matter. Religious enthusiasm was scarcely more desirable than the political variety; all emotions in excess of official requirements were as reprehensible as they were baffling, and in a word, they alarmed him. The Archbishop of Vienna, Cardinal Josef Othmar Rauscher, used to tell the story of an audience at which his mother told the Emperor that young Othmar, instead of pursuing his legal studies as his parents wished, was fired with the desire to become a priest. 'Good woman,' was the instant reply, 'if you agree I will have the matter investigated by the police.'

Franz I looked upon the clergy as a body of men closely resembling a branch of the civil service. But the fact that they themselves had long since begun to think and act like civil servants was due much less to the Emperor's policy or to that of Metternich whose attitude towards the Church was equally utilitarian, than to the clerical reforms of Joseph II, the effects of which were in some ways the reverse of what had been intended. The dissolution of monasteries and convents not belonging to 'active' orders engaged in teaching or the care of the sick was intended as a measure of rationalization, a pruning operation which would enliven the whole Church in Austria. Great numbers of communities in which religious were living out their lives in a gentle, harmless manner were dispersed, and a few were certainly no loss to the community. But while discipline varied, it has never been alleged that in general the Austrian monasteries, still less the convents, were sinks of iniquity. Yet leaving aside the spiritual impoverishment caused by the loss of the contemplative orders, the intellectual trend of the reign of Joseph II was unfavourable to the religious life, and slowly the heart went out of the monasteries. Members of a teaching order in Vienna felt themselves to be nothing more than schoolmasters; they wore secular clothing, could go out as much as they liked and received women in their rooms. In effect, therefore, the last stage was worse than the first, and during the reign of Franz I the post-reform situation bore a distant resemblance to the pre-Reformation era.[1] Hofbauer's reputation in Bohemia as a saintly man preceded him to Vienna, but in the ears of Franz Hager's successor, Count Sedlnitzky, the message had a different ring. 'The Apostle of Vienna', as his followers called him, was watched as carefully as any agent of a foreign power, and he appears in the archives as 'an exceptionally dangerous person', an 'erring priest' whose 'machinations and proselytizing activities' called for strict and intensive surveillance. (Julie Zichy had been deeply influenced by the preaching of Clemens Maria Hofbauer. When Metternich, to distract his mind from Sagan, switched the formidable battery of his charm onto Julie and her heart responded she fell into an agony of remorse, and from this conflict she never entirely extracted herself. After her death the ashes of Metternich's letters together with a broken ring were sent to Metternich in a casket.)

The beginnings of the most significant, because most truly seminal, element in the intellectual life of the Biedermeier era also lay in the reign of Maria Theresa's son, which is to say in the age of the Enlightenment. The men and women who were young in the twenties carried in their hearts, just as older men such as Hammer-Purgstall did, a slightly idealized picture of that Emperor and his government. They had forgotten his mistakes such as the shaven-headed prostitutes and the way that aristocrats guilty of fornication were made to clean the streets. These things had turned people against him at the

[1]Professor Erika Weinzierl-Fischer, *Visitationsberichte Österreichischer Bischöfe an Kaiser Franz I (1804–1835)*.

time, but since his day too much had happened, and it represented an ideal of freedom of the press, of tolerance, freedom for the universities, against which the educated classes continually measured the 'System' and, finding it wanting, lapsed into resignation. What happened when idealism was constantly rebuffed by reality, when not creativity but renunciation was called for, Grillparzer described as flight into an inner world, a flight which could be infinitely enticing: 'He who has once enjoyed the sweetness of communion with his own self, will not return. Thus he lives in a world of his own making, ungainsaid, ordering all matters, thinking all thoughts according to self-made laws. So pleasant a rule leads to the last fountain-head of this evil: a need of powerful impressions ... having no vigour for deeds, yet full of thirst for action, full of relish for delight yet lacking the capacity for it, crammed full with thoughts yet with no willpower; this is the situation of such a person ...'

A profound conflict between his ideals and reality, humble resignation, a wistful longing for great deeds, followed by renunciation; a turning towards domesticity, nature and the simple life; flight into fancy or introspection: this is bourgeois, early Biedermeier man in Vienna—and not only there but over a far wider field within the Habsburg Empire. That a foreigner should have decided that the Viennese were in the highest degree unrevolutionary is not surprising. When driven beyond endurance the poor may riot, they do not initiate revolutions; Vienna's intelligentsia had withdrawn from a position of influence to one of impotence before the end of the eighteenth century. It was inevitable that, as a German historian noted in the 1840s, between 1815 and 1830 no one in Austria should have put up any real resistance to the 'System'. If even one man of intellectual distinction had voiced a protest, circumstances might, he thought, have been very different.[1]

Why did no one do so? Absolute, unconditional, unquestioning loyalty to the crown was such a striking characteristic of most sectors of the Viennese population that it might almost be diagnosed as an essential ingredient in its self-assessment as a group and as a psychological need in individuals. Criticism of the monarch of a kind so common in England during the Georgian era was scarcely ever

---

[1] A. Wiesner, *Denkwürdigkeiten der österr. Zensur vom Zeitalter der Reformation bis auf die Gegenwart*, Stuttgart, 1847.

heard; it was channelled off into criticism of almost any other person or institution. If the Emperor could not afford to be criticized because he personified the state, so the population had no concept to fit the state other than the person of the Emperor. In both Archduke Karl and in his brother Johann we seem to see veneration for the sovereign colliding, sometimes with considerable violence, with rational considerations or, alternatively, with idealism of an entirely different description. The gallant fiasco of the Alpenbund conspiracy, Archduke Johann's endless patience and self-abnegation while he waited, for years on end, for the Emperor to give the permission to marry which he had once given in writing and then rescinded verbally, add up to a portrait of Biedermeier man which gains in truth the closer one scrutinizes the details.

The Emperor Franz's irrationally suspicious nature occasionally gave birth, as was really to be expected, to bouncingly tangible offspring, but he was to be spared the discovery—it was reserved for posterity—that Archduke Johann had all the time been involved in the monarch's favourite nightmare.

Enough has been said about the tedious struggle which all clubs and societies, however innocuous and open to inspection, had to wage with the *Polizeihofstelle*. An élite order of knighthood, *Zur Blauen Erde*, with its headquarters at Seebenstein castle in the Pitten valley was no exception. It had many highly placed members, and in 1811 the Emperor visited Seebenstein himself, announced himself as satisfied, and with Archduke Johann as its Grand Master —he joined in 1813—it began to seem as though if not both, then at least either he or the society, would acquire enhanced respectability from the association. During the Congress of Vienna, however, several personages joined, including Prince Wilhelm of Prussia, the Grand Duke Karl Auguste of Weimar and the future King of the Belgians, Leopold of Saxe-Coburg. Franz I became restive. The one thing that he disliked about the Congress was that it brought a great number of men into Vienna who were either suspected or known to be Freemasons—Prince Hardenberg, for example, and Freiherr vom Stein—and now he got it into his head that the Knights of the Blue Earth might be Freemasons in disguise. In 1820 he closed it down. The Emperor's irrational fears had a way of turning out to be remarkably well-founded.

Biedermeier Man: an Introspective Society

With the same all-but unanimity with which, during the Reformation, for a time nearly all the leading families of the Austrian aristocracy became Protestant, in the late eighteenth century they flocked into the masonic lodges. They were joined by not a few senior members of the Catholic Church hierarchy, who for the most part were noblemen; for example, the Bishop of Gurk Count Salm, the Prebendary of Salzburg and Passau Count Spaur, Prince-Bishop Johann-Baptist Count Auersperg, and Abbot Urban Hauer of Melk: without the acquiescence of these and other influential men Joseph II's church reforms could hardly have been carried through. Freemasonry was not merely a secret society for members of the upper classes who liked to dabble in such things, but one of the main pillars of the Enlightenment. In Austria where it was introduced by Maria Theresa's husband Francis of Lorraine, such men as the scientist and physician van Swieten, and Freiherr von Sonnenfels who achieved the abolition of judicial torture and compulsory labour were masons. It was easier to outlaw Freemasonry than to eradicate it, since a former mason might swear, as every civil servant had to do, that he belonged to no secret society, and yet, as the years went on, he was carrying the old philosophy, the old ideals, into the nineteenth century and forming a link with early liberalism. That there was no question of it having been eradicated root and branch can be seen from Caroline Pichler's entry (her father was a mason): 'The Order of Freemasons is going about its business with almost ridiculous openness. Masonic songs are printed and sung. It is however not disadvantageous to belong to this brotherhood which knows how to draw supervisors, chairmen, governors everywhere unto itself.'

Franz I must have seen or known of the letter which Marie Antoinette wrote to her brother the Emperor Leopold in August 1790, the year of his succession: 'Beware of all Masonic associations, you will surely have been warned, it is in this manner that the scoundrels think to achieve their goal in every country; may God preserve my Fatherland and Yourself from a like misfortune!' As the years passed, imperial displeasure was heavily reinforced by pressure on the part of the Church, and a time was to come when no practising Catholic in Austria was to find it easy either in practice or in conscience to be a Freemason. For Archduke Johann the conflict with the Church was not yet acute, but what of his position *vis-à-vis* the Emperor? It was always the opinion of Franz Hager that it was in 1815, when the Archduke was in England to acquire industrial know-how, that he came into contact with Freemasonry and as a result brought back a burning enthusiasm not only for technology but also for the ideals of the brotherhood. It is a justifiable assumption that Archduke Johann, coming from a country where Freemasonry had gone underground, must have enjoyed what amounted to a refresher course in England where it had flourished unhindered since the foundation of the first lodge in 1717.

In 1818 three intercepts were laid before the Emperor. They were in a cipher which the censorship was unable to break,[1] but surrounding evidence showed beyond doubt that Freemasonry lived on and that no less a person than the Chancellor of State Count Saurau played a leading part in it. Archduke Johann's closest confidants were his secretary and bailiff Johann Zahlbruckner and the foundry owner Vinzenz Huber; one of his very few intimate friends among the nobility was Count Saurau who spent as much time as possible on his estates in Styria. The connection is unlikely to have been overlooked, but the Chancellor of State was an adept at covering his tracks (his policy towards early liberalism in Bohemia was repressive), the cipher remained intact and there for the time being the matter had to rest. However, the existence of the three intercepts was not forgotten and various unsuccessful attempts were made to break it. Nearly 30 years after their discovery, when the Emperor Franz Joseph had been on the throne for nine years, the Freemasonry question was raised by the Vatican in connection with the Concordat which was finally signed on 23rd November, 1857, and now the Minister of Police, Kempen, shut himself up with the unsolved riddle and at last broke the cipher. The authorities were appalled at what they found. Freemasonry, banned for so many years, was not extinguished but lived merrily on, not in a formal sense but in spirit, and this in spite of the compulsory oath taken by nearly every man in public life. Worst of all—Franz was spared the knowledge—Archduke Johann emerged as the patron and protector of Freemasonry during the 1820s. What was the imperial title, All-Highest, beside the one which the Emperor's most

[1] See p. 144.

august subjects had bestowed upon Archduke Johann: *'der Aller-heiligste'*, the All-Holiest? This then was the true standing in the minds of some of his contemporaries of the prince whose attitude towards the central government had been demonstrably equivocal, yet whose submissiveness towards his elder brother as his sovereign, his feudal lord (he always referred to Franz I and even to Ferdinand in these terms) was unconditional.

When the cipher was broken and the implicating letters were read Archduke Johann was 75. Some 18 months later, on 11th May, 1859, he died in his town house in Graz. During most of his life he had lived in a state of mental conflict arising from his attitude towards his elder brother who personified authority, the law of the land, and, in a mystical union, the lands and peoples of the monarchy. Discordance arose where the interests of these personae appeared to clash. In his unostentatious way of life Archduke Johann was the typical Biedermeier man, but far more significant than this was the swing of the pendulum between action and resignation. In the case of Archduke Karl the picture is strikingly similar: the man of action, repeatedly hampered and frustrated by the framework within which he must organize this activity and, in consequence, alternating between powerful bursts of energy and doubt-ridden lethargy. In him a characteristic recurred which was typically Austrian: a lack of ruthlessness in following up an advantage, a tendency to throw in his hand, to be content with small results, difficulty in maintaining a sustained effort. The pure Biedermeier element in both men was the moral-philosophical scruple over the onus attached to deeds.

The events of July 1830 in Paris set fire to a fuse in Vienna which lay at some distance from the powder-barrel. Few visitors noticed the difference, but a Superintendent of Police, Baron Waldstätten, who had only recently been describing the Viennese as phlegmatic ('this most treasured characteristic of the nation'), childlike in mind with a 'lively feeling for obedience and subordination', was now talking of a prevalent mood which he defined as irritable and unpropitious. Metternich himself took time to recover from the shock: 'My most secret thought', he wrote to Nesselrode after a meeting with him in Karlsbad, 'is that the old Europe stands at the beginning of the end. Determined to perish with it, I shall know how to do my duty. The new Europe, on the other hand, has not reached its beginnings. Between the end and the beginning there will be chaos . . .' But in the meantime, an event took place which for a short time caused the hearts of the intelligentsia to lift. On 2nd March, 1835, after a short illness, Franz I died.

Those who thought that the death of the Emperor might be followed by a relaxation of the grip in which officialdom held the intellectual life of the monarchy were soon disillusioned. In his will, the Emperor had left his subjects his affectionate regards but nothing more. If anything, it seemed that the machinery of government would be more rigid than ever. The booksellers of Vienna, however, thought it worthwhile making an attempt to put a toe in the door in the hope that the late Emperor's over-sensitivity on the score of the sovereign's prerogative—only administrative matters might be called in question, matters of principle never—had gone to the grave with him. They were hoping to bring about the repeal of the censorship edict of 14th September, 1810, which, as its date shows, was part of the machinery created to stamp on the popular patriotic movement of 1809, and marks the official end of the booksellers' boom during the French occupation when there was a rush to fill the home shelves with all the standard authors such as Goethe, Schiller and Kleist. It was a most odd document, notorious for the elevated tones with which it begins and the chill that follows!: 'No ray of light, from whatever source in the monarchy it may spring shall remain unremarked and unrecognized, nor hindered in its potential usefulness and effectivity'; Now came the but: 'but heart and head of immature persons must be preserved with cautious hand from the corrupting products of a depraved imagination, from the poisonous breath of self-seeking seducers, and from the danger-ous phantoms of perverted minds.' Was this purple passage the loosening of their intellectual fetters which the peoples of the mon-archy had been promised after the Peace of Pressburg?

By contrast, one of the principal landmarks in the reign of Franz I lies in the sphere of legislation. Only months later, on 1st June, 1811, after half a century of revision and recodification, the Imperial *placet* was given to the *Allgemeines bürgerliches Gesetzbuch*, the Aus-trian statute book which, influenced in its latter stages of growth by the Kantian philosophy of natural rights, was an intellectual triumph of the highest order. In its statement on the rights of the individual it carries forward the ideas of the Enlightenment. On the status of women it was in some vital respects 60 years ahead even of British legislation, and there is a case for saying that even if most contemporaries were unaware of the fact, the 'A.B.G.B.' was a cohesive factor in the relationship between the peoples of the monarchy and their government as well as among themselves. It immediately became valid throughout the Empire.

As the restiveness of the educated classes of the population under the weight of censorship grew, so the need for it increased. Postal censorship was still in full swing, and at the beginning of the thirties it was still possible to keep a firm grip on the mails entering and leaving Vienna, as a letter from Gentz written shortly before his death to Baron Wessenberg, who was in England at the time, clearly shows: 'You must realize that the mistrust towards one and all, the espionage against one's own confidants and the opening of all letters without exception has here reached heights for which there can scarcely be a parallel in all history; thus, for example, I should never have dared to write you a letter such as the present one via one of our couriers . . . every other channel (other than the British courier) is unsafe, even Rothschild's.' It was a different matter altogether to control the movement of information and comment in Galicia, Lombardy or the Kingdom of Naples. As early as 1823 Metternich was feeling the shortage of intelligence from this source, and as general mobility increased so did his difficulties. The intake of registered letters during the heyday after the Congress was about a thousand a day, but it was gradually reduced to a mere trickle, and by the end of the Metternich era was less than a tenth of the peak number.[1]

Count Josef Sedlnitzky became Vice-president of the Police and Censorship Department at the end of 1815 and succeeded Baron Franz Hager as President in May 1817. The story goes that he was sent to Vienna from Galicia to report on a charge of neglecting his duties, but the Emperor liked him so much that he kept him. True or not, from then until 1848 Sedlnitzky becomes the villain of the piece in a way that Hager never was. While Hager is not known at all today except to specialists, every reasonably well-read Austrian has

[1] Josef Karl Mayr, *Metternichs Geheimer Briefdienst, Postlogen und Postkurse,* Vienna, 1935.

heard of 'Metternich's poodle'. He is a curiously colourless figure, a wizened, lantern-jawed man whose reputation has come down in such a form that a mention of his wife's presence at a tea-party in memoirs of that time at once casts a chill over the proceedings, and it is highly probable that the poor woman did have this effect. Yet two historians[1] have believed that he was better than his reputation, and he is said to have possessed a pleasant, slightly urbane manner, and to have been slow and over-punctilious in his work. Both Franz I and Metternich liked to use Sedlnitzky as a scapegoat, hinting or saying straight out that he was a man whose over-enthusiastic devotion to what he supposed to be his duty they could do nothing to quench. But then neither would have dreamed of calling Sedlnitzky to heel, while he was convinced that he was carrying out both his sovereign's explicit instructions and his implied intentions. In this he was quite right. Baron Hormayr called him 'Metternich's ape', Hammer von Purgstall 'the dust on Metternich's shoes', Grillparzer 'that miserable Police President', and Heinrich von Srbik went so far as to hold him responsible in large measure for the public's hatred of Metternich. Srbik's bitter antagonist, Viktor Bibl, disagreed and said of Sedlnitzky that he was at heart a benevolent character 'who secretly may often' (a phrase more becoming to a historical novelist than to a scholar) 'have rebelled against the hardships and the foolishness of censorship which were laid exclusively at his door.' Well-disposed he may have been, but he assented to the system of priorities laid down by the régime, and these rested on the principle that any inconvenience to individuals—and this might be considerable—must be endured without complaint where the state's interests were involved. It was the sheer impossibility of saying where these interests began and ended which prevented educated, humane civil servants from making up their own minds and made them, while they served this self-perpetuating, self-justifying apparatus, more cowed, more timorous by far than those members of the public into whose lives they brought bitterness.

Taken over a period of half a century, the inland postal censorship was staggeringly unproductive. It invented a few conspiracies, but where plots did exist it failed to uncover them. The rest was tittle-tattle and file-pushing. Censorship of books was not unlike the atti-

[1] Viktor Bibl and Julius Marx.

tude of twentieth-century British justice towards obscenity in the pre-Lady Chatterley era: if it's expensive enough you can have it. Metternich answered a query about a book held up in transit thus: 'Forbidden, yes, to the extent that it may not be publicly advertized and offered for sale; not, however, to readers to whom no detriment is to be feared. The Austrian censorship has a regard for persons.' Leather-bound volumes of Goethe, Schiller and so on were less dangerous than cheap editions, collected works were better still. These would receive an ungrudging *admittitur*. Conditional categories in tortured Latin followed: *transeat, erga schedam conced.*, and at last *damnatur*. Among this last lamentable group vast quantities of light romances, stories of knightly chivalry and haunted castles were withheld from their public. That political pamphlets of a radical nature were *verboten* goes without saying, and in 1847 *Punch* was confiscated because of its caricatures. It was never easy to subscribe to foreign newspapers as personal application had to be made for permission to do so, whereupon the subscriber's name was placed on a list held by Censorship Chancery. On the whole, the Censorship preferred to avoid sensational measures such as confiscation of foreign papers which were critical of Austrian foreign policy or internal affairs, and it was better to allow a subscription to lapse and then to turn a deaf ear to requests for a renewal. In spite of the lively demand for foreign papers, as political awareness and unrest grew, by 1848 their number had actually sunk.

The censors' daily task did at least bring variety. Inscriptions for gravestones, memorial cards, badges, cuff-links and tobacco boxes —all had to be scrutinized in the light of some possible hint of a secret society. Not even goods in transit were immune, but here a censor might burn his fingers. A consignment of china boxes en route from France to Trieste, on the lids of which the word *Liberté* was painted, was impounded and the offending word erased. Not surprisingly, the furious buyer refused to take delivery of the goods and sent in a protest and a demand for damages through the French Ambassador. The claim was successful, and compensation was paid.

The theory has been put forward in recent years[1] that in this field we depend too much on hearsay, since contemporaries told what they had heard at second or third hand, and writers on the period

[1] By Julius Marx.

have been copying each other's reports ever since. If, the argument runs, publishers' actual output is compared with the number of manuscripts by home authors which were rejected or sent back for revision (they were never confiscated), the first group is overpoweringly the larger. If Austria (to use the term coined by the Frankfurt man of letters Ludwig Börne) had really been surrounded by a 'Great Wall of China', private libraries would not have been as well equipped as they very commonly were, and Grillparzer would not have seen a cab-driver on his box deeply engrossed in a banned pamphlet as he waited for a fare. Scientific periodicals and works of scholarship, on the other hand, were withheld if Count Sedlnitzky looked upon the addressee as a 'political' professor; here too he was acting in perfect obedience to the intentions of Franz I and of Metternich, who, to be doubly sure, had a separate censorship department of his own in the Chancellery; this is the salient factor in Metternich's personal responsibility for the intellectual climate of the capital. Where intercepts were concerned, the material handled was evidently not always on the ministerial level. Martha Bradford wrote home: 'The Police of Vienna equals that of Paris. . . . Think of the Prime Minister, Prince Metternich, amusing a few selected friends the other evening with *every thing* that passed in the interiour of a family of English travellers, more remarkable for their wealth than their refinement, and who little imagined that all their proceedings were reported to such a man and discussed in such a circle! He was off his guard probably at the time he let the cat out of the bag for a little fun, but I suppose we never cough, sneeze nor turn a child into the Nursery to blow its nose without the events being reported to the Government!'

Thousands of people were only acutely aware of censorship and of the presence of informers in the context of the theatre. The regulations were strict, and, given the circumstances, not always unreasonable. Five theatres were open all the year round. The Hofburgtheater and Kärntnertorheater staged grand and comic opera, tragedies and comedies. The Theater an der Wien went in largely for romantic farces and 'magic'; all three had ballet as well. The two smaller theatres in the Josefstadt and Leopoldstadt districts presented popular entertainment, chansons, burlesques, folk comedy and so on. The Imperial theatres were subsidized out of the privy purse, and it is not to be expected that any monarch of the time would willingly have paid large sums out of his own pocket to watch, say, *Richard II*. Other European sovereigns were no less touchy than the Habsburgs in their lack of enjoyment of Shakespearean royal tragedy, but here the operative word was *staatsschädlich*: nothing was allowed that could be interpreted as damaging to the interests of the state. Not only *Richard II* and *Richard III*, but *Hamlet, Macbeth, King John* and *Henry VI* were held at bay for years in order not to accustom the public to unhealthy thoughts of the murder and deposition of kings. *King Lear* would give the audience the idea that a king, if he were too unhappy, might go off his head, while Schiller's *Maria Stuart* put one in mind of Marie Antoinette who lost hers altogether. German standard works such as *Egmont, Wilhelm Tell, Wallenstein* involved rebellion and military insurrection; *The Merchant of Venice* might create a 'hepp-hepp tumult', an outbreak of antisemitism.

This was the official policy, this was the trend against which directors and producers had to fight, but to conclude that therefore none of these plays were performed would be to fall into a trap in company with a number of writers on that period. Austria was an autocracy tempered by inconsistency: on 28th March, 1822, Heinrich Anschütz played his first great tragic role on the stage of the Hofburgtheater—as Lear. He also played Shylock and in his memoirs, describes another actor's performance of Macbeth. These victories, and the high standards of the Burgtheater during the Biedermeier era, were very largely the achievement of the Director,[1] Joseph Schreyvogel, who with great patience raised the taste of the audiences and dispelled some of the fears of the censors.

But it was in its role as guardian of religion and public morals that the paternal state shows itself at its most remote from the actual atmosphere of the theatres in the Josefstadt, Leopoldstadt and on the banks of the Wien, whose audiences for the most part did not consist of pop-eyed virgins. Some of these regulations were wholly baffling, such as the one which reserved the name of God for sole use in the imperial theatres, leaving 'Heaven' for those beyond the Glacis. The Devil—this of course has always been the case the world over—was cut down to size with a nickname. But suicide and

---

[1] Actually *Sekretär*, but the title is misleading.

adultery were banned altogether. Stage directions were watched for innuendo, and regardless of circumstances the juvenile leads were never permitted to leave the stage together. No tripping off hand-in-hand, but boy off right, girl off left, and they might not, even for a minute, find themselves accidentally locked in a room together. Unquenchable optimist that he was, the poet and playwright I. F. Castelli submitted a manuscript which contained the statement: 'She possesses a white, voluptuous bosom.' This was scaled down to: 'She is very well built in front.' Nestroy fought with the censors all his life, and we find him still at it in 1851:

> Stage directions: *Jennifer is sitting on a rock in a cave in the woods. Her young, slim body is covered over and over with fresh green leaves which supply her sole drapery.*
> N: Ah, now look at that—fresh green leaves! *(pause)*
> This is a play I'll come and watch in the autumn.

Passage blue-pencilled.

The general atmosphere favoured by the authorities was one of cheerful *Kraft durch Freude*; world-weariness and all pessimism were undesirable. For fear of nationalism, even nationality as an appellation was forbidden. Thus: no mention of Italian singers, Spanish dancers, Slovakian or Hungarian thoroughbreds was admissible, not even English horse-breeding. The peoples of the Habsburg monarchy—and this was perhaps the greatest sin among a great deal of nonsense—were presented exclusively on the level of folk-lore.

The principles never changed, but here and there laxity crept in, and there were signs—a well-known prelude to judicial reform—that the machinery was not working as it should; the censors were becoming inclined to turn a blind eye. One cannot, either, be quite sure whether or not Nestroy spoke those lines. At every first night of his 83 plays a police agent was certainly in the house. But were his eyes glued to the text? With the greatest comedian in Europe before him, with the house crackling with tension, is it not more likely that he would keep glancing at the stage, would gradually forget to follow the script, and—had the wretched man spoken this word or that, or had he not? And what proof was there? At subsequent performances Nestroy often smuggled censored lines back into the play. He had—where the theatre was concerned—a highly sophisticated audience before him, able to interpret an almost imperceptible pause, or the discrepancy between the spoken word and facial expression. In the Hofburg and Kärntnertor theatres a well-read audience sometimes noticed a different discrepancy: between the actors' words and the text which stood on the shelves at home. Nestroy offered his audiences a further delight for which they may be envied. Hardly had polite society found the opportunity to see the latest straight play on the stage of the Hofburgtheater (it was likely to be one of those pieces based on classical mythology which German literature has so heavily overworked) but they could already go across to the Theater an der Wien and see a devastating parody in which the whole sublime paraphernalia was brought smartly down to the level of Viennese lower-middle class *mores*. Nestroy was an exceptionally hard and rapid worker and never sat about in coffee houses. And as though this were not insult enough, the box office frequently gave the victory to the parody over the original. The première of *Der Zerrissene* on 9th April, 1844, presented Nestroy's version of *L'homme blasé* by Duvert and Lauzanne. It ran for 50 performances and has had its modern revival, whereas Kupelwieser's translation at the Josefstadt theatre was a flop.

Throughout his long life on the stage, Nestroy was forever in trouble for extemporizing, which was strictly against the regulations. The actor-playwright Ferdinand Raimund thrashed his mistress, the actress Thérèse Grünthal (the chronicle reports that two strokes with a cane or stick were administered on the staircase up to the boxes in the Leopoldstädter Theater), for refusing to name the man with whom he had seen her sitting in the stalls. Repenting of this unseemly outburst of jealousy, Raimund made a public apology from the stage which is believed to have been well received by the audience. But not by the police, who were so humourless as to sentence him to three days *in irons*, including one day's fast, for 'wilfully transgressing the prohibition against extemporizing on the stage'. The severity of the sentence, the court hoped, would act as a deterrent. The courts were at least consistent. In the autumn of 1835, Nestroy, driven frantic by the ignorant and impertinent comments of a young critic called Franz Wiest who had been troubling him for weeks like a swarm of gnats, hit back from the stage in an uncensored couplet. The result was again three days, though there is no mention of irons. Nestroy appealed but was overruled and sat out his time during the following January, plus two days, presumably a suspended sentence. The experience upset him to such an extent that on leaving the lock-up he went straight to Pressburg, declaring that he would never return, but he allowed himself to be persuaded by an emissary from his director and slave-driver, the actor-manager Karl Carl.

These incidents show Raimund and Nestroy in conflict with the authorities, but they do not capture the essence of Nestroy's personal situation. Nestroy fought against the Metternich system much as a farmer struggles as a matter of course against the elements, but his real battle to the death was with his audience. Leaving Franz Grillparzer aside for the moment, all the playwrights of the time, Eduard von Bauernfeld, A. Bäuerle, Ferdinand Raimund, and the literary maid-of-all-work Ignaz Franz Castelli ('Just live! suffer! but live!') were essentially conformists. They disliked the police state but they nestled in its downy warmth like chicks under a broody hen. As professionals they were concerned with the reactions of their audiences, writing to please them, measuring their applause.

No one could have been closer to his audience than Nestroy. Of Shakespearean virtuosity in his use of the vernacular, an artist in words as weapons of satire, he bit into his audiences' self-esteem as no playwright had dared to do before him. The Viennese, a living critic has said, are a race of character actors who like to drop in to the theatre to see what sort of a job their less talented colleagues are making of it. What Nestroy handed to them was a picture by no means in accordance with the stereotype reflection to which they had accustomed themselves from time immemorial. It was a bitter wit, a searing satire which poured across the footlights, and it was not just the easy targets—the philistine bourgeois—whom he turned inside out. In *Zu ebener Erde und im ersten Stock (Ground Floor, First Floor)* (1835), an ambitious construction in which the action takes place on two levels, the ground and first floors of the title, with very effective correlation between the two, it soon turns out that the members of the poor, simple family below are every bit as corroded as the people upstairs. In *Lumpazivagabundus* (1833), a story which has become a classic of three wandering journeymen who come into money, Nestroy not only proclaims his rejection of the Biedermeier ideal of sober domesticity, he protests against the rules of good behaviour, law and order and conformity.

There is bound to be a particular tension in the house when an actor, and one of Nestroy's calibre, is the author of every word he speaks and for that matter of the whole play (Nestroy wrote big parts for his lifelong friend Wenzel Scholz and also for Karl Carl). Nestroy's performance might be punctuated by bursts of applause, he might have a score of curtain calls, but he and the rest of the cast frequently had to act through a tumult of hissing, catcalls and stamping, of such proportions that some who were present were amazed at their being able to carry on at all. His plays lack all sentimentality, and if he produces the stock figures—wise old men, virtuous, loving daughters—by the second act he will have turned them inside out. He had no illusions about human nature in general or about the Viennese in particular, and his wit is as fresh as ever, both facts which explain the extent of the Nestroy revival since the last war. His technique for getting past the censor with so much desstructive criticism of contemporary conventions has been compared with the way in which the Strauss family brought their waltzes to a close.[1] A waltz essentially has no end and ought to go on for ever, but as end it must, this is brought about by some unrelated device. The result is stilted banality. In this analogy Nestroy's happy ends are equally forced. Family life, authority and the rights of property are reinstated, filial obedience, duty, modesty, hard work, honesty and sobriety carry the day, and all join hands for the final chorus in which these virtues are extolled and, above all, declared to reign supreme right there in the capital of the happiest of all monarchies. It would all hardly convince a child, let alone these audiences, but the conventions had been observed.

Johann Nestroy, 'creator of the tragic farce',[2] had his part to play in 1848 and the years which followed. He died in 1862, and as his hearse moved in a procession along a route which took one and a half hours to cover, the people of Vienna lined the streets in

[1] Hans Weigel, *Flucht vor der Grösse.*
[2] Rio Preisner, *J. N. Nestroy—der Schöpfer der tragischen Posse.*

unbroken ranks all the way to the graveside where his coffin came to rest not far from the graves of Beethoven and Schubert.

Franz Grillparzer met Katharina Fröhlich in the house of the banker J. H. von Geymüller during the winter of 1820–21. They soon fell in love, and became engaged. He was then 30, she was 20. Shortly after his eightieth birthday he asked her to come to St. Stephen's Cathedral at six in the morning in order that they might be married. The old lady's indignant comment, through a flood of tears, was: 'That would be to imprint a stamp of vulgarity on the sacrifice of a long lifetime. I am not some aulic councillor's old cook.'[1] It was probably the longest engagement on record.

'Grillparzer,' Byron noted in his diary in 1821, 'a devil of a name, to be sure, for posterity, but they *must* learn to pronounce it.' Theatregoers in Vienna already knew his name owing to the sensational success of *Die Ahnfrau (The Ancestress)* in 1817, followed by *Sappho* which Byron had read in translation. He himself hated it, and as a young man he still reddened and stuttered when addressed by name.

Katharina was the third of four gifted sisters. Anna, the eldest, taught singing, Barbara painted, and the youngest, Josefine, was a professional singer. Katharina wanted to go on the stage and it is very likely that she would have made a career, but Grillparzer forbade it. Kathi was the most lively of the four sisters, a dark-eyed girl whose good looks and gay, natural manner have been convincingly described. This was no passive young rosebud waiting to be married off but a person the force of whose emotional life can be guessed from her rapt absorption in music. 'She becomes drunk on music', Grillparzer wrote in 1822, 'as a tippler on wine. She is no longer her own master when she has been listening to good music.' Through his own powerful musicality this strand became the most enduring element in their relationship, and he said more than once that they were never closer to one another than when they were playing or discussing music.

By now Grillparzer had had other affairs, he had plunged into erotic experiences of an almost violently intoxicating description, and there is not the faintest trace of Ruskin in his gradually hardening determination not to go to bed with Kathi. He knew that he

[1] 'Ich bin keine alte Hofratsköchin.'

suffered from two disabilities which would kill any marriage: there was a lack of co-ordination between mind and body in which reality, the affections, and therefore the personality of the partner, were permanently at risk. '. . . That one should have to *wash* in front of one another!' The second disability is related to the first, or the consequence of it: exceptionally rapid satiation. Hardly had the woman yielded, and this might mean no more than the realization that the barriers were down, but the erotic tension sagged. The tragedy of Franz Grillparzer and Katharina Fröhlich is perhaps this, that she who was in many essential respects his equal would have been able to hold him. For it was not that he loved her too little, on the contrary it was his terror that sexual intercourse would bring his love for her to an end that caused him to place both himself and her in a situation of permanent stress.

It is possible, though not certain, that they did indulge in one experiment which misfired owing to his state of tension. Whether they did or no, the underlying factor was surely his mother whose suicide robbed him, in his middle 20s, of the warmth, the stillness, the undemanding companionship that he needed. And the music. Grillparzer's father was, almost to the degree of caricature, a cold, stern upholder of moral principles with a complete inability to show, if he felt it, any sign of affection, a man whose standards no boy could hope to attain, in whose eyes he could scarcely hope to see approval, still less to discern love. His mother had only one escape route: music, but her way of passing on this treasure to her son was rough and insensitive, and his natural musicality had to be considerable to have survived the early years of soulless practice. Yet for years they made music together, playing not only compositions for piano but all those adaptations for piano of operatic and orchestral music which were so popular at the time. The question of whether there was in Grillparzer's relationship with Kathi a tabu in connection with his mother must be asked, though it cannot be answered. But the classical Biedermeier spirit of withdrawal, encapsulation, self-denial and resignation is all too apparent.

Before long he had fitted himself up with not one *ersatz* mother but with four. Kathi, in the meantime, had many admirers, and escape from her neurotic playwright would have presented no difficulties. She did make one attempt to break away, and there was talk of an engagement to the bailiff of an estate in the country. But it was a half-hearted affair or the result of desperation, because on another occasion she said to a friend: 'Don't people realize that there is only one man in my life?' The dilemma was insoluble, as well she knew, and the strain wore her down until in 1830 she became seriously ill. It really, Grillparzer thought, might be the best thing if she died, because there was no way out. On the evening when the doctor told him that she might not outlive the night he paced the streets for hours, beside himself with agitation, and came at last to the Volksgarten where he threw himself down, sobbing, on the steps of the Temple of Theseus. She recovered, and everything went on as before. There were quarrels, and outbursts of jealousy on his part; in these matters there is no place for logic. During one of their reconciliations he drew Katharina on to his knee, and to console them both began to make a little gentle love to her, only to discover: 'All sensation is extinguished. I should so dearly love to rekindle it, but it is no use . . . she has faded. We have both grown older.'

He was not so blind as not to know what he had done to this once so gay, desirable and sensitive woman, in denying her sexual fulfilment and motherhood, exposing her to a lifetime of slights and innuendo, though he was certainly able to banish the thought from his mind for long periods of time; no one can live permanently with a load of guilt and it is usually possible to shift part of it on to the victim. She became nervy, suspicious and occasionally waspish, the whole basis of the relationship, renunciation of physical love for the sake of the things of the mind and soul, was threatened, and it was fortunate that her sisters were able to take some of the strain. Katharina knew what she had done and that her reckoning had not paid off: she had given him the one gift which she could not afford— time.[1] But ought she to have given in over her career? Grillparzer does not appear to have counted this among the deprivations which he in effect demanded of her. The actress Sofie Schröder, who once saw Kathi acting in an amateur performance, went up to her afterwards and said: 'Fräulein, if you don't become an actress you will be committing suicide.' But Grillparzer 'didn't like actresses', and that was enough.

[1] Heinz Politzer, *Grillparzer oder das abgründige Biedermeier.*

Biedermeier Man: an Introspective Society

When he was 56, Grillparzer and the Fröhlich sisters moved into a flat in the Spiegelgasse where they all lived together until, one after the other, they died. The writer Marie von Ebner-Eschenbach[1] who often visited them mentioned, although she loved and revered Grillparzer, a particular refinement of torture practised on Kathi; that he never singled her out in any way, but referred always to 'meine Damen', and 'the ladies with whom I live'. And in return they addressed him as 'Grillparzer'. Remembering his almost pathological rejection of his own surname, it is a minor curiosity to find them, in this memoir, cajoling him: 'Come, Grillparzer, eat up!' Perhaps this was all part of the self-punishment.

In his earlier years, when he was less often morose and sunk in melancholy, he was an artist at satire, and before it was closed down in 1826 he was a lively member of the club known as the *Ludlams-höhle* where, after the theatre, he and his friends would improvise parodies of the latest new play. His *Eight Critical Letters* dissect *König Ottokar's Glück und Ende*; there was the satire *The Magic Flute Part Two*, and a letter supposedly dashed off by a girl to her lover in which she tries to describe one of Grillparzer's tragedies. This is such an exquisite piece of deadpan wit that it suddenly seems to close the gap between the Burgtheater and the Theater an der Wien: perhaps Grillparzer could have been a most able assistant to Nestroy in some of those parodies of the deadly serious productions at the Court theatres.

If it were possible to ask Kathi Fröhlich whether her 'sacrifice of a long lifetime' had been worthwhile, her answer would have to include some assessment of Grillparzer's place in literature, whereupon too the question would arise: to what extent was he a victim of the Metternich régime?

Three out of the four vestal virgins lived to see Grillparzer hailed as the greatest living writer in the German language, they were inseparably part of the celebrations on his eightieth birthday when Vienna wore a path to his door to bring the nation's homage, when the Emperor Franz Joseph honoured him as no writer had been honoured in Austria before, not without reason as since Walter von der Vogelweide in the Middle Ages there had been none so great to

[1] Marie von Ebner-Eschenbach, *Meine Erinnerungen an Grillparzer.*

honour. But he hated every moment of it and sat at home muttering, 'Too late, too late.'

Austrian literature begins with Grillparzer, and he cannot have
been unaware of it. The explanation of his loss of nerve when he
went to call on Goethe and fled, sobbing, from the room, and also
of the sequel, the talk during which, in spite of Goethe's kindness,
little rapport was established, was not youthful shyness. It was a
mixture of rending desperation, not fully conscious resentment,
and a touch of patricidal fury which the genius of Weimar aroused
in him. Karl Kraus said of Grillparzer that he became a classic because the Austrians needed one of their own for the school books,
and also: 'One line from Nestroy's *Talisman* is worth more than the
whole of Grillparzer.' Egon Friedell and Hans Weigel are two more
Austrians who have dared to chip away at the memorial.

It is another Austrian phenomenon that a number of the leading
creative minds of mid-nineteenth-century Austria have not travelled
well or not at all: Ferdinand Raimund, Johann Nestroy, Franz
Grillparzer, Adalbert Stifter, and Anton Bruckner. The flow of
Grillparzer's dramatic verse sweeps along in the grand style, but
much is written between the lines, and perhaps it takes an Austrian
to hear this. Many theatre addicts in Vienna will admit today that
they can think of nothing more dreary than an evening watching a
Grillparzer tragedy, but in his own time this was anything but true.
His profound, almost extrasensory comprehension of the psychology of the Austrian monarchy, the Habsburg myth, added to his
grasp of politics which was apt to emerge in the guise of prophecy,
struck awe into the hearts of his more perceptive contemporaries.
He wrote hastily, grudgingly, and what he wrote was seldom his
thought put into words but an approximation; his ideal, a play
without words, taking place in the mind. His own most characteristic attitude transferred to the stage: the hero turns away with a
weary gesture of dismissal, the awaited words are left unspoken. If
Grillparzer never quite attained his full potential stature, if a veil
sometimes seems to fall between imagination and action, this is less
the result of his fear of Sedlnitzky than of his own words made
flesh. To lay bare one's soul in public, he believed, was as indecent as
to expose one's body. Unremarkable in itself, this feeling of embarrassment was a disadvantage to a dramatist who was setting out to

analyse the deeds, with their underlying motives, of historical characters and to reinterpret the figures of classical antiquity. And when all has been said about outside pressures, not forgetting inevitable self-censorship, for this reluctance to rip off the last mask, to push his anti-heroic characters into total commitment, into action, the responsibility of the police censorship is questionable.

As literature his plays have to stand alone and cannot, as is essential for an understanding of the man, be complemented by his voluminous journals and the rest of his creative works, but in their very limitations they are Grillparzer and they are Austria. The relentless mediocrity of Rudolf von Habsburg, as painted in *König Ottokar's Glück und Ende*, who defeated King Ottokar of Bohemia on that uniquely bloodstained plain to the north-east of Vienna, the Marchfeld, is not a portrait that every royal dynasty, or every nation in the nineteenth century, would have cared to accept of its founder. But any visitor to Vienna, so crammed still with the results of centuries of patronage of the arts by the Habsburgs, who has seen the head of the founder of the dynasty, Rudolf IV (probably the earliest royal portrait from life north of the Alps) will have to admit that Grillparzer's interpretation cannot be wholly false.[1] The evasiveness, however, is Grillparzer. In *Ein Bruderzwist in Habsburg*, the historical parallel to the political inaction of the Biedermeier era is the situation before the outbreak of the Thirty Years War when the Emperor, faced with two alternatives, knows that any action whatever will precipitate disaster. It reaches out to the second half of the twentieth century in its vision of the victory of violence over humanity. This was one of Grillparzer's prophetic visions, of a Europe in which civilization would be engulfed by a new barbarism from within. *Ein Bruderzwist* was written before 1848 but he laid it aside and it was not performed until 1872, the year of his death.

Grillparzer is central to an understanding of the Austrian Biedermeier as he holds the key to so much that is too elusive to bear the crudity of expression in words. *Der Traum ein Leben*; life is a dream; the end, silence. He embodied and acted out so much that is

---

[1] Grillparzer asked one of the censors what was wrong with this play. The reply was 'Nothing really, but—you never know.' The censor was right: great offence was taken by the citizens of Bohemia.

characteristic of the period, while in his plays Austria itself and the Habsburg dynasty are present in all their profound complexity. He himself certainly believed that his creative period was one constant struggle against the Metternich régime and that he was broken on the rack of dour incomprehension and political suppression. 'Medals here let none await/ For the régime forbids it, / Here hangs no cross on genius' breast, / Nay, on the cross hangs genius.'[1] In his *Recollections of 1848* he recorded: 'Despotism has destroyed my life, at least my literary life.' His subjective impression must be taken as decisive, but it would be a mistake to accept this without a look at the circumstances.

The political régime was not the whole of life, and to be a meteorically successful dramatist enjoying the wholehearted support of the Director of the Hofburgtheater, Schreyvogel, at a time when the theatre was the focus of intellectual life in Vienna, was scarcely a tragic fate. Many theatres in the German states, said Heinrich Laube, had richer financial resources, but the best actors were in Vienna, and it was 'not to be denied that a performance at the Burgtheater is the greatest pleasure to be had in a German-language theatre.' There was no star cult, it was always the ensemble, and the play came before everything. The première of *Der Traum ein Leben* on 4th October, 1834, brought Grillparzer the homage not only of the boxes and stalls, but of the general public. No one knew better than Ferdinand Raimund what Grillparzer had done: he had taken the traditional components of popular Viennese theatre and raised them to Burgtheater level. 'You see,' said poor Raimund, 'that's what I always wanted to do and actually my *Bauer als Millionär* is the same idea . . . only, I have not all those fine words, and they wouldn't understand them out there. It's a thousand pities about me!'

It must have seemed to Grillparzer that in this wicked world nothing can be depended upon, not even failure. His diaries are filled with self-denigration and self-hatred, with bitterness and clouds of melancholy: 'As a person not understood, as a civil servant passed over, as a poet tolerated at best, my life drags on its monotonous way.' And: 'My natural condition is one of inward brooding

---

[1] Auszeichnung hier erwarte nie, / Denn das System verbeuts, / Das Kreuz hängt hier nicht am Genie, / Nein, das Genie am Kreuz.'

interspersed with distraction. Preferably without an object but with a lightening flash of thought now and then.' He never quite lost the wit of his youth: 'Inside my head the state of affairs much resembles Hungary. Raw materials in abundance, yet diligence and industry are wanting; the substance is not processed.' It was inevitable that he should think of suicide, and it was not the least Biedermeier trait in him that he drew back from the brink of disaster with a gesture of despairing futility. Fortunately he was not always sunk in gloom. In England he seems most of all to have enjoyed his talks with Bulwer Lytton and the roast beef, and he found an inn near the Thames where an ox was roasted whole. 'A day without beef', he noted, 'is no day at all.' The change of scene may have given him a rest from his interminable digestive upsets. But he was one of that breed of men who away from home are forever in trouble with their passports and luggage. Accident-prone to a degree, he fell downstairs and off ladders, and one day he was able to write with grim satisfaction: 'Thank God, I cut my finger while shaving.'

Grillparzer was the most musical of poets, with whom, when language would no longer carry his meaning, music took over. Adalbert Stifter, the master of German narrative prose, thought that he was a painter. Born in 1805 in Upper Austria, he went to Vienna in 1826, but it was not until 1840 that he began to publish the short novels about that part of Austria which one thinks of as the Stifter country. They are not everyone's fare, the description is interminable and far too detailed, and yet this is their strength. His contribution to Austrian Biedermeier began with the self-inflicted and enduring wound of a loveless marriage, which in a man of his ethical purity induced a spirit of quiet renunciation, acceptance of the inevitable divorce between ideal love and reality, and premature acceptance of middle age. *Nachsommer*, Indian summer, in one word this title of one of his novellas summarizes it all. It is the autumn of life, all passions are—spent is not the word; the fires have died down, but the sinking sun throws a golden light across the landscape; it is a glow coming from within, a scene by Ferdinand Waldmüller in words. It is a culture for the middle-aged. But Stifter also wrote of Vienna, and it was perhaps still in the firm belief in his destiny as a painter that he took to mounting the spire of the Cathedral to watch the dawn. To do this he had to go up in the evening and spend the short summer night at his observation post. His description of Vienna as it slowly comes to life is simple and precise but so evocative that the reader holds his breath for fear of dispelling the magic as girls appear with brooms, yawning and stretching, at doorways, and as the light strengthens, over the Wienerberg past the Spinnerin am Kreuz, down the road from Trieste, covered waggons trundle, bringing food to the still sleeping capital.

It was a city in which Austrian literature was born at last, and it would expand and receive tributaries and come down without the least interruption to the present day. Writers in German in various parts of the monarchy, above all in Prague where the Habsburg 'mission' to a subject people turned Slavs into writers and poets in the German language, would immeasurably enrich that literature with the myths of those peoples. Not only the Northern and Southern Slavs, but also the peoples of Venetia and Lombardy formed organic links with Austrian literature. Ironically enough, during the second half of the century, Vienna was at the same time to become the principal centre of the intellectual development of the Slav peoples.

Grillparzer and many others in his time believed wholly in the 'German' cultural mission in the Austrian Empire, and this belief was in no way identical with pan-Germanism. German romantic nationalism left him cold; all attempts by German nationalists to arouse enthusiasm for a common cause he rejected absolutely, seeing in their efforts a lever which could wrench Greater Austria apart, whereas he believed in a supranational organism consisting of Northern and Southern Slavs, Hungarians, Italians and so on under the cultural leadership of the German language. In this, Grillparzer was of one mind with Metternich, among whose motives for maintaining a vast censorship apparatus directed towards control of the free flow of thought between Germany and Austria, his struggle against pan-Germanism in Austria was not the least in importance.

While Austrian literature was coming to life during the Biedermeier era, principally on the stage of the Hofburgtheater where 'Burgtheater-Deutsch' became synonymous with purity of diction, the artists had little to offer beyond charming genre paintings, and music was almost equally limited. 'How petty was the world of publicly performed music at the conclusion of the thirties and beginning of the forties!' wrote the critic Hanslick. 'At once luxuriant and superficial, it bore the character of a sensual life seesawing between dim sentimentality and effervescent wit . . . predominant were the Italian opera, virtuosity and the waltz. Strauss and Lanner were worshipped. I should be the last man to underestimate the brilliant talent of these two men who in their very unpretentiousness were nevertheless the most original, in their way the most perfect and enchanting phenomena of that musical epoch. Every nation may envy Austria its Strauss and Lanner.' By 1839 each had published more than a hundred 'works' and the periodicals were going into ecstasies over each new waltz as it appeared. 'That this sweetly narcotic three-quarter time which ruled all heads and feet, combined with the *wälsche* [in this case Italian] opera and the cult of virtuosity makes listeners ever more incapable of intellectual effort, goes without saying.' He goes on to talk of the bad influence of the notorious critic Saphir and of Heinrich Proch. Proch was a composer of songs which were adored by the Viennese. They were sung in every house and were on every concert programme; Schubert's *lieder* were as good as forgotten. By 'cult of virtuosity' Hanslick meant, first and foremost, Franz Liszt whose technical fireworks set the pattern during the forties in a way that Hanslick wholly disapproved of. Liszt, Thalberg and Paganini were the star performers at musical *soirées* which were given at intervals by Prince and Princess Metternich on the Rennweg, but here Schubert's *lieder* were sung as well as *bel canto*. Like all fashions, virtuosity carried all before it for a time, the exceptions being the philharmonic concerts of Otto Nicolai, until the public was exhausted not only by the performers' superficial panache but by its own enthusiasm. In the autumn of 1846 Hanslick went to see Liszt. 'He sat at the piano clothed in a black velvet blouse and wide Turkish trousers, not playing, but writing. He had a notebook on his knee and wrote, at an angle, his thin extended notes. As he wrote he talked to me and, from time to time also, to a circle of four or five young people who lounged on the divans, smoking and chatting as though they were in a coffee-house.'

Although in 1846 Lortzing was conducting at the Theater an der Wien, no one at that time was taking any notice of what was going on in Germany. Wagner, Schumann, were of little interest, and Mendelssohn was performed in the United States before he was heard in Vienna. During this same year Robert and Clara Schumann, with their young daughter and accompanied by Meyerbeer, came to Vienna for a series of concerts, and the Schumanns stayed with Professor Josef Fischer of the Konservatorium. Hanslick describes Clara Schumann's concert on New Year's Day 1847, her third in a series. Like Beethoven, said Hanslick, Schumann was a bad conductor, his beats were small and uncertain, his eyes were riveted to the score and he was evidently hearing the music more as it was written and as it sounded in his mind than as it was played by the orchestra. Attendance was very thin, the applause chilly and obviously intended only for the pianist and not for the conductor's Concerto in A minor; nor did the Symphony in B flat fare any better. The Schumanns and their friends walked home in silence, until at last Clara broke out into lamentations over the coldness and indifference of the public. Schumann was philosophical: 'Calm yourself, Clara dear, in ten years it will all be quite different.' They were not to have to wait as long as that. Jenny Lind, however, 'passed through Vienna like a comet', the Viennese were at her feet and her carriage was drawn through the streets by enthusiasts. All this astonished her: nowhere, she said, had she been so fêted. Jenny apart, and not even she could save the Schumanns' last concert, qualitatively speaking, music was at a low ebb, but there was no lack of it. 'Opera and theatres are overflowing,' said Stifter, 'we are flooded with concerts, the virtuosos' crusade is about to be launched, Strauss and Lanner make music in places of public entertainment and in a thousand houses fingers are hammering upon the pianoforte.'

Sacred music on Sundays, too, was not for the most discriminating, and the scene in the Augustinerkirche was certainly the same as it was when Charles Sealsfield saw it in the late twenties; as it would hardly change for decades to come. 'Bells are ringing at all the side altars and the largest crowd is by the priest who can say Mass in the shortest time, about twelve minutes. The fashionable world occupies the pews, and in the nave are the dandies of Vienna, walking to and fro, ogling and conversing. There is a bustling, a running, a crossing, a noise, which excites anything but serious reflection.

Hardly is the concert over, now the whole crowd hastens to the doors, leaving priest, divine service, everything, to its business unmolested and alone. Hardly a soul remains for the sermon.' (This of course was why the Catholic Church in its infinite wisdom moved the sermon back to a central position in the Mass.)

A less revolutionary people than the Viennese could hardly be imagined. Each in his or her own way, how many people, Austrians as well as foreign visitors, had said this. On the other hand: 'He is a kind of cosy *frondeur*, ready to oppose everything under the category of "government" or "the law".' 'Things have got to change', they cry, 'there must be an improvement'; how, no one asked. This was how Eduard von Bauernfeld saw the opposition in Vienna: content to sit around in coffee-houses, watching other nations struggle for freedom and hoping that a scrap might fall their way at no cost to themselves. In the meantime it was business as usual. Bauernfeld, however, is only seeing the circle in which he moved. Among the working classes unrest was considerable, and growing, the current wave should probably be dated from 1839 and was due as always to rising prices. These facts were known to the central government since they figured in the police reports. The mood of the prosperous middle classes was indeed anything but revolutionary: for all those who were engaged in the business life of the monarchy these were good times, new faces were to be seen in the best seats of the theatres, and in 1842 Carl at the Theater an der Wien, recognizing the situation, put up his prices. Suddenly, the small tradesman and his wife found themselves effectively shut out of their own theatres, not that they cared for the new Vaudeville from Paris which the new *parvenu* class preferred to Nestroy. Perhaps this was a small matter, but it was one more pebble thrown into a pool which would ultimately overflow.

10

The Political Awakening:
'Tell my people I consent to everything!'

As the social drama develops which will end in the anti-climax of 1848, we might perhaps turn back to watch the political scene, in particular the struggle for power at the court of Vienna after the death of Franz I.

As the funeral cortège of Franz I wound its way through the narrow streets to the church of the Capuchin Fathers on the Neuer Markt, many of his more elderly mourners can be assumed to have been indulging in inner monologues appropriate to the occasion, containing equal parts of self-congratulation on having survived the deceased, mild apprehension arising from claustrophobia among the densely-packed crowds, and resentment over personal physical discomfort. Some, a very few, of those who followed the coffin were grieving; how many can have been sustained by that feeling which often accompanies the death of kings, that a dead era is going to its grave but a new freshness is in the air, that leading the chief mourners is one under whose aegis, or at least, during whose reign, a national renaissance may gush forth? For a few days, no longer, many of the bystanders did think so. No one alive on that day possessed the necessary perspective to be able, as we can, to assess the historical importance of the one truly significant action of the dead Emperor: his laying down of the crown of the Holy Roman Empire as a sequel to his assumption of the Imperial crown of Austria.

Having reached the end of his reign, it may perhaps be worthwhile to return to the subject for a second look. Did his action matter? Was not the Holy Roman Empire a mere pious fiction, a joke, an excuse for occasional picturesque and expensive pageantry? Even if Franz had come through the Napoleonic wars still wearing the crown of Charlemagne, what would it have signified amidst the turmoil of the industrial revolution, in the new mobility of the railway age?

Apart from an interval of five years from 1740 to 1745 during the War of the Austrian Succession a Habsburg had worn the crown since the time of Friedrich III in the fifteenth century. From then on the *Reichsgedanke*, the idea of empire, had lived in Vienna, being lent tangible expression by the Imperial Chancellery and by the presence of the Vice-Chancellor as representative of the Imperial Arch-Chancellor, the Archbishop of Mainz. They might have been cardboard figures, but were brought to a semblance of life by the fact that down the centuries, owing to their existence, Habsburg policy could never be dissociated from, nor conceived independently of, imperial concerns. This crown before which every monarch of the present day has stood, visibly gripped by the extraordinary charisma of the supranational symbol before him, was for centuries the only unifying force capable of holding the German peoples together—the sovereign princes, the estates and commons. Quarrelsome the liege lords of the Empire may have been, but to them the coronation in Frankfurt had the validity of a divinely appointed sacrament and was indissoluble.[1] In practical terms, the bond between the Emperor and the German states involved Austria in the defence of the Rhine against France, and this concept never lost its relevance. Perhaps, then, the old Empire did count for something. But after the end of the Napoleonic wars the chief significance of the *Reichsgedanke* lay in the last two words of the name borne by the Empire in modern times: the Holy Roman Empire of the German Nation. This was the old idea in a new guise: the German nation in search of the state form which would become modern Germany. The Imperial crown had become a symbol of German unity. It is understandable therefore if, as Professor Golo Mann argues,[2] men should have begun to refurbish, in retrospect, the old costumes and props of the Empire to suit a new ideology and a new

[1] Heinrich Benedikt, 'Die Casa d'Austria, das Reich und Europa', in *Spectrum Austriae*, Vienna, 1957.
[2] Golo Mann, *Deutsche Geschichte des 19. u. 20. Jahrhunderts*.

set of circumstances, in terms which that interminable epic had hardly warranted. In this way the symbolism of Charlemagne's crown acquired a power which formerly it had lacked.

After Napoleon's withdrawal behind the Rhine, the allied head-quarters was at Frankfurt am Main, and here the proposal was raised that Franz, Emperor of Austria (to whom the word 'nation' was anathema)[1] should again assume the crown which, acting with dubious constitutional legality, he had put from him eight years earlier, dissolving the *Reichstag* and releasing its members from their allegiance. Favourable public opinion apart, this was no mere fancy; the statesman vom Stein was for it and he was not a man to indulge in fancies. Nor was this an isolated occasion, as the issue remained a live one to be raised again when the Emperor Franz had been in his tomb for five years. In 1840, Austria's reputation as a *Völkerkerker*[2] notwithstanding, King Frederick William IV of Prussia offered Metternich the imperial crown for the Habsburg dynasty, and in 1849 after the accession of the Emperor Franz Joseph, the offer was repeated. There is a certain piquancy about this picture in which Prussia offers the crown to a reluctant Austria. Since the days of Maria Theresa's great foreign minister Prince Kaunitz, it had been a secret axiom of Austrian policy that the balance of power in Europe would not tolerate too close a relationship between Austria and Prussia. England and France prevented a marriage between Maria Theresa and Frederick II when she was still a child: in personal terms a singularly fortunate intervention.

In 1814, this insistence on the Habsburg presence in Germany, the prevalent feeling that although Austria had withdrawn from the Netherlands, to abandon its responsibilities in the defence of the Rhine almost amounted to treachery, found their echo in Metternich's wish to maintain Austria's position of power in Germany, centred on Mainz. But the Emperor Franz, with that inflexible stubbornness, the unwillingness even to discuss the pros and cons which he so often brought to complicated matters of state, presented

[1] Hence the name of the Burgtheater in Vienna, which Franz I changed from Hof- und Nationaltheater to Kaiserlich-Königlich Hofburgtheater.

[2] The theory that the peoples under Habsburg rule were incarcerated in a vast gaol. But it would be more accurate to speak of gaols, so eager were they all to adopt the role of gaoler towards the others within their boundaries.

Metternich with a simple alternative. He could take it or leave it, accept the Emperor's decision or go. As Franz I saw it the German crown was nothing but a burden and a menace to the stability of the Habsburg monarchy; he would not, perhaps, have agreed with the Emperor Franz Joseph's celebrated statement 'Ich bin ein deutscher Fürst.'[1] The Hohenzollerns evidently failed to see the difficulty of embodying the entire Habsburg monarchy in Germany, or of creating a league, a body of nations, call it what one will, containing such dissimilar cultures and stages of civilization.

Franz I saw his duties with blazing clarity. They were to act as a court of appeal for each of his subjects, as their protector against the civil servants who were *his* servants. The Emperor Franz Joseph was to see his function in the same light: when the first population census was held he wrote under 'occupation'—'self-employed civil servant'. Franz I ('he bores his way through documents like a drill', said Metternich, 'and comes out at the other side without having done more than create a hole in a file)' mistrusted his civil servants on principle, and to some extent because not one of them, however junior or however remote his location, could be quite sure that his memoranda would not land up on the desk of the *Allerhöchster Herr*, the monarchy acquired a body of public servants who, while intimidated and bureaucratic, were as incorrupt as any that the world has seen. The type found its apotheosis in Bancbanus in Grillparzer's *Ein Treuer Diener seines Herrn (A True Servant of his Master)*. As a concept of statecraft it was the logical realization, even if an almost maniacal logic, of the idea 'l'Etat c'est moi'; it was not one to hold much appeal, if only on account of the drudgery involved, for the Georges of England.

Franz I had had a serious illness just nine years earlier, and Grillparzer was moved to describe how the angel of death, hovering over the Hofburg and seeing the assembled crowds, said, 'I was sent to break one heart, I cannot break so many.[2] That was as might be, but the Emperor's nearly mortal sickness forcibly brought to mind the question of the succession. Must the law of primogeniture prevail in all cases, even when the heir to the throne was mentally

---

[1] 'I am a German prince.' This was not literally true: it has been worked out that Franz Joseph was exactly 3 per cent German.
[2] Last lines of *Vision*, 1826.

handicapped? The law had certainly not worked out wholly to the advantage of the Empire in the case of Franz himself, and it became visibly perilous in combination with close in-breeding: Franz I and his second wife, the mother of Archduke Ferdinand, were first cousins twice over, as her father, Ferdinand I of Naples-Sicily, was brother to Franz's mother, while her mother was a sister of Franz's father. But such was the Emperor's reverence for precedent that the possibility of an exception to the rule was never seriously entertained. To put aside Ferdinand in favour of his second son Franz Karl—his mind too was something less than rapier sharp—would be 'revolutionary', and that was the end of it. The controversy never lost its interest, but once Archduke Ferdinand had been crowned King of Hungary in 1830 it became irrelevant.

It was natural that the Archduchess Sophie's opinion should coincide with her own interests. She saw no advantage to anyone in putting a feeble-minded epileptic on the throne, and certainly great advantage for herself in her husband Archduke Franz Karl being placed there. Did it, in the long run, really matter? Which alternative was in the best interests of the state: Ferdinand plus Regency Council, or Franz Karl without, but with a very strong-minded wife? One answer very swiftly emerged: it all depended on the Council. Another comes to mind in retrospect: if the Archduchess had really held the power and the supreme position for which her soul craved, is it not possible that she would have been a little kinder, later on, to her daughter-in-law Elizabeth, and helped her, at first only as wife of the heir to the throne, to find her feet gradually, to the great advantage of her marriage and perhaps even of the emotional stability of her children?

The Chancellor's interests were diametrically opposed to those of the Archduchess. Ferdinand plus an inevitable Regency Council: in his own eyes this was the only possible solution, since with his flair for diplomacy he would very soon dominate the Council. Were Franz Karl to come to the throne he would instantly rush into the arms of Count Kolowrat, but in any event this powerful Bohemian nobleman must be eliminated. The whole problem had clearly been exercising Metternich's mind for some time as a draft will of unknown date existed which was set up by Gentz, and Gentz died in March 1832. But when it came to the point, when the vital question of the redistribution of power in the Austro–Hungarian Empire called for an answer, no one was ready.

The political testament of Franz I gave rise to an infinite amount of speculation, largely owing to the stringent precautions taken to prevent its contents from becoming fully known. This alone caused many people to doubt its authenticity. For generations the document even seemed to have vanished, and it only came to light when the most long-lived of the interested parties, the Emperor Franz Joseph, and indeed the Empire itself, had died: in 1918. But the suspicions of persons close to the throne at the time were specific: did Metternich perform a feat of sleight of hand with the will? The principal reason for their uneasiness was the bitter struggle for power between Prince Metternich and Franz Anton Count Kolowrat.

At this time, said Varnhagen von Ense, 'Metternich's power and reputation were at their peak, he was looked upon as without question the first man in Austria, who had defeated, removed, outdistanced or paralysed all his rivals and opponents, and who, while possessing almost no power at home, yet in external affairs he held the whole in his hands, and even the Emperor would not have dared to defy him for long.' As Franz I saw it, Metternich was the conqueror of Napoleon, the man to whom, in the final reckoning, he owed his own crown. He was grateful and a little over-awed. At many of the courts and in the chancelleries of Europe Metternich was the witch doctor who, 1830 notwithstanding, had—if any man possessed it—the patent cure for revolution. 'More than ever', wrote Charles de Mazade,[1] 'the Chancellor of the Court and State felt himself to be at the summit of his ascendancy, master of Austria, governing Germany still, containing Italy, keeping a watch everywhere upon revolution, manipulating with dexterity the affairs of Europe.' His visits to foreign capitals resembled a royal progress, a fact which Metternich noted in tones of preening satisfaction. An extension of his fire-extinguishing activities was the dialogue between himself and King Louis Philippe. It was carried on through diplomatic channels and was as overlaid on both sides with the usual flowery language as a sunny wall with creeper, but its political significance was far from negligible, and the Sardinian Minister

[1] Charles de Mazade, *Un Chancellier d'ancien régime.*

279

in Vienna reported: 'The Chancellor of State has adopted towards Louis Philippe the role of pedagogue and political mentor. He furnishes him with advice, exhortation and admonishment . . .'

Varnhagen's reservation that Metternich possessed almost no power at home is, however, the key to the situation in the Hofburg. The appointment of Count Kolowrat to the post of *Staats- und Konferenzminister*, distantly approximating to the function of a Prime Minister, was made on 29th September, 1826. In addition he assumed responsibility for the political Section B of the State Council. In January of the following year he took over the Finance Department, and he was also privileged to advise the monarch in his private financial affairs. Although 1826 has to be seen as the watershed in Metternich's power in Austrian home affairs, even before then it was not as unlimited as it has sometimes been represented. His replacement of Count Philipp Stadion as Foreign Minister by no means removed that rival from the scene. As Minister of Finance from 1816 to 1823 (he died in the following year), Stadion was the man who, with the most active assistance of the Rothschild brothers, rebuilt the Austrian economy after the financial chaos in which the Napoleonic wars had left it. All his life Stadion was the darling of the Austrian aristocracy, and Metternich's lack of understanding of finance and economic policy was a weak spot in his statesmanship which aggravated the two men's personal relationship. Metternich's weakness in this field was never overcome; nor was his ignorance of Austrian home affairs as a whole, which was largely the fault of the framework of government—the lack of a Cabinet— but partly too because the Emperor simply did not divulge to him all matters of state. The Chief of Police, however, reported both to Kolowrat and to Metternich, and under the Chancellor's aegis there was a second, and stricter, censorship department. Even the supreme office of *Haus-, Hof- und Staatskanzler* to which he was appointed in 1821, and even his responsibility after the death of Count Karl Zichy as chairman of the 'ministerial conferences', failed to give him that overall picture which, for years past, it would arguably have been very much in the interests of the monarchy for him to have possessed. If his power at the time of the Emperor's first illness was nevertheless immense, by 1834 Kolowrat had managed to narrow down Metternich's field of vision to a remarkable degree.

Public opinion, informed and otherwise, was wholly on the side of Kolowrat and against Metternich, and in this it did the Prince an injustice, Kolowrat a little too much honour. Count Kolowrat was not entirely the jovial, liberal-minded, disinterested grandee of popular belief and as he has been painted by one school of historians. It is a misfortune that Kolowrat kept no diaries and wrote no memoirs, but he was not really the type of man to do either. Heinrich von Srbik sees him as an unusually gifted man, possessing a first-rate knowledge of civil administration but lacking clarity and constancy of mind. A positive lust for power warred against an aristocratic distaste for the burdens of office and usually won; it certainly did so during those five or six years before the death of Franz I, when, with the hard-won serenity of the Biedermeier era turning sour in all classes from peasant to priest, the two central figures—Field-Marshal Count Bellegarde saw them as the two heads of the imperial eagle, one looking left, the other right—were fighting for possession of the Emperor. And Kolowrat carried the day.

How it was done, how Kolowrat managed to gain the Emperor's ear, is something of a mystery since Franz I felt little if any warmth towards him and he undoubtedly was fond of Metternich. Throughout the reign of Franz I questions of ministerial competency are particularly baffling because titles of office came and went or were altered, and departments also came and went, without these designations necessarily providing a reliable guide to the power which went with them. Now Metternich's title of office availed him little: suddenly he found himself Minister of Foreign Affairs and very little more, dogged and hedged in at every corner by an opponent as resourceful as he was resilient. In the absence of any departmental integration and without that control of the various departments of state which Franz I had been so reluctant to permit to any subject, Metternich had to recognize that he had been isolated, while Kolowrat was to all intents and purposes Prime Minister. Suddenly he would get bored, fed up or ill and would retreat to Prague or to his estates in Bohemia (there are echoes here of the Franz/Karl relationship), and Metternich would at once spread a rumour that his sickness was of the mind. But after a while back he came in bouncing health and ready to check Metternich's every attempt to regain a foothold on the home front. The Emperor enjoyed the spectacle, it strengthened his own position. It may in fact have been his own intention. Franz I has been seen[1] as the last practitioner of a policy laid down for his son by the Emperor Charles V: the sovereign should choose his advisers from among the protagonists of opposing camps, hear both sides and make his decision. The Emperor Franz Joseph was taught never to listen to the opinion of anyone on a matter outside his sphere of competence, and throughout his long reign he never departed from this practice.

There was another factor in the power structure, the importance of which Metternich had never overlooked: the Church.

Clemens Metternich was a rationalist, and in this he never altered much, even in later life under the influence of his bigoted rather than devout third wife. His attitude towards the institutional Church underwent a phase of development in which he grew increasingly to value the influence of the Church as a bastion against revolution, but in this he went further than the Emperor. The blank hostility of Franz I towards the Jesuits never wavered, and their petition to be allowed to set up a noviciate in the neighbourhood of Vienna was refused, even though it had not been possible to prevent members of the Society of Jesus from settling within the Empire after their final expulsion from Russia. The Emperor Franz abominated the Jesuits for the same reason that he disliked and feared all organized groups, but Metternich—he could do nothing for them yet—was looking for allies, and now he turned ultramontane, hoping to find in the clerical party at Court some degree of backing against Kolowrat.

Three women led the strictly Catholic party—Catholic not only in the sense of strict religious observance but of opposition to the ideas of the 'new liberalism' which created far from negligible spiritual conflict in the minds of a great many educated Catholics. There was, firstly, the Empress Caroline Augusta, Franz's fourth wife, who brought to the Hofburg a deep religious faith not without elements of bigotry, while her unassuming, direct approach, her kindness and charitable activities did much to raise the Court in public esteem during the last years of her husband's reign and beyond. To her marriage she brought vigorous health, but while this

[1] Heinrich Benedikt, 'Die Casa d'Austria, das Reich und Europa' in *Spectrum Austriae*, Vienna, 1957.

was to bring no dynastic benefits, her piety did in time faintly illumine the Emperor's total incomprehension. Secondly there was the Archduchess Sophie, and, last of the trio, Ferdinand's consort Maria Anna, soon to be Empress of Austria, a title in her case of such clanging emptiness that it is doubtful whether even one of Vienna's celebrated young washerwomen would have been willing to change places with her.

At 38, the heir to the throne was still unmarried because it had always been the view of the Court physicians that sexual intercourse would endanger his health. Metternich's reversal of this policy formed part of his gradual preparation for the coming reign. It was essentially a simple decision, and the Court physician Dr. Stifft was easily brought to change his opinion, but to discover a suitable princess was not easy. The field was small, there would be few takers even for a position of such brilliance, and the Archduke Ferdinand could not be hawked around Europe, courting refusal and mockery. Metternich could think of only one prospective candidate who would dare neither to decline the offer now nor to get in his way in time to come. Princess Maria Anna of Sardinia was the niece of King Karl Felix, of the senior line of the House of Savoy, a man in whom as an autocrat with a passionate dislike of all forms of popular representation Metternich had a willing pupil. He was known to be eager, if not avid, for a further link by marriage with the imperial house, and the delighted consent of his sister-in-law Marie-Thérèse, the Queen Mother of Sardinia, who as sister of the late Empress Maria Ludovica was also sister-in-law to Franz I, was soon obtained. The King wrote to his niece immediately.

Probably not since the days of Marie Louise had any princess been presented with such an ultimatum. That very morning on which she received her uncle's letter her mind had to be made up and her answer given. She consented because she had been brought up to unconditional obedience, and it is possible that the indescribably dreary prospect before her had not yet taken shape in her mind. The diplomat Baron Wessenberg's heart was filled with pity for her. 'God alone knows', he wrote in his diary, 'what conflicting feelings have warred in her heart, she to whom no hope, no prospect of a happy life remained. God alone knows also, how she may have struggled within herself until she reached the point of submission to her destiny. . . . If renunciation of all that lends charm to life . . . makes a person worthy to enter the Kingdom of Heaven, then no one in the world today has more right to do so than the princess who will now soon be Empress of Austria.'

How infinitely more distressing, because more lonely, was the situation of a royal princess compared with that of her male relations: they at worst had a choice, and refusal was just possible; for the women there was no escape. Marie Anna was refused permission to bring with her, as she would have liked to do, her own father confessor and two of her ladies who would have helped to lessen her homesickness. The mealy-mouthed words of the Ambassador in Turin, Count Friedrich Senfft, dictated by Metternich, make distasteful reading. 'It would create an unfavourable impression if, contrary to the prevailing custom, Princess Maria Anna were to disdain in advance the undoubtedly most excellent clergy of her future fatherland and were to bestow her august confidence solely upon a priest from her former homeland. . . . It is the tender concern of His Majesty the Emperor as Father and as Sovereign which prevents H.M. in this context also from complying with the wishes of the Sardinian Court. . . . Concerning the further desire of H.R.H. the bride to take with her two Ladies, the Duchess of Lucca has undertaken to write to H.R.H. and in the light of her own experience and conviction, advise against it.' She was caught up in the net like a thrush in a fruit cage.

After the marriage by proxy at Turin, her uncle's capital, on 12th February, 1831, her wedding in Vienna took place on 28th February, and on the following day Ferdinand took to his bed, 'making', in the words of E. C. C. Corti, 'the worse possible impression'.

As Franz I lay dying, more important than any of these august ladies was the Emperor's father confessor, Bishop Wagner.

The overriding importance of the Emperor's political testament lay in the constitution of the Regency Council, and he would have been a naïve man who supposed that the names of the two Archdukes who, each in his own way, had done more for his country than most others of their rank before them, would naturally figure in it. Archduke Joseph too, who had never agreed with the policy whereby Hungary was enclosed behind tariff barriers and excluded from industrial development so as to remain the corn belt of the monarchy, was unlikely to be a docile member of the Council, and even Franz Karl was apt to come up with ideas of his own—or his wife's. The testamentary dispositions must be couched in such terms as would exclude from influence over state affairs every member of the imperial family who possessed even in rudimentary form a mind of his own. This was sufficiently important in itself, but there was a corollary: the least degree of independence of the Chancellor's will would form a vacuum which would at once be filled by Count Kolowrat.

Prince Metternich made a second draft based on the first. It named as chief adviser to the heir to the throne Franz's youngest brother, Archduke Ludwig, a good-natured, well-intentioned but intellectually undistinguished man who would thankfully follow the advice of his brother's Chancellor—and not only in foreign affairs. Now came the paragraph which Metternich could not well complete without inevitably being accused of overstepping his prerogative, if not of manipulation. 'I hereby nominate and urgently recommend to My Son as His most loyal adviser, worthy of His entire trust . . .' Bishop Wagner could be relied on to see that there was no slip up over the insertion of the name. The text goes on: 'Assign to the Prince Metternich, My most faithful servant and friend, that same trust which I have bestowed upon him over so long a span of years . . .'

Passages followed which were to have an almost hypnotic effect throughout the coming reign and even beyond it: 'Displace no part of the foundations of the state, rule, change not . . . Place Your entire trust in My Brother Archduke Ludwig. Call upon His counsel henceforth in all major internal affairs.' Kolowrat was not mentioned at all, nor were the Emperor's other brothers.

Did Metternich fiddle the will? At the time many people were convinced that he had, and that when the Emperor signed it he was too weak to take in its contents. The historian Viktor Bibl, a very biased critic as the title of his book, *Metternich der Dämon Österreichs*, sufficiently demonstrates, was convinced that undue influence was at work. On the other hand the absence of the name of Kolowrat, in whom Franz I had full confidence, is striking yet not decisive, and with this exception, in the light of the history of the Emperor's relations with his brothers and his consistent refusal to˘allow them any hand whatever in political affairs, there is no denying that the will reflects the mind and assumed intentions of its signator.

Among those who knew the condition of the Emperor's mind at the crucial time was Bishop Wagner, but what he knew and thought we shall never know. In any case, the Bishop would not have spoken a word against Metternich. He himself was busy with a document, the second to leave the sickroom shortly before the end. It was addressed directly to the heir to the throne and it set the seal on the gradual cancellation of Joseph II's programme of clerical reform.

The will did not go so far as to name the members of the Regency Council, and in view of Metternich's now wholly restored and indeed greatly enhanced power, and the elimination of Kolowrat, it must have seemed wiser to take one step at a time. There would in fact have been nothing to prevent Metternich from taking the Council into his own hands if it had not been for the determined action of Archduke Johann. In his headlong rush to Vienna the Archduke was following a sure instinct which was at once confirmed when he learned that Metternich intended to take the chair in the Council and, apparently, govern the Empire as he wished. Shortly after his arrival he was closeted with Metternich for three hours. He accused the Chancellor of attempting to seize power in a form which would be tantamount to making himself President of Austria, and of wanting to bring back the days of the Merovingians and appointing himself to the role of a latter-day Pippin. Evidently shaken by the determined stand of the one man who wanted no part in the power structure for himself, Metternich gave in. After the death of the Emperor, the Emperor Ferdinand himself took the chair of the Regency Council at meetings of the State Conference, and in his absence, Archduke Ludwig. Metternich, Kolowrat and Archduke Franz Karl were permanent members and on occasion other ministers could be brought in, but Metternich could only take the chair in the absence of both Ferdinand and Ludwig.

The new Emperor, crowned by a happy coincidence on St. Simplicius's Day, did at least enjoy his coronation. He loved every minute of it and would like to have been crowned every day. The public was less enthusiastic. 'We are ruled', the saying was, 'by thirty men: a council of three plus a nought.' The Archduchess Sophie was to make repeated attempts to enduce the 'nought' to abdicate in favour of her husband, but her chances of success were nil. 'What I hold against your husband', she told Metternich's wife, 'is that he wanted an impossible thing: to run a monarchy without an emperor, with an idiot on the throne to represent it.' As a senior civil servant, Baron Kübeck, put it, Franz and Metternich between them had created an absolutist monarchy without a monarch: a *monstrum horrendum cui lumen ademptum*. Ferdinand was a signature machine, no more.

Was Archduke Johann right to check the would-be nineteenth-century Pippin? His impetuous intervention prevented Metternich from having the last word in the affairs of every department of state, a position not far short of dictatorship, and in doing so he would have had the entire support of public opinion. But this action too had its consequences. The Emperor's will required Archduke Ludwig to 'hear' Metternich on all internal affairs; it did not require Metternich to listen to Archduke Ludwig on foreign affairs—if the Chancellor had written such a *passus* into the will it could merely have been for his own amusement. Meanwhile, however, Count Kolowrat had by no means disappeared from the scene; he had remained just where he was. All along, knowing nothing about the will, his plan had been to leave foreign affairs to Metternich and to run everything else himself. The Chancellor, baulked of that accumulation of authority which would have enabled him to purge the civil service of Kolowrat's favourites and, at last, to gain the influence over home affairs which the nobleman from Bohemia had denied him for so long, now had to content himself with a series of minor but none the less embittered skirmishes. Kolowrat always had this one weapon: resignation; while Metternich, in the last resort, could only call upon his rival either to comply with the will of Franz I or to go. This he was reluctant to do, both because of Count Kolowrat's supporters at Court and among the nobility, and because it was inadvisable altogether to neglect public opinion which looked on Kolowrat as a liberal. Kolowrat in fact shared the deep pessimism of so many leading members of the society of his time. To Baron Mareschall, Austrian Minister to Brazil, he wrote words which might have come from the pen of Franz I, Metternich or Gentz: 'If we advance with the *Zeitgeist* our agglomerate of countries will fall apart; if we do not march with it we shall be crushed.'

Kolowrat's agglomerate, a word which the *Oxford English Dictionary* defines as 'a collection of things rudely thrown together', was now to be ruled until 1848 by a deeply disunited oligarchy. 'These gentlemen', said Baron Kübeck, 'have devoted their lives to paralysing all the organic institutions in order to bring their personal influence to bear upon the deceased Emperor. All have grown grey in the pursuance of their intrigues. They will find it hard to create a well-regulated body politic. So accustomed are they to deceit and dissemblance, that they lie to themselves, and intrigue against the fruits of their own labours.' They were 'a monstrous regiment of geriatrics'.

On the question of Archduke Johann's intervention it is possible to reach the disappointing conclusion that it might have made little difference either way. The need at that time for a co-ordinating mind at the centre is undeniable, and the vision of a clear and subtle mind reorganizing the machinery of government is tempting. Metternich wanted supreme power. That, having it, he was the man to carry out fundamental administrative or even constitutional reforms and to re-set the softened paste which held the mosaic together[1] is another matter altogether. His ignorance in the all-important sphere of finance bordered on insouciance even when no specialized knowledge whatever was required. An example of this was his inept handling of the repayment of British government subsidies. In the mid-1820s the conclusion was drawn in London that if Austria could afford to mount an expedition against Naples it could repay an old debt outstanding since the end of the eighteenth century which, with compound interest, now came to the attractive sum of £4 million, the equivalent in Austria of 40 million gulden. (In 1823 the Austrian state deficit was 34 million gulden.) No one in London seriously supposed that the Austrian government would ever pay up, and it was greeted as a happy windfall when Metternich, going behind the back of the Minister of Finance, Count Stadion, committed his government in a statement to the Duke of Wellington. The money was advanced by the Rothschilds. His action has been considered a notable diplomatic blunder[2] because

---

[1] 'The monarchy is a mosaic of which the paste has become soft and it only needs a knock to fall asunder.' Baron Karl Friedrich von Kübeck.
[2] By Heinrich von Srbik.

in the past the British government had more than once referred to the loan as a bad debt which had been written off, and because it would have been easy to dispose of it at some juncture in the course of peace negotiations, for example at the time of Austria's entry into the coalition against Napoleon.

One of the supreme diplomatic talents of all time, a statesman who could see every conceivable potential combination of approaching political events and never lose his grasp on his main design; nevertheless his deep-seated distaste for clear-cut decisions, for closing down all alternative options and taking irreversible action, would arguably have played its part whatever the extent of his freedom of movement. Had not he himself written those ominous words into the will of Franz I, the monarch whose hand he had guided for 26 years but behind whom he had always sheltered: '*Verrücke nichts . . .*'[1] Which is to say that even had he possessed that unlimited power which the general public believed that in effect he had, he would not have used it to modernize the state. As it was, the ship of state could only drift, driven by nothing but its own impetus, according to the law of inertia. Somehow, it had to be kept afloat until the heir to the throne came of age: this motive has been ascribed to the genius of Metternich but it may contain more than a touch of hindsight. He, for the time being, was satisfied. 'Here, things continue as though nothing had happened', he wrote to one of his ambassadors. 'The art consisted in not being taken unawares . . . I did a great deal, and I acted rightly.'

To Metternich nothing might seem to have happened, but not everyone shared this impression. Those archdukes of the older generation who performed viceregal functions on the periphery: Palatine Joseph in Hungary, the Archduke Ferdinand in Transylvania, Max in Galicia and Rainer in Lombardy-Venetia, had a relatively free hand. But now that the family was without a head, Karl and Johann, who had both been excluded from office in the state for many years, felt their situation to be doubly humiliating. Archduke Johann could at least feel that he led an active and useful life. Surprisingly enough, Archduke Karl believed that he might again be of service to the state, and it was a hope shared by Lord Palmerston, who thought that under the present constellation

[1] 'Displace nothing . . .'

Metternich's influence might sink sufficiently to allow that of Arch-duke Karl to grow. This was not the case. In October 1835 Karl wrote a memorandum which was placed before the State Conference. Pointing to the lack of unity and order in the army he put up the proposal that the Emperor should appoint him (once more) Supreme Commander and permanent adviser to the crown on military affairs. Perhaps he felt that one can but ask. It was an embarrassing move for Metternich since it would be hard to say why he should be denied the post. Yet it was abundantly clear that it must be pre-vented, because the appointment, apart from placing the strongest weapon in the state in his hands, would automatically bring the old soldier on to the Regency Council. The two men had been secret enemies from the very outset—since 1809 when Metternich was working for war, a fact which Archduke Karl had never forgiven him, any more than Metternich had ever forgiven Karl for the fact that Napoleon offered him the crown. But Archduke Ludwig too had no intention of admitting his prickly brother to the Council. The usual Austrian solution was adopted. A flowery letter was written, the substance of which was that his valuable advice would be called for from time to time; he could give the Emperor all the benefit of his great experience—and so on. Archduke Karl with-drew, defeated, his memorandum was filed. It would be unjust to say that the subjects it dealt with—the defence of the realm and military organization—were filed away with it. Count Clam-Martinitz, for many years past Metternich's informant on defence, has sometimes been dismissed as a '*Salongeneral*'. In the new reign he became Adjutant-General to the Emperor, and in his further capacity as head of the military section of the State Council he did a great deal for the army. He also tried to build a bridge between Metternich and Kolowrat, and if he could have succeeded, the bene-fit to the country would have been considerable; the effects of the antagonism between them bit deep into the machinery, such as it was, of government. Within six months Archduke Karl and Prince Metternich were to cross swords once again.

The events of the full span of a man's life had lent to the royal dynasty of France an air of instability, and worse: paradoxically, a whiff of the *parvenu* hung about the incumbent in his own house. During the course of King Louis Philippe's extensive correspondence with Metternich it was natural that the thought of inter-marriage with the Habsburgs should come into his mind. Not that the marriage bond with an archduchess had ever provided a guarantee of tenure; conversely, the experiences of Austrian ladies at the side of rulers of the French had not been such as to form encouraging precedents. However, one would like to think that a new era had dawned, and like Archduke Karl, the King may have felt that there was no harm in asking.

This was the very direction in which King Louis Philippe, and for that matter Queen Marie Amélie as well, was looking, as the Archduke now had a daughter of marriageable age whose name was Thérèse. The customary moves through diplomatic channels began while Franz I was still alive, and while there was no confirmation from the Ballhausplatz it seemed that Archduke Karl was more than willing to consider the heir to the throne of France as a son-in-law. But he had married for love, and he would never push his daughter into a marriage against her will. There, with a rather odd silence in official quarters and with the Archduke's favourable attitude known to Louis Philippe, for the moment the matter rested. At the beginning of May 1836 the Duc d'Orléans and his brother the Duc de Nemours left Paris for a tour of Europe. They were a great success wherever they went, particularly in Berlin, and in Vienna expectancy grew. The salons were not disappointed. The younger brother was quiet and reserved, clearly aware that he must not only allow his elder brother precedence but must keep to a lower key; the Duc d'Orléans was strikingly good-looking, tall and spirited. The Archduchess Thérèse was impressed and her father was delighted: these were two thoroughly nice young men, a view with which the girl's brother Albrecht fully agreed. They were all reckoning without Metternich.

The Chancellor's motives for preventing the engagement were not solely governed by personal spite although he can hardly have forgotten the way in which the Archduke had outmanœuvred him in connection with his own marriage. For reasons of policy, he was disinclined for a marital union with France which would involve political commitment. But he now handled the affair with what looks like deliberate clumsiness, pausing for too long before he intervened, and then placing the whole onus on Archduke Karl: it was to be supposed that he had had second thoughts; the victims, not the Chancellor, were to carry the can in what had now become an embarrassing situation. The French Ambassador, St. Aulaire, was told that the Archduke feared the possibility of physical assault, a danger to which the royal family of France was always exposed. And the young Archduchess was shy and timorous by temperament, and it would be better, therefore, if the matter were pursued no further. By the time the Archduke fully realized what was going on it was becoming rather late to intervene, but he could yet have done so. He fell a prey to one of his moments of vacillation: perhaps other people knew best; who knew how it might turn out? If anything went wrong it would all be his fault—and so on. But he and his family felt that Metternich had deliberately and publicly humiliated them.

King Louis Philippe was offended, and although the dialogue with Metternich did not dry up altogether, it became more formal and entirely lost that confidential touch which it had possessed before this unfortunate interlude. It soon transpired that the Archduchess Thérèse was not so timorous that she could not be given in marriage to King Ferdinand of Naples.

There can be no doubt that the incident decided Metternich to put an end once and for all to any nonsense of this kind, and that it gave birth to a document which would add to the difficulties of archdukes and their sisters in time to come: the Habsburg *Familienstatut*. This law, the authorship of which tends to be overlooked, lays down that, 'The Emperor and Head of the Family possesses not only sovereignty and jurisdiction over all members of the Family, but in addition the right of particular supervision, especially with respect to tutelages, trusteeships and marriages, and applies also to all such actions and circumstances of the All-Highest members of the Family as might impair the honour, dignity, calm, order and welfare of the Most Illustrious Arch-House ...' After a brief glance at the rights of these persons, and a declaration that marriages contracted without imperial permission are null and void, the document returns to the first theme and develops it further. 'It is needful that, henceforth, the Head of the Family shall exercise the right of exact and careful surveillance of every action of Family members which might exert a detrimental influence upon the Imperial House. Therefore, it behoves the Head of the Family also to watch over their upbringing and education, in such a manner as shall ensure that they be appropriate to the exalted station and vocation of the House. To that end be added also the choice of persons in close proximity to them and the supervision of journeys undertaken by members of the Family, especially to foreign countries.' The document is signed by the Emperor Ferdinand, Prince Metternich and Baron Franz von Lebzeltern-Kollenbach and dated 3rd February, 1839.

It may be objected that all this document did was to codify normal practice. True, but for 'the Emperor' etc. the name of Metternich must be read throughout the text. And while Archduke Karl's attempt at an independent exercise of parental rights provided the irritant, the sting lies in the tail. The matter of the education of the Archduke Franz Joseph was causing Metternich some anxiety. As we have seen, Ferdinand's brother Franz Karl was normal but a trifle dim. He had never wished to ascend the throne and his son Franz Joseph was fast emerging as the heir presumptive. His education was clearly of the first importance, but it tells us much about Metternich's personal standing that he found it necessary to bolster his enormous power and prestige as Chancellor by creating to this end legislation enabling him, as well, to intervene in the affairs of every single member of the family and its collateral branches, to the extent of removing from their circles of close friends and advisers all those of whom he disapproved.

Metternich himself had never been anything else but free to follow his own inclinations.

From the point of view of posterity, the most important development in Metternich's private life during his middle years was his encounter with Dorothea Lieven, since a love affair followed which was conducted largely by correspondence. Dorothea Lieven had none of the haunting allure of the Duchess of Sagan. With her almost overlong neck, sharp features and rather skimpy hair, her looks were debatable, nor was she by the highest standards of the time a well-educated woman; as the Germans would have said, and did, she lacked *Bildung*. What she did possess was intelligence in high degree, the kind of mind which can range over a wide field, which assimilates rapidly and grasps essentials. She was also perfectly equipped to play a part in the highest ranks of society, could impart a sufficient illusion of beauty, had charm, spirit and tact. Politics were her passion, and as the wife of a Russian ambassador she was able to embark on a career of political intrigue in which she has had few rivals.

Metternich met Countess Lieven, the wife of the Russian Ambassador to London, two years after the death of Julie Zichy.[1] At once she began to fill what had become a yawning void and in his letters to her Metternich found the totally receptive audience of one that he needed. This need is one of Metternich's most fundamental characteristics. Neither diaries nor memoirs were for him ideal vehicles of self-expression, both perhaps being too closely related to the official memoranda to the Emperor and to the flood of instruction and political analysis which streamed from the Chancellery. He needed a dialogue, and it must be with a woman, one with sufficient intelligence and grasp of affairs to be able to toss the ball back. Up to a point he had always had this. It was not that he sought the company of intellectual women as such: Germaine de Staël had horrified him—she was too ugly, and her awkward, unfeminine movements threw him into a kind of panic, making him long for only one boon, to be spared her overwhelming physical presence. With Dorothea Lieven he could have a sexual relationship, to be indulged in when opportunity offered. For Metternich, however, it probably consisted not so much in a violent physical and emotional desire, a desperate yearning for physical intimacy, as a *mise-en-scène* from which all else followed, a bodily encounter the memory of which set the scene for the intellectual dialogue. It may well be doubted whether Dorothea Lieven was the great passion of his life, whether, sexually, she was as profoundly disturbing a woman as Wilhelmine Sagan who had had the power to blow him right off course for weeks during the climax of his career, the Congress of Vienna. Into his letters to Dorothea there creeps a note of false sentiment and of rationalization. Here is self-expression, but the writer is also busily arranging the mirrors and lights so as to create a favourable image. Little correctives to past history have to be under-

---

[1] Metternich first met the Countess (in 1826 she became Princess Lieven) in London, but they fell in love and the affair actually began during the Congress of Aachen in 1818. Further opportunities of this sort were their only means of meeting.

taken, just as Sir Thomas Lawrence had to be asked to paint out the sardonic twist to his lips in the portrait made after the Congress—it was completed in 1819—a request with which the artist complied. In the private sphere, they contain those little infidelities towards the past to which men seem to be so much more prone than women. Fully aware as he must have been that even in the unlikely event of his confidence being respected at the time, publication of his letters was only a matter of time, he now betrays Julie Zichy. The story of the casket, the ashes and the ring is told, but with an addition: in her will—it contained, says Metternich, various terms and references which only a certain woman friend and he himself could understand—she had explained to her husband that she had never been able to love him, and why. It may have been true, but it seems most unlikely that a woman who is always described as the soul of kindness and tact would have informed the father of her five children in her will that she had never loved him.

Usually, Metternich floated on a higher plane. He would speak of 'the strange and melancholy drama which history presents . . . that I may contemplate it the best-placed and most distinguished box stands at my disposal. No noise disturbs me. And the great masses of mankind are no hindrance to my views of the panorama, for I survey affairs from a higher point of vantage than they.' For this he had the Emperor to thank. 'Heaven has placed me at the side of a man who might have been created for me, just as I was for him.' Meanwhile, the affair between Metternich and the wife of the Russian Ambassador to the Court of St. James had no more escaped the attention of Viscount Castlereagh than had the fact that she had become a political agent of the first importance. She amused the Prince Regent and he enjoyed her company; it was clear that Dorothea Lieven was now an invaluable link between the Prince and Metternich. It seemed a good idea to bring all parties together on the occasion of a royal visit to Hanover in the autumn of 1821. The two lovers were entranced at the prospect, and the meeting was a success in every way, though George IV, as he now was, so fell over himself in his flattery of Metternich that even the man who could write that the Emperor of Austria might have been created for him was faintly nauseated. The King named all the great men of classical antiquity who came into his mind, added those of the

Middle Ages and of modern times, and wound up with the rider that all these men had supposed themselves to be of consequence, 'yet they were nothing by comparison with yourself. Since the world began, there has only been one single really great man, and you are he!' 'Who says too much', Metternich wrote to his wife, 'says nothing.'

The love affair lasted for seven years, and it was he who tired of it first, she whose last letters contain a nostalgic note, a plea for a fresh start. Soon she would turn on him with violence, intriguing against him in England with the bitterness of a rejected mistress. The relationship had had one weakness which slowly acquired a cumulative effect: they saw too little of one another. In such a case the danger is that one or both will create the lover in their own image, that they will make one another up. In Metternich's sense of drama, the fluency of his style which tended to create a momentum of its own and above all in his narcissim, this danger was inherent from the outset. But to these factors, and their disagreement over political issues—how strange it is that the statesman whose most consistent line of policy was to keep Russia out of central Europe should have loved two women who, if they were not precisely Russian agents, were obliged to side with that country's interests—another was suddenly added. Never in all their married life had Eleonore Metternich taken any steps to bring an affair of her husband's to an end. In 1825, however, this is just what she did. She died.

In his early 50s, Clemens Metternich was still as handsome a man as could be found in any salon in Europe. He had not put on a pound in weight since his youth, his fair hair was only now touched with silver, the Kagenegg nose gave interest to his regular features. Hormayr, who of course loathed him, saw something sybaritic, voluptuous and at the same time crafty about the ever-half-smiling mouth of the courtier. No one who ever saw him failed to record their impressions, few see him with the eyes of a Hormayr or a Sealsfield,[1] but every one speaks of his cold, stiff graciousness, the

---

[1] Karl Postl emigrated from Austria to the United States, adopted the name Charles Sealsfield and lived on his writing. His *Austria As It Is* was the most famous of all attacks on the Metternich/Franz régime—blistering polemic, and very funny, it is naturally more than a little overblown.

faintly ironical twist to his mouth which the painter's eye of Lawrence at once spotted. Some visitors remembered to add that they
had been surprised by a switch to an expression of genuine-seeming
amiability and kindness. He always had an unattractive voice, a
hollow-sounding, nasal drawl which with advancing age killed all
spontaneity, all the quick cut and thrust in conversation which
people so loved before that art died out, and in time his monologues
at dinner became notorious. He laughed like a jackass. All the same,
a more eligible bachelor it would be hard to imagine, and the salons
of Vienna rustled at the thought, nowhere more so than in the house
of Molly Zichy-Ferraris, widow of Franz Zichy and mother of
Mélanie.

It will be remembered that Molly Zichy's house was a centre of
diplomatic and amorous intrigue, that during the Congress no
delegate could afford to overlook the least of her entertainments,
even kings if boring were not invited. The younger princes met once
a week in her salon. Yet, according to Lulu Thürheim, she was no
beauty and of limited intelligence, and her hips reached half way
up her back. But she believed herself to be elegant, influential,
piquant and witty, and probably this was half the battle. She dominated Viennese society for years. Czar Nicholas did not declare war
on her, all the same during the 1830s her finances were in such a
state that Metternich decided there was nothing for it but to put her
out to grass, and this was done with the assistance of Baron Rothschild. Her old age cannot have been altogether a happy one. 'Poor
Molly lives today', wrote Lulu, 'old, nearly blind, and forgotten,
on the charity of her children. She endures her loneliness and her
misfortune with stoical calm, and thereby proves that her soul has
a larger capacity than her mind.'

In the meantime her star was still in the ascendant, and it was
generally thought that, such was the friendship between Metternich
and the Zichys, it could only be a matter of observing the decencies,
the usual year of mourning and a bit to spare—few of his subjects
would have dared to imitate the precipitancy shown by Franz I in
his marital affairs—before the luscious and fiery Mélanie would fall
like a ripe plum into the Chancellor's arms. Meanwhile, his cousin
Flora Wrbna-Kagenegg acted as hostess in the palace on the Rennweg. Herself one of the élite among the Congress beauties, a lively,

outspoken woman, she too had made up her mind that it was to Mélanie that she would soon be handing over the reins of the household. They were all quite wrong. The death knell of Metternich's love for Dorothea Lieven was rung, not by an antagonist whose power she would have recognized, but, in all innocence, by a 21-year-old girl. Baroness Antoinette Leykam, pretty, sweet-natured, inexperienced: she must have held a very powerful appeal for Metternich or he would not have wanted to marry a girl (who knows, perhaps this too had its attractions) who was not his social equal, whose mother moreover had been a Neapolitan singer *née* Pedrella. The Leykams were therefore, at a pinch, *Zweite Gesellschaft*, the second layer of society, and the Zichys, immensely caste-conscious as they were since they belonged to one of the oldest families in Hungary, felt for this reason doubly injured. The general opinion was unfavourable. But the Emperor was all sympathy, and he solved the problem by bestowing on Antoinette the style and title of Countess Beilstein, although in the eyes of the rulers of society this action only aggravated the situation by emphasizing that she was not good enough for him as she was. They clearly wanted to have it both ways.[1]

In spite of the obvious disadvantages, the marriage was undoubtedly a happy one; the memory of the cheerless wedding at Hetzendorf where an icy wind blew through the chapel, and the priest, upset by the age gap between bride and groom, fumbled in his search for suitable words, was soon forgotten. Hetzendorf, now a school of fashion, was an imperial residence, lived in at the time by the Duke of Württemberg and his wife who was Metternich's sister. In such company the bride's parents felt a little out of it, and Metternich quickly bundled them out of sight. They were not much in evidence thereafter. On 17th January, 1829, after 14 months of marriage, ten days after giving birth to a son, Antoinette too was dead. The baby, Richard Metternich, was the future husband of the celebrated Pauline Metternich *née* Sándor. As he lay in his cradle, the eldest of Lorel's children, Viktor, was dying in Naples, the last of the beautiful and talented Metternich-Kaunitz brood to succumb

[1] So says E. C. C. Corti. Against this: according to the strict rules of the Habsburg Court, Antoinette Leykam was not *hoffähig*, or entitled to appear at Court. Franz I simply exercised his prerogative in presenting her with a dignity in her own right before she adopted her husband's station by marriage.

to the fatal sickness which, in giving them life, Lorel had implanted in them.[1] Melanie Zichy was waiting, but Metternich took time to get over the death of Antoinette, and it was two years before *le besoin de ne pas être seul* overcame him once more and, on 30th January, 1831, he married his third wife. Czar Nicholas's wedding present was unsuitable for public display: he cancelled Molly Zichy's debt. Metternich was now 58, and it speaks for his vitality that he felt he had the energy, mental as well as physical, to marry a girl of 26 who was the opposite in every way of the gentle, calm and modest Antoinette Leykam. Melanie's extreme conservative views, the volubility with which she gave voice to them and her almost fanatical defence of Metternich's policies sometimes had the opposite effect to the one she intended, but her influence was confined to the drawing-rooms. In the country at large, as resentment built up against Metternich, two factors can be laid, one wholly, the other partly, at the Chancellor's door.

The Academy of Sciences was a recurrent issue during the reign of Franz I. Of the attitude of the Emperor towards the sciences and scholarship enough has been said: it was clear to all that during his lifetime nothing could be done. Count Kolowrat, and this contributed a great deal to the support which he enjoyed among the intelligentsia, was wholly in favour of the foundation of an Academy, referring to it in 1837 as 'a question of honour'. Kolowrat's partisanship was, perhaps, the kiss of death, but Metternich had other reasons for dragging his feet which he continued to do up to the end. First of all, he saw it as a potential stumbling block for the Jesuits whom he wished to make responsible for the entire system of education in Austria. His second reason was closely related to the traditional prejudices of the Emperor. Metternich was warmly interested in the natural sciences—medicine, geology and archaeology—and he was glad to support enterprises such as the botanical and zoological expedition to Brazil in 1816–1817. He lent his support to Daguerre, and to the introduction of gaslight. When

[1] Eleanore Metternich (Lorel) had seven children. Two boys died in early childhood, and the others all inherited from her (she died of it herself) a tendency to tuberculosis. Metternich's adored eldest daughter Marie married Count Joseph Esterházy; she was one of the beauties of the Congress. Clementine, an ethereal beauty painted by Lawrence, died in 1820, aged fifteen, and Marie followed a few weeks later. Viktor first showed signs of the disease in 1819.

Archduke Johann went to England after the Congress he asked him
to bring an exact description of the gas lighting system in London so
that he could try it out in his garden on the Rennweg. Metternich
undeniably had a positive thirst for knowledge, particularly where
it had some practical application. But the word *Wissenschaft*—and
an *Akademie der Wissenschaften* was the matter at issue—covers a
broader field than the English word 'science', and in this gap lay the
stumbling block. The feelings of the deputation of learned men,
the great orientalist Baron Hammer von Purgstall among them, can
be imagined when Metternich assured them that, in his own eyes,
an Academy would only be 'a suitable means to steer its scientific
endeavours into those channels' which suited himself. He empha-
sized that 'the welfare of the state takes precedence over the interests
of the sciences', consequently, here too, the President of Police must
be in charge of its supervision. The scholars were perhaps aware of
Metternich's prophecy that the foundation of London University
would bring about the downfall of England.

It was an extraordinarily late manifestation of massive religious
intolerance, a last wave that had originated in the ground-swell of
the Counter-Reformation, that forced 500 Protestants to emigrate
from the Zillertal in 1837. The most immediate effect of the Edict
of Tolerance promulgated on 13th October, 1781, by the Emperor
Joseph II had been that by the end of 1782 73,000 people declared
that they were Protestants. It was to be a long time before Protestants were admitted to public service; at the time under discussion
there were still none in the civil service and there was just one
Protestant grammar school master in Vienna.[1] The sovereign Archbishop of Salzburg, Prince Schwarzenberg, could scarcely expel
nearly 500 men, women and children for their religious beliefs.
Friction, however, was inevitable in the sphere of taxation for, as
his title shows, the Archbishop was more, when he was not less,
than the spiritual father of his people, and it was not hard to see in
his Protestant subjects a dissident element in the population. But
for their expulsion and despatch to Prussia the concurrence of the
State Council was required, where, to his credit, the Councillor for
Church Affairs, Prebendary Jüstel, identified the group as adher-
ents of the Augsburg Confession. It was Metternich who declared

[1] At the Annagymnasium.

that they were 'anarchists', political revolutionaries, gin-swilling ruffians to whom the Edict of Tolerance did not apply. The Chancellor's heavy share in responsibility for this affair can therefore hardly be denied. Whether or not this was known up and down the country, it must have been the general impression that had he wished to do so he could have prevented the expulsions, so that the Austrian Protestants may be listed among those who had a specific and, as it were, up-to-date grudge against Metternich.

The booksellers' petition in 1839 was technically a revolutionary act because it was a request not for a more liberal interpretation of law, but for a change in the law, for which they were not entitled to ask. After 1840, with seething unrest in other parts of Europe and with the censors unable to hold back the flow of printed polemic into the country, the first urgent call for reform came from a different quarter altogether. Paradoxical though it may seem, it came from the castles of the nobility out in the provinces, to some extent too from prosperous middle-class aldermen—ironmasters, gunmakers, tradesmen—in the country towns. Yet this was a natural course of events. The inhabitants of the capital consisted broadly speaking of Court and society and the satisfiers of their needs, of civil servants trained in unquestioning loyalty and obedience, and intellectuals: scholars and writers whose social function was at that time in no way understood by authority. There were the university students, an unorganized, totally unrevolutionary working class and finally a highly explosive but equally unorganized and leaderless proletariat. The *Landstände*, the delegates to the provincial Diets, were exceedingly tired of having to climb into fancy dress and drive in state once a year 'like a set of buffoons' to their seat of government just so as to append their signatures to documents sent down to them from the capital. While they held conservative opinions, many members of the aristocracy were aware that the almost feudal conditions on the land (these were far more severe in, for example, Bohemia than within the area of present-day Austria) were so out of tune with the spirit of the times that if they were not changed the land-owning classes would be swept away by revolution.

Heinrich von Srbik says of these noblemen and other members of the reform movement that with their 'utopian ideas' they had no conception of the way in which the students and the masses would snatch the rudder from their hands. Nor, it may be added, were they the only ones who refused to see the force of Metternich's theory about the uncontrollable pressure exerted by the masses, who, once the dam was breached at any point and the way was shown to them, would sweep all before them. To these landowners it seemed to be a matter of bringing in the hay before the deluge. They had, at least, a legal platform of sorts under their feet. The two conditions of peasant tenure which had to be abolished were *Robot*, compulsory labour and services in lieu of rent, and *Zehent*, literally that tenth-part of the harvest to which the landlord was entitled; in practice the proportion varied. These questions had been raised again and again in one area or another, but they now began to gather momentum, and at last a new section of the Chancellery was formed, charged with working out new conditions of tenure and appropriate compensation. Meanwhile Count Sedlnitzky was alerted: he was to pay close attention to the activities[1] of the leaders of the reform movement in Lower Austria and to uncover their contacts with persons in other parts of the monarchy. What it amounted to was that the whole reform movement was placed under police observation.

The next active step was the appearance in 1843 of a pamphlet called *Austria and its Future* written by Baron Viktor von Andrian–Werburg in collaboration with members of the provincial Diets. It openly accused the government of having wasted the twenty-five years of peace since the Congress when it had stood in a position of unparalleled strength, so that in the assembly of nations Austria was now near the tail end, enjoying the sad reputation of a European China and facing internal disintegration. Owing to a deliberate policy of divide and rule, its peoples faced one another in bitter hostility. A mistaken Eastern policy had presented Russia with the control of the Balkan countries and above all with possession of the Danube delta. And what was the essence of the Metternich system? 'A man should be merry, get drunk, talk smut, possibly set up a cotton mill and read Adolph Bäuerle's *Theaterzeitung*. But every interest in his community, in his province, in the state, in the most important questions of the day, however closely they may affect his

---

[1] *Umtriebe*, the favourite police word to denote machinations, intrigues, goings on, anything of which authority disapproved.

moneybags, to all these matters he will kindly pay no attention, so as not to incommode the gentlemen of the government.'

The pamphlet—this was the forbidden publication which Grillparzer saw a cab-driver reading on his box—became a bestseller. The dramatist wrote a review of it in which he spoke out his own prophecy about the future of the monarchy. 'In my opinion, Austria will go to its doom if it does not carry out three things: namely an improvement in the finances, the liberation of Hungary from its stubborn isolation, and the ascendancy of the German principle by voluntary means as guarantors of unity.' Of these three problems the German ascendancy was the most intractable.

The Austrian Ambassador to the Court of St. James, Count Joseph Maurice Dietrichstein (the son of l'Aiglon's tutor), found it difficult to uphold the official Austrian point of view that to introduce modern 'constitutional Utopias' into an organism formed of such heterogeneous components as was the Austrian monarchy, was an impossibility. Lord Palmerston failed to see it. 'Why don't you give differing constitutions to the various provinces of the monarchy?' he asked. 'I confess to you, I see the salvation of the peoples and of the thrones also, only in representative régimes.' The Prince Consort told Count Dietrichstein that the intellectual and moral currents now moving through the world were so emphatic in character that Austria, alone, could never hold them at bay. It could not cut itself off, relying entirely on traditional principles instead of introducing reforms throughout the Empire. The Ambassador must sometimes have wished that his chief were there to defend his own policies. In fact, he soon would be, but by then few politicians would find it worthwhile to listen to him.

To some extent Metternich's precise degree of responsibility for home affairs must remain open to differences in emphasis. His own opinion was unequivocal. 'I do indeed preside at the conferences of Ministers, but am unable to exert any influence over internal affairs, because in this Council each matter is already cooked and is merely served up at mealtimes. If, then, the soup is salt and the dish spoiled, I become aware of it, but I cannot alter the state of affairs. . . . Hence the quantity of complaints and slanted judgments laid at my door . . .' More than anything else, it is his personal isolation that this remark makes abundantly clear. Notwithstanding his intellectual superiority over all those contemporaries who, with him, had 'grown grey in intrigue', and however much his reputation as the 'coachman of Europe' might reflect his personal power as a statesman, by temperament he was disinclined for and unsuited to total independence. He was not a Bismarck. The working partnership with Franz I provided just that degree of shelter which his character needed, but ten years and more after the death of his patron, to dominate the State Council would have called for a resilience, a strength of will and also a will to act which Metternich either no longer possessed or never had. The two futile Archdukes on the Council were neither a spur to action, nor did they offer shelter, except in the driest legal sense, since no one within or without the country believed in it. Nothing could have been further from the mind of Kolowrat than to assist Metternich in any way; the Archduchess Sophie was convinced that if there was to be any chance of saving the monarchy—she never forgave him for putting Ferdinand on the throne—Metternich must be removed from office with the least possible delay. Her hostility, strangely echoing the feelings of the Empress Maria Ludovica so long before, had its part to play in the events of March 1848.

Abroad, Austria's past or potential allies offered little comfort. In the appraisal of her own expansive policies and of Austria's efforts to hold her peoples together, England was inclined to apply double standards of morality, and few members of the British government would have cared to place much money on the Empire's chances of survival. France's instability gave little promise of help in holding the situation in Italy; Austria's interests and those of Prussia were not identical. This left Russia, on whose support against revolution Metternich had been able to rely during the reigns of two Czars. Now, with the threat of revolution imminent throughout Europe, among nations and peoples with whom the Russians were related and those with whom they were not but who were dangerous enemies, and with the ever-present danger of contamination to be borne in mind, Russia quietly withdrew from her alliance with Austria into an attitude of monolithic indifference, and waited. Both at home and abroad Metternich's isolation was oppressive. In his middle 60s, the Chancellor was ageing fast, and the change in him between October 1847 and February 1848 was particularly noticeable. Now almost stone deaf, he is described[1] as having shrunk to a shadow of his former self, endlessly repeating the political banalities of a past era.

At the news of the revolution in Paris and the deposition of King Louis Philippe there appears to have been a Habsburg family council at which Archduke Johann was present. The Prince, he said later, was the only one with whom it was possible to talk sense, only he always believed that matters could be settled by talking. The rest (probably excepting the Archduchess Sophie with whom Archduke Johann was basically in agreement) were all, as regards morale and behaviour, beneath criticism.

A curious incident which happened on 4th March in London gives an idea of the clouds of intrigue now forming around the greatest master of the craft. On that evening Lady Palmerston gave a dinner party at which members of the Rothschild family revealed that they had news from Vienna that the Chancellor had resigned. The unfortunate Dietrichstein was bombarded with questions but could only deny the rumour. It was afterwards believed that if the story emanated from Vienna, the motive may have been to undermine Metternich's standing abroad; if born in London it was probably a Stock Exchange manœuvre.[2]

If there was going to be trouble in Vienna, so much was common knowledge, it would inevitably break out on 13th March when the Estates of Lower Austria were to meet in the Landhaus in the Herrengasse. Members of the opposition (the Estates consisted of nobles and senior clergy) were to press for action on their motion to introduce social reforms over a wide field. Apart from the abolition of *Robot* and *Zehent*, they were demanding representation of the middle classes and the peasantry in the provincial Diets, publication of finances, reforms of the jurisprudence and in primary education, religious tolerance and alleviation of the severity of the censorship leading on to the gradual granting of freedom to the press. They were also to call for the instant removal of Metternich and Sedlnitzky. These demands were to be passed up as a petition to the throne. Thousands of signatures had been collected among the citizenry and deposited with the Diet; a petition from the

---

[1] By Count Vitzthum-Eckstädt, Saxon diplomat.
[2] Heinrich von Srbik, *Metternich, der Staatsmann und der Mensch.*

students of the University was handed by a deputation of professors to the Emperor himself.

The Diet was in session. Crowds of young men began to collect in the Herrengasse and in the courtyard of the Landhaus, where speeches were made, and soon the throng was swaying this way and that all the way from the Michaelerplatz to the Freyung and the Ballhausplatz. It was an entirely middle-class crowd, but groups of artisans and labourers were beginning to appear from beyond the Glacis, though in no large numbers because the gates of the city were then closed to prevent such an influx. The general tension, the excitement, the anxiety on this day, were of a kind and an intensity which had probably never been known in Vienna before. Many a civil service or army family was racked with dissension, shocked beyond recovery at the knowledge that sons and grandsons were creating a ruction in the streets, insulting by implication if not in fact, the sacred person of the Emperor. They would have been more shocked still if they had realized the state of demoralization which was fast seizing most members of the imperial family.

Among the crowd, leaflets were passed from hand to hand: it was the speech of the Hungarian nationalist Ludwig Kossuth to his country's *Reichstag* on 3rd March in which he called for a constitution. As the hours passed, the crowd, irritated by the long wait and inflamed by Kossuth's words, pressed forward and began to force an entry into the conference hall. It was a situation in which a very small sector of a crowd, largely owing to a series of misunderstandings, was getting out of control, but the remainder presented no menace whatever. It was upon this unarmed crowd of students, middle-class citizens and a few workers that Archduke Albrecht ordered his Italian grenadiers to fire and to assist its dispersal with blows from rifle butts and with fixed bayonets. (Archduke Karl had died in April 1847, and was therefore spared the knowledge that his son had turned his fire against defenceless men and women.) It was an act of savage brutality and had the effect of altering the whole quality of the conflict, bringing thousands into it whose sanguine temperaments had not been aroused so far. It was brutal, but it was a most suspect action as well.

It must be said again: the authorities, that is to say all who read the police reports and everyone else with ears to hear, knew that the saying was 'on 13th March *geht es los*'—'we're off'. Then where were the police? Waiting quietly on the Glacis and in barracks were anything up to 14,000 troops, but in the city and around the government buildings and the Hofburg there was not a policeman to be seen. The presence of even a handful of *Polizeisoldaten*, Franz Grillparzer believed, could have stifled the whole revolt before it started. To wait for the first explosion and then to smother it by force of arms was an act which looks very much like deliberate provocation, particularly in view of the Viennese public's well-known antipathy towards the army. The demands for Metternich's resignation were now backed up by the threat of armed rebellion.

For his part, Metternich could have done his country a great service by resigning in the morning. An account exists of the decisive meeting in the Hofburg at which the State Council debated the petition laid before it by the Estates of Lower Austria, the most urgent item in which was the resignation of the *Haus-, Hof- und Staatskanzler*, Fürst Clemens Metternich.

They had just two hours. Among those present were the Archdukes Ludwig, Johann and Franz Karl, Kolowrat and Metternich. During this time the Estates had to hold the crowd at bay. And now for one and a half hours Metternich held a peroration on constitutional theory which contained nothing at all of any immediate relevance. At last Archduke Johann pulled out his watch. 'Fürst, we have half an hour left and we have not yet discussed the reply which we are to give to the people.'

Count Kolowrat interrupted. 'Your Imperial Highness! I have sat in this Cabinet with Prince Metternich for 25 years, and have always heard him speak like this without ever arriving at the point.'

Archduke Johann: 'But today we must arrive at it immediately.' [To Metternich]: 'Do you know that the leaders of the people demand your resignation?'

Metternich: 'On his deathbed the Emperor Franz I made me swear on oath never to abandon his heir. But if the imperial family wishes for my resignation I should consider myself released from my oath.'

The Archdukes assented and Metternich declared his resignation.

The Emperor Ferdinand, suddenly: 'I, after all, am the Sovereign. Tell the people that I consent to everything.'

Epilogue: The End of an Era

At the news that Metternich had resigned the Viennese lit up the town, banners were hung from every window, there was music and song and the inns were full. In due course they buried their dead with the joint assistance of a Catholic priest, a Protestant pastor and the Chief Rabbi—an unprecedented and never-repeated scene. They cheered Ferdinand the Good, and all those thousands who had never known or cared whether Schiller was being performed with cuts or not at all believed that a free press and the end of censorship, now promised to them, were fine things. For a few days it seemed as though that most un-Viennese infectious sickness, revolution, had been shaken off like any other passing fever. It had in fact scarcely begun.

During the coming months Vienna was to drift through a condition of peaceful anarchy into spasms of violence ending in anticlimax. To a considerable extent the revolution was imported, having been fed and stoked by pan-German ideas which remained to sow disunity for generations, and by Kossuth in Hungary, who emerged as the banner-bearer of a mystical Magyar nationalism as conceived by the smaller landed gentry. These matters meant nothing to the Viennese; what caught their attention was Kossuth's call for a constitution. Vienna seemed to become a republic, as in the summer and again in October, the Emperor and his Court fled the capital. This too was basically a misunderstanding as the revolution was not intended to unseat the Habsburgs, and no republican movement acquired impetus at any time.

Now that, at last, Biedermeier man found himself standing on the

Epilogue

edge of the ravine, the purity of his ideals in imminent danger of being sullied by translation into action, many leading figures drew back, among them the physician and poet Baron Ernst von Feuchtesleben. Grillparzer wrote a poem in praise of Radetzky in Italy, Bauernfeld suffered a physical and nervous collapse. Adalbert Stifter's comment illustrates the mind of the Biedermeier intellectual to perfection: 'The ideal of freedom has been destroyed for a long time to come.' Back on his feet again, Bauernfeld went to see Archduke Johann and found him in a deep depression from which he was unable to arouse him. The Archduke had one more scene to play in the Habsburg drama, as the Emperor's representative in Vienna. He was welcomed with flaming torches and thunderous cheers, and at his meeting with the members of the revolutionary committee his unassuming, friendly courtesy and understanding of their point of view won their trust immediately. He stayed long enough to open the Vienna *Reichstag* in July (this was a genuinely constituent assembly, the only imperial parliament in the history of the monarchy) but then left with his wife to take up office as Imperial Administrator, *Reichsverweser*, to the *Reichstag* in Frankfurt. Had he stayed in Vienna there is no saying how much evil might have been averted: Prince Windischgrätz might not have done the hat-trick in firing in turn on the inhabitants of Prague, Vienna and Budapest.

Archduke Karl was not the only contemporary who believed that —as he said in 1802—'Among all its enemies, Austria has none more dangerous than its own government.' Nearly a century later his words were echoed by the Emperor Franz Joseph who, when asked by President Theodore Roosevelt what he considered to be his primary function as a monarch in the modern world, answered without a moment's hesitation: 'To protect my people from their government.'

The trouble was that the Habsburg Emperor *was* the government. During the reign of Franz I the head of the *Casa d'Austria* personified the empire over which he ruled in a way which now existed nowhere else. Nearly 20 years after the French Revolution, roughly at the point where this story begins, Austria was fast becoming an anachronism. Later, in the thirties and forties, at a time when England had long since conquered the oceans of the world, when North America was becoming a commercial and intellectual power, Austria was still being run as though it were the private estate of an eighteenth-century *grand seigneur*—which in a sense it was—while the general atmosphere and scale of values were a little like those of a Victorian nursery.

The literature on the Metternich era is so vast that an amateur historian can hardly hope to master it, but some of the diaries and memoirs, to say nothing of the censorship intercepts and reports by secret agents, are so fascinating that the reader happily wastes time wallowing in superfluous and often misleading detail. But even the basically essential memoirs, biographies and historical studies display a wide variety of opinions. Archduke Karl, the 'Saviour of Germany', the 'Hero of Aspern', has sometimes been treated with unscholarly partiality. His relationship with his brother Franz, last Emperor of the Holy Roman Empire, first Emperor of Austria, is of great historical significance until after the Battle of Wagram, when this thread of the narrative recedes into the background, only re-emerging from time to time in moments of national crisis. It is easy to be carried away by affection for this complex individual and in so doing to create prejudice against the Emperor and, later, against Metternich, where this is not wholly deserved. Where the younger brother Archduke Johann (born in 1782) plays a historical role there is the same danger. But while the roots of discord between brothers are always bound to go back to their relations with one another as children, it is hardly to be wondered at if attempts by Karl or Johann to play at foreign affairs on their own account aroused the implacable hostility of both the Emperor and his chief minister.

To be a Habsburg archduke was not, as we have said before, an easy destiny. Not even mental deficiency was a guarantee of freedom; to be greatly superior to the Emperor in intelligence and force of character meant a lifetime of friction and frustration, not only in relations with him but with the men whom he chose as his advisers. Just how difficult it was is borne in on one with increasing force as the two Archdukes struggle to do what they believe to be in the interests of their country, while they become ever more thickly engulfed in clouds of displeasure from the throne whose incumbent was possessed by a searing mistrust of the two men in his entourage who would most certainly have sacrificed their lives for him.

Franz's third wife, Maria Ludovica, was, he complained, 'too brainy' for him *(zu viel Geist)*. Her political involvement as leader of the war party exposed her to much criticism, and Napoleon was rude about her. But she was a devoted stepmother, caring untiringly for the mentally retarded heir to the throne, she was loved by everyone who really knew her and her death from tuberculosis was certainly hastened by her exhausting duties as hostess to the Congress of Vienna. Her wit is still fresh and she is the only person on record to have administered a public snub to Metternich. She considered the Habsburgs to be on the whole a difficult lot, and, herself affectionate by nature, she found their emotional awkwardness unappealing. Of one of her brothers (their father was also a Habsburg, a son of the Empress Maria Theresa) she remarked: 'He is satisfied and happy, and I believe he is in love . . . in an archducal sort of way, which is not mine.'

Knowing the Empress Marie Louise as well as she did, her comments on the character of the Archduchess who was 'sacrificed' to Napoleon are of value. History has perhaps been a little unfair to Marie Louise. If her intelligence was not of the brightest, she was certainly a genuine professional, who, so long as she had a leading part to play, usually played it well. Having learnt that she was indeed expected to marry the devil, the anti-Christ in person, she dried her panic-stricken tears and got on with it; she even mopped up the tears of Franz who was profoundly moved at the spectacle of himself in the role of a father who did not hesitate to offer up his own daughter for the sake of his people. Was she disloyal to Napoleon afterwards? Of course she was. But she was not a free agent, their correspondence was impounded, there was no way by which she could tell truth from falsehood. The psychological gymnastics which royal princesses could be called upon to perform were enough to strain sanity, and Marie Louise was an extreme example—perhaps the last—of marriage as a weapon in international relations. Once she got away from Schönbrunn and settled down in Parma with her General Neipperg, she was able to edge away from the spotlights into the wings. Though not altogether, because she remained the mother of Napoleon's son, the Duke of Reichstadt. The scene where she stands wringing her hands beside the deathbed of the young Aiglon is affecting. But why did she delay her arrival? Was it the fault of Metternich? It was her own fault, and Reichstadt knew it. It was not only that she had always placed her interests before those of her son. After the death of Neipperg she took as her third husband Count Bourbelles who, as governor of Parma, swiftly undid all the good done by Neipperg's highly capable and humane administration. (He was later to be appointed as tutor to Franz Joseph by Metternich.) But at the same time, she was much pre-occupied with the physical beauty of junior officials about her Court and it was more by luck than her own good management that Reichstadt was able to see his mother before he died.

If it was never easy to be a Habsburg archduke, to be the son of Napoleon was certainly torment. But it was not, I believe, so much the sense of being a prisoner which tormented Reichstadt; it was more the wearing uncertainty in his mind, whether or not he was destined to wear the crown of France. Parallel with this was the lack of an assurance that he had any future in the service of his grand-father or his heir on the throne of Austria. No one seemed to be able to tell him anything, and if ever the young man was mentioned in Metternich's presence the look of distaste on the Minister's face, as though a smell of warmed-up cabbage had trailed past his nostrils, was warning enough not to pursue the subject.

Any attempt to summarize the character and achievements of Metternich in a page or two must be rejected at the outset: this most scintillating character cannot be pinned down in this way, and the last word has not been said on him; unpublished sources exist. He bristles with contradictions. To his liberal-minded contem-poraries everywhere, Clemens Wenzel Lothar, Count (after Leipzig, Prince) Metternich-Winneburg-Beilstein personified everything that was conservative and reactionary; he was the most hated man of his time. But no woman who became his mistress, however exalted her station in life, ever left him; the only possible exception was the Duchess of Sagan. It was always he, inwardly at any rate, who left them. He held the reins for nearly 40 years, which for a statesman is a record hard to equal, and that he managed to keep his seat after the death of Franz I was one of the most brilliant and carefully planned coups of his long career. And yet: there, as on so many other occasions, his actions contained self-interest but they were not frivolous.

The present-day assessment of Metternich's ability as a statesman still rests, where Austro-German historiography is concerned, largely on the judgment of Heinrich von Srbik. But this distinguished historian has been accused of taking Metternich too much at his own word; as even the Emperor noticed, Metternich developed a highly refined technique for covering his bids, and he rewrote history as he went along. It was often said of him that he was bone lazy, that during the Congress he would lie in bed half the morning, spend the rest of it 'sighing in the salon of the Duchess of Sagan', while in the afternoon he might find time to receive three or four individuals of rank who thronged his antechamber before drifting off to change for the evening's entertainment. This also was a half-truth, and he certainly infuriated the Prussians. But never at any time would he have left the Emperor not knowing what to do or say.

The secret of his influence over Franz I lay in the method of presentation. He did the Emperor's thinking for him in advance and laid the pre-digested material before him in such a way that Franz found his own unclear ideas formulated, his prejudices confirmed, his fears rationalized and personalized. He never permitted himself to display his own power, but filtered it through the Emperor, who for his part liked to make a 'boo-man' out of Metternich, creating just that little space between them which allowed him to court popularity on his own account. Franz would listen to petitioners with evident signs of sympathy, saying very often: 'Well, I'll do my best, but I don't know that we'll get anywhere', so that the agitated subject, now deeply moved, would feel that in some way the Emperor too was a victim of the bureaucratic machinery; *der gute Kaiser* really would help if only he were able to, if those hard-hearted ministers . . . and Metternich . . . The technique almost amounted to a confidence trick, and while it astonished the few who saw through it, it deceived thousands, even among members of his entourage.

It would be absurd to reject the evidence left by these two men's contemporaries on the subject of Metternich's notorious police state, the spies, censorship and the rest; for the most part it is a

Epilogue

chorus of condemnation. And yet—there were men in his time who insisted that Metternich was neither illiberal nor intolerant, he simply believed that the country could not afford these luxuries. Intellectual life suffered, that much is certain, scientific development was hampered and the growth of democracy arrested. To some extent, of course, Austrian inefficiency, *Schlamperei*, acted as a compensating factor, tempering the police state. The most charitable view of Metternich's home policy—it has often been put forward—is this: he was gaining time for the country to recover its strength after the Napoleonic wars, and the humus, accumulating almost imperceptibly during the years when Vienna was largely cut off from the intellectual life of the rest of Europe, protected the exquisitely delicate, often introspective intellectual climate, some prefer to call it the swamp culture, of the Biedermeier era. Looking beyond Metternich's time, in this walled garden the seeds were swelling which in the second half of the century would burst out into an explosion of genius which ushered in the twentieth-century world.

But to the people living at the time, perhaps the whole thing looked quite different. Did the Austrians really feel so cut off from every intellectual stimulus? A present-day literary historian believes that the Great Wall of China image has been somewhat overworked. It is no use: the contrasts, the contradictions, remain. Austrian society used to be among the most rigid and hidebound in Europe, the first and second ranks and the bourgeoisie floating one above the other like so many layers of plankton. For a considerable number of years Vienna was the social centre of a continent, its drawing-rooms the most dazzling, witty and extravagant of all, and it would be a mistake to suppose that after the Congress was over the great families pawned their jewellery to pay their debts and settled down to a couple of decades of introspection and picnics in the Helenental. The middle-class world described by Schönholz—households run with clockwork precision, infinitely respectable, disciplined, stuffy and tedious—co-existed with the 'sensual uproar' recorded by Sealsfield and others. It is all true, allowing of course for the shifts in emphasis and degree which must occur in a period of this length: from 1805 to 1848. But in all the reading which must be got through before a historical survey can be undertaken, one factor

Epilogue

recurs again and again: the pessimism among the thinking men of the time. In Archduke Karl and his brother Johann one remembers their recurrent attacks of black depression: 'Your Majesty stands alone . . . in the midst of chaos . . .' There were quite a number of those memoranda which were so disliked by the Emperor. In their case heredity may have played a part, but they shared their view of the scene with a great number of the most influential men of their day. It is an almost pathological gloom, a despairing *après nous le déluge* which was not general in other western European countries and in England would have been unthinkable.

In the international field, all that Metternich most dreaded has happened. He opposed Prussian-dominated pan-Germanism as implacably as he fought the nightmare of a Russian breakthrough into eastern and central Europe. Metternich's Europe died in 1866 at the Battle of Königgrätz (Sadowa) with the defeat of Austria by Prussia, and the logical sequel was that the Austro-Hungarian Empire went up in flames in 1918. Both Metternich and Gentz would have been surprised to know that their world lasted as long as it did. 'Well', Gentz had said, 'it will see us out.' Still greater pessimists than Archduke Karl had been prophesying the imminent disintegration of the Empire even before the close of the eighteenth century. In all this *Weltuntergangsstimmung* there was more than a trace of irrationality and nightmare. The diagnosis was correct, the prophets knew which symptoms would prove fatal. But they underestimated the elements which, for a while yet, would hold the Empire together. Countries so inexhaustible in their potential wealth could survive in spite of governments, and after the thirties and forties of the nineteenth century the Austro-Hungarian Empire was held together, not by constitutions, but by a grid-iron of railway communications, by its industries and commerce. Yet only for one more lifetime. The revolution, such as it was, over, the Emperor Ferdinand abdicated and on 2nd December, 1848, his nephew ascended the throne as Franz Joseph I. A reign of 68 years had begun, the Indian summer of a more than 600-year-old dynasty, the House of Habsburg.

Bibliography

Anschütz, Heinrich, *Erinnerungen aus dessen Leben und Wirken,* Vienna 1866.

Bac, Ferdinand, *Vienne aux temps de Napoléon,* Paris 1933.

Barea, Ilse, *Vienna, Legend and Reality,* London 1966.

Bartasch, Robert, *Wiener Gerichte im Vormärz,* Vienna 1912.

Bauernfeld, Eduard v., *Erinnerungen aus Alt-Wien,* Linz 1948.

Bibl, Viktor, *Der Herzog von Reichstadt,* Vienna 1925.

Bibl, Viktor, *Die Wiener Polizei,* Leipzig-Vienna 1926.

Bibl, Viktor, *Erzherzog Karl,* Vienna 1942.

Bibl, Viktor, *Metternich, der Dämon Österreichs,* Leipzig 1943.

Bibl, Viktor, *Kaiser Franz. Der letzte römisch-deutsche Kaiser,* Leipzig-Vienna 1937.

Bietak, W., *Das Lebensgefühl des Biedermeier,* Vienna-Leipzig 1931.

Boguth, W., 'Die Okkupation Wiens und Niederösterreichs' in *Jahrbuch für Landeskunde,* Vienna 1908.

Böhmer, Günter, *Die Welt des Biedermeier,* Munich 1968.

Bourgoing, Jean de, *1809,* Vienna 1959.

Bourgoing, Jean de, *Vom Wiener Kongress,* Vienna 1964.

Bourgoing, Jean de, *Le Fils de Napoléon,* Paris 1932.

Brandis, Clemens, *Österreich und des Abendland an der Wende des XIX Jahrhunderts,* Innsbruck 1953.

Castelot, André, *l'Aiglon,* Paris 1959.

Charmatz, Richard, Article in *Neue Freie Presse,* 10th June 1909.

Cooper, Duff, *Talleyrand,* London 1932.

Corti, Egon C. Conte, *Anonyme Briefe an drei Kaiser,* Salzburg-Leipzig 1939.

Corti, Egon C. Conte, *Metternich und die Frauen,* 2 vols., Vienna-Zurich 1948.

Corti, Egon C. Conte, *Der Aufstieg des Hauses Rothschild,* Vienna 1949.

Ebner-Eschenbach, Marie von, *Meine Erinnerungen an Grillparzer,* Vienna 1955.

317

Bibliography

Fournier, August, *Die Geheimpolizei auf dem Wiener Kongress*, Vienna 1913.

Gentz, Friedrich von, *Tagebücher* (relevant vols.), Vienna 1920.

Glassbrenner, A., *Bilder und Träume aus Wien*, Vienna 1942.

Gräffer, Franz, *Franzisceische Curiosa*, Vienna 1849.

Gräffer, Franz, *Kleine Wiener Memoiren*, Vienna 1845.

Hanslick, Eduard, *Aus meinem Leben*, vol. 1., Berlin 1894.

Helfert, Joseph-Alexander, Frh. von, *Marie Louise*, Vienna 1873.

Hertenberger, Helmut, *Die Schlacht bei Wagram* (PhD thesis), Vienna 1950.

Hobsbawm, E. J., *The Age of Revolution*, London 1962.

Hormayr, Johann Frh. von, *Lebensbilder aus den Befreiungskriegen*, Jena 1845.

Kahl, Kurt, *Johann Nestroy, oder der Wienerische Shakespeare*, Vienna 1970.

Kaiser, Friedrich, *Ein Wiener Volksdichter erlebt die Revolution*, Vienna 1848.

Kissinger, Henry A., *A World Restored*, London 1957.

Klopfer, Hans, *Aus der Franzosenzeit*, Vienna 1959.

Langsam, Walter Consuelo, *The Napoleonic Wars and German Nationalism in Austria*, Columbia U.P. 1930.

Laube, Heinrich, *Reise durch das Biedermeier*, Vienna 1943.

Leitich, Ann Tizia, *Wiener Biedermeier*, Bielefeld 1940.

Leitich, Ann Tizia, *Metternich und seine Sybille*, Vienna 1960.

Magris, Claudio, *Der Habsburgische Mythos in der österreichischen Literatur*, Salzburg 1966.

Mann, Golo, *Friedrich von Gentz*, Zürich-Vienna 1947.

Marx, Julius, *Die österreichische Zensur im Vormärz*, Vienna 1959.

Mayr, Josef Karl, *Metternichs geheimer Briefdienst*, Vienna 1935.

Mayr, Josef Karl, *Wien im Zeitalter Napoleons*, Vienna 1940.

Mazade, Charles de, *Un Chancellier d'ancien régime*, Paris 1889.

Mellach, K. & Fritsch, G., *1848. Protokolle einer Revolution*, Vienna 1968.

Menzel, Wolfgang, *Reise nach Österreich im Sommer 1831*, Stuttgart 1831.

Nicolson, Harold, *The Congress of Vienna*, London 1946.

Pichler, Caroline, *Denkwürdigkeiten aus meinem Leben*, 4 vols., Vienna 1844.

Politzer, Heinz, *Grillparzer oder das abgründige Biedermeier*, Vienna 1972.

Pölz, Karl, *Die öffentliche Meinung in Wien 1848*, Vienna 1948.

Preisner, Rio, *Johann Nepomuk Nestroy—der Schöpfer der tragischen Posse*, Munich 1968.

Rauchensteiner, Manfried, *Kaiser Franz und Erzherzog Carl*, Vienna 1972.

Bibliography

Reeve, Henry, *Journal of a Residence at Vienna . . . in 1805–1806*, London 1877.

Reisenauer, Jeanette, *Grillparzer und Frau von Stael*, Vienna 1946.

Reiss, Josef, *Die österreichischen Freimaurer*, Vienna-Leipzig 1932.

Richter, Josef, *Briefe eines Eipeldauers über d'Wienstadt*, Munich 1970.

Schmutzer, Anna, *Stephan Edler v. Wohlleben, der Bürgermeister des von den Franzosen besetzten Wien* (PhD thesis), Vienna 1955.

Schönholz, Friedrich Anton von, *Traditionen zur Charakteristik Österreichs . . . unter Franz I*, 2 vols. Munich 1914.

Schrail, J. N., *Unbekannt gebliebene Kriegsereignisse aus den Jahren 1805 und 1809*, Vienna 1891.

Schulmeister, Otto (ed.), *Spectrum Austriae*, in particular 'Das Phänomen Wien' by Anton Böhm, and 'Die Casa d'Austria, das Reich und Europa' by Heinrich Benedikt, Vienna 1957.

Sealsfield, Charles, *Austria As It Is*, London 1828.

Spiel, Hilde, *Fanny von Arnstein, oder die Emanzipation*, Frankfurt 1962.

Spiel, Hilde, *Der Wiener Kongress in Augenzeugenberichten*, Düsseldorf 1965.

Srbik, Heinrich Ritter von, *Metternich, der Staatsmann und der Mensch*, 2 vols, Munich 1925 & 1954.

Steiner, Herta, *Das Urteil Napoleons über Österreich* (PhD thesis), Vienna 1946.

Stifter, Adalbert, *Aus dem Alten Wien*, Vienna 1926.

Thürheim, Countess Lulu, *Mein Leben*, 3 vols, Munich 1913.

Trollope, Frances, *Vienna and the Austrians*, 2 vols, London 1837.

Turnbull, Patrick, *Napoleon's Second Empress*, London, 1971.

Vancsa, Kurt, *Der Geist der Grillparzerzeit*, Vienna 1942.

Varnhagen von Ense, K. A., *Denkwürdigkeiten und Vermischte Schriften*, Leipzig 1859.

Wandruszka, Adam, *Das Haus Habsburg*, Vienna 1956.

Weckbecker, Wilhelm, *Die Weckbeckers*, Graz 1966.

Wecke, Ilse, *Der Österreichische Pressekampf gegen Napoleon* (PhD thesis), Vienna 1950.

Weigel, Hans, *Flucht vor der Grösse*, Vienna 1960.

Weinzierl-Fischer, Erika, 'Visitationsberichte Österreichischer Bischöfe an Kaiser Franz I (1804–1835)' in *Mitteilungen des österreichischen Staatsarchivs*, Vol. VI, Vienna 1953.

Wertheimer, Paul (ed.), *Alt-Wiener Theater*, Vienna.

Weyr, Siegfried, *Wien, Magie der Inneren Stadt*, Vienna 1968.

Weyr, Siegfried, *Wien, Zauber der Vorstadt*, Vienna 1969.

Wilmot, Martha, *More letters from—Impressions of Vienna 1819–1829*, London 1935.

Winter, Eduard, *Romantismus, Restauration und Frühliberalismus im österreichischen Vormärz*, Vienna 1969.

Index

Index

Index

Index

Index

Index

Index

Index